The Collector's Catalogue

Country-store Americana, a nostalgic collection of old signs and canisters interspersed with sentimental Victorian paintings, patterns the walls of designer Ray Kindell's living room.

THE COLLECTOR'S CATALOGUE

Thousands of the most sought-after collectibles you can order by mail, from coins and stamps to miniatures and Art Deco – something for everyone, ideas and tips for displaying collections

By José Wilson and Arthur Leaman, ASID

HOLT, RINEHART and WINSTON   NEW YORK

Library of Congress Cataloging in Publication Data

Wilson, José.
 The collector's catalogue.

 Includes index.
 1. Collectors and collecting—Directories.
I. Leaman, Arthur, joint author. II. Title.
AM213.W54   069′.5   78-10168
ISBN Hardbound: 0-03-042756-8
ISBN Paperback: 0-03-042751-7

First Edition

Designer: Helen Barrow
Printed in the United States of America
10 9 8 7 6 5 4 3 2 1

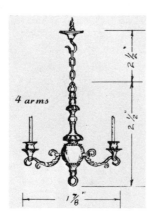

Miniature silver, exact replicas of the originals.
Miniature Silver, M-20.

Court cards from Shakespeare's King Richard to the
Empress Josephine. Sallie's, S-2.

ACKNOWLEDGMENTS

We gratefully acknowledge the kind cooperation of the many galleries, museums, shops and companies that sent us catalogues and photographs. We particularly wish to thank our Associate Editors, Ralph Pomeroy and Martin Kreiner, for contributing their knowledge and writing abilities. Ralph Pomeroy, our art authority, also wrote the short pieces on framing, hanging and displaying paintings and prints. He is the author of several books, was Contributing Editor on Arts for *House Beautiful,* and has been on the editorial staffs of *House & Garden, Art News* and *Art and Artists.* Martin Kreiner is a composer, lyricist and puppeteer with an extensive background in music, theater and publishing. Our thanks also go to Johnnie Dinstuhl for expert manuscript typing and, most of all, to Helen Barrow for her advice and counsel and for planning, organizing and designing this book.

J.W. and A.L.

Introduction

Japanese netsuke miniature reproduction. Peabody Museum of Salem, P-7.

COLLECTING has become the great American pastime and, not coincidentally, a hedge against inflation. While stocks or the price of gold may rise or fall, the value of limited-edition works of art and collectors' plates, antique cars, porcelains, silver, furniture and Persian rugs, coins, stamps, autographs and similar collectibles can only increase with time, demand and scarcity. Limited-edition plates by well-known artists that cost $100 or less on issue may be worth five or ten times as much within a decade. One French crystal plate issued in 1965 at $25 was fetching almost $2,000 twelve years later, a truly spectacular jump. Antique Persian rugs have been known to increase tenfold in value in ten years, and we certainly don't have to tell you about the skyrocketing prices of other antiques.

Yet while collecting can be more profitable (and certainly more fun) than playing the market, investment alone is not the motivation behind the current interest in collecting. In an increasingly impersonal and chillingly technological age, collections are cherished for their warmth and human value. Collecting can put you in touch with different cultures, new art forms, the lovingly crafted, esthetically satisfying things that are vanishing from our everyday lives. The joy of collecting and the exhilaration of the search are enriched by the educational process of learning about something in depth — whether it be history through old books, autographs and manuscripts; geography and currency through maps, stamps and coins; natural history with minerals, fossils and shells; or the heritage of our own country, revealed through the crafts of the settlers and American Indian and Eskimo art and artifacts. Visiting museums, attending lectures, reading specialized books (one of the listings in this book is a mail-order house with a catalogue of over 1,400 books on antiques and collectibles), joining collectors' clubs, societies and organizations, and getting together with fellow collectors at forums and conventions can broaden your horizons and bring new interests into your life.

Collecting is also a simple and direct way to express your individuality and personal taste. Many famous people are collectors, and you'll be in such good company as Truman Capote (paperweights), Pauline Trigère (turtles), artist Theodoros Stamos (Art Nouveau and American furniture classics), Raymond Burr (books on boxing) and James Beard (wine rinsers, majolica and Chinese porcelains).

The range of collections is unlimited. A collection is anything that appeals to or interests you, and you don't have to spend a lot of money on it. Offbeat collections are all the vogue—toothpick holders, comic-book art, old Coke bottles, matchcovers, marbles, locks, keys, cash registers, campaign buttons, mechanical banks, newspapers, milk bottles, tin containers, wooden nickels, even barbed wire. *The Encyclopedia of Associations,* published by Gale Research, has pages and pages of collectors' clubs and organizations (see page 208).

A word of caution, though, on collecting things that were originally mass-produced and of no intrinsic value, such as Depression glass and Shirley Temple spoons, part of the current boom in twentieth-century ''junk.'' Factories are now turning out replicas of these sought-after and easily copied objects, and there is no way of knowing whether you have bought something made forty years ago or yesterday. Such acquisitions should be made for fun rather than profit.

If you are collecting things of value with a view to their appreciation, learn what to look for and how to spot a fake or a copy. If you are making expensive purchases, buy from reputable dealers, firms that have been in business for a number of years and/or belong to accredited professional organizations. Follow the auctions conducted by such famous houses as Sotheby Parke Bernet and Christie's, in spirit if not in person, through their auction and sale catalogues, and place bids by mail (you'll find details of their catalogues in our listings). Small collectibles that are easy to ship—stamps, coins, autographs, books and so on—are often auctioned by mail. Look for advertisements of auctions in collector's magazines and newsletters or notices in newspapers.

If you buy from sources abroad, remember that antiques made more than 100 years ago, original works of art, handmade copies of paintings, and handcrafted objects made by a ''primitive people'' at least 50 years ago are not dutiable, while china, silver and other collectibles of more recent date carry different rates of duty. These are subject to change, and you should get the most up-to-date information from your Regional Commissioner of Customs, or by writing to the Department of the Treasury,

Bureau of Customs, Public Information Division, Washington, DC 20229. You may wonder, as we did, why music boxes carry an 8 percent duty while bagpipes are free, but those are the vagaries of the system.

Some general advice on ordering by mail. Most mail-order companies have their regular shipping methods, but if this is not spelled out in the catalogue, it is always wise to find out how merchandise will be sent — parcel post, UPS or, in the case of large pieces, by motor or air freight—and whether shipping charges are included in the price of the item or extra.

Always keep a record of your order with all pertinent details: the name and address of the company, the description of the item (and catalogue number, if any), date ordered, any required sales tax and handling and shipping charges included with your payment and the number of your personal check or money order to prove that you paid. When your cancelled check is returned, clip it to the record of the order so you don't have to waste time hunting for it if any query should arise. Many mail orders, especially those purchases you make from large companies and seasonal catalogues, can be charged to major credit cards, often by merely calling a toll-free number. In this case, hang on to the monthly statement from the credit-card company in case you have to return the merchandise and request a refund. Check the mail-order company policy on returns, substitutions, and guarantees, and whether there is any time limit on returns. In any case, if your order arrives damaged or proves unsatisfactory or not what was represented, it is best to return it within ten days of receipt with a letter (keep a carbon) stating concisely what was wrong and whether you wish a replacement, exchange or refund. If you don't hear within thirty days, send a second letter by registered mail and request a return receipt. Should the contents of a package arrive damaged or broken, explain this and ask the company what they want you to do with the package. Be sure you *save* the original packaging. This is your proof that the damage occurred in transit and through no fault of yours. While we don't anticipate such problems, it is advisable to be prepared.

Should you be starting a collection, here are some principles to guide you. First, find a subject that reflects your tastes and interests and is within your financial scope. Buy to please yourself; don't just follow a current fad. There's no point in cluttering up the house with something you don't really care about, so make sure that whatever you collect will be a source of pleasure and something you can live with. Good places to investigate the wide range of collectibles are museum shops that sell high-quality reproductions of works of art in the museum's collection, or if you are interested in Americana, Colonial Williamsburg's Craft House, the Edison Institute's catalogue of reproductions from Greenfield Village and the Henry Ford Museum and small, regional museum shops of historical societies, many of which you'll find in this book.

There are two new publications that would also be extremely helpful. One is Time-Life Books' *Encyclopedia of Collectibles,* a lavishly color-illustrated series of volumes packed with information from successful collectors. With the first (trial) volume you get a paperback *Collector's Handbook* that tells you about buying at auctions and flea markets, detecting fakes and protecting against fire and theft. The other, a 280-page *Price Guide to Country Antiques & American Primitives* by Dorothy Hammond, published by the American Antiques & Crafts Society, Fame Avenue, Hanover, PA 17331, costs $6.95 or is free if you join the Society. Annual membership is $12.

Look on your collection as a personal form of decoration, something you can use, as many people do, to initiate a color scheme, provide a focal point for a room or just bring beauty and individuality to your home. Because we believe that collections are an integral part of good living at home, we have included in this book many examples of ways in which they can be used and displayed; also included are sources for china cabinets, vitrines, display cases and stands, and lighting that enable you to show them off to best advantage. There is also advice on matting, framing, hanging and grouping prints and paintings.

This book should be regarded as a guide to what the various galleries, shops and companies have to offer, and their usual price range. Catalogues, especially those for the one-of-a-kind collectibles subject to prior sale, are revised and reissued as merchandise is sold and new things added. Other catalogues are updated seasonally or yearly and, in these days of rising costs, the new editions will often cost more than those we list. Business, too, is volatile. Between the time we received the information and the time this book is published, some businesses may have changed their addresses or their names — or simply disappeared. These things happen, and there is no way we can alter the printed word once the book goes to press. Furthermore, we do not claim to have covered all the shops and companies that sell collectibles, for they number in the thousands. Many of those we approached did not reply to our repeated requests for information, and there are undoubtedly others we did not hear of in time to include them in our listing. For instance, a major offering of art, objects and furniture from the Nelson Rockefeller Art Collection has just been announced.

We would appreciate your recommendations and suggestions for future editions. Send them to Collector's Catalogue, c/o Holt, Rinehart and Winston, 383 Madison Avenue, New York, NY 10017.

JOSÉ WILSON and ARTHUR LEAMAN

Contents

Federal Girandole
Looking Glass
reproduced from
the Philadelphia original.
Edison Institute, E-4.

Note:
All sources for collectibles
are in numbered alphabetical sequence.
To find the source for any object illustrated,
turn to the given letter and number.

A wall niche, well above eye level, directs attention to folk art and framed American Indian necklaces in a small guest room designed by Evelyn Jablow. An American Indian rug is hung on one wall like a tapestry. Photographer: Grigsby.

A-1
ADDISON GREENE, Dept. CC
480 Second Avenue, L.B. #153
New York, NY 10016

Metal Sculpture: Original and Limited Edition Pieces, free, published annually, illustrated, black and white.

Addison Greene specializes in abstract designs, "junk art" and figurines. New designs are constantly being created, and the company welcomes special commissions. All designs can be scaled to specification, and most finishes are interchangeable. There are wall, table and standing sculptures; wall console and mirror; sculptured fountains and cocktail-table bases of brushed stainless, natural oxidized, gold- and silver-leafed steel with copper, brass and bronze accents. Prices range from $35 to $1,500.

A-2
ALASKA ARTOGRAPHY, Dept. CC
Box 993
Anchorage, AK 99510

Information on request.

Trent Swanson, the owner of this small company, specializes in finding unusual Alaskan art for his customers from a want list. Among the items he does carry are an 82″ mastodon tusk for $9,700 and a scrimshawed fossil walrus tooth for $165. Among the items he will search for are alabaster, soapstone and ivory carvings of such things as Eskimos, bears, owls and walrus as well as fossilized ivory jewelry. Prices for most items range from $150 to $2,500.

A-3
THE ALBANY INSTITUTE OF HISTORY & ART SHOP, Dept. CC
125 Washington Avenue
Albany, NY 12210

List of publications, free, published annually.

The publications, which range in price from 10¢ to $15, include such subjects as Hudson Valley Paintings, 1700–1750; New York Furniture Before 1840; Grandma Moses, history and catalogue of exhibit, 1950; and Ammi Phillips, Portrait Painter, 1788–1865. There are also fifteen postcard views of Old Albany in black and white, $1.50 the set, color reproductions of various paintings, and slides of paintings.

A-4
ALBRIGHT-KNOX ART GALLERY, Dept. CC
Buffalo, NY 14222

The Gallery Shop, free, published annually, 10 pages, illustrated, color.

The small fold-out catalogue from this fine museum devoted to contemporary art is beautifully designed and full of fascinating things. For collectors of pins, there are some whimsical pop art pins created by Barbara Feldman—bagel, watermelon, plate of bacon and eggs, slice of cake, lips, rainbow, shooting star, loony-looking birds, 22 different designs—and made of German plastic in vibrant multicolors ($5 and $7), some equally fanciful toys and mobiles, and color reproductions of exhibition posters—Mark Rothko, Max Bill, Jasper Johns and Robert Rauschenberg. A Rauschenberg *R. R. Survey*

Poster: Most Northern Outpost, limited printing, offset lithograph, 30" x 40" unframed, is $20. *Modular Images,* four aluminum shapes designed by Stephen Godzisz that can be arranged in any number of ways, to stimulate personal interaction with the work, are $38.50 the set. Authorized reproductions in Alvastone from works in the Gallery collection include a seventeenth-century memorial king's head with beaded collar, 13" high, Benin Culture of West Africa ($75), a thirteenth-century Mexican Totonac ceremonial axe head, a stylized representation of the symbolic jaguar and snake, 12½" high ($45) and a small sculpture of a girl bathing by Pierre Bonnard. On the cover is an especially attractive Alvastone reproduction from the ceramic original of Fernand Léger's *La Fleur Qui Marche* (Walking Flower) in two sizes, 8" high for $25, 16" high for $85. Shipping charges are extra. There are also some interesting catalogues, one being the newest comprehensive Gallery catalogue, *Painting and Sculpture from Antiquity to 1942,* 528 pages, 32 color and 450 black-and-white illustrations, $35 in cloth, $18.95 in paper.

A-5
AMERICAN CRAFTS COUNCIL, Dept. CC
44 West 53rd Street
New York, NY 10019

American Crafts Council Publications, *free, published annually.* ***Your Portable Museum,*** *free, published annually.*

The museum publications include the bimonthly *Craft Horizons* ($3.75 per issue, special subscription rate available) and catalogues of their own exhibitions such as *Clayworks: 20 Americans,* 1971, 36 pages, 47 illustrations of contemporary ceramics with social, political and humorous themes, $2.15 to members, $2.40 to non-members. *Fabric Collage* is a collection of American quilts, hangings and San Blas molas, 1965, 20 pages, 10 illustrations, $1.40. *Your Portable Museum* covers the slide-film service of the Research and Education Department of the Council. The 35 mm slide kits may be purchased or rented and cover a variety of subjects such as *Coffee, Tea and other Cups* by thirty-nine American ceramists, 50 slides, $62.50 purchase price or $11 rental fee; *Soup Tureens 1976* from the Campbell Museum exhibition of contemporary American ceramic tureens, 75 slides, $93.75 purchase price, $13.50 rental fee; *The New American Quilt,* contemporary quilts of innovative design and techniques by twenty-five American craftsmen; *Forms in Metal,* metalsmithing in America from the 1700s to the present. The 35 mm filmstrips cover such subjects as *The Music Rack,* 25 minutes in color and

sound of Wendell Castle designing and making a laminated wood music rack, $30 rental, and a study of workshops held at six West Virginia glass factories in 1976, titled *New American Glass: Focus West Virginia,* 28 minutes of color and sound, $30 rental fee.

A-6
AMERICAN EXPRESS COMPANY, Dept. CC
Special Offer Headquarters
P.O. Box 754
Great Neck, NY 11025

Expressly Yours, *no charge to card holders, published biannually, 34 pages, illustrated, color.*

Like most of the major gift catalogues, this always has some one-of-a-kind or handcrafted items of interest to collectors. A current catalogue showed antique blue-and-white porcelains from the People's Republic of China—a ginger jar with rosewood lid ($100), cachepot, bowl, and classic vase, 9" tall ($160)—a painted brass and copper sculpture of African violets, mounted in natural gray stone, by Demetrios ($50) and a tapestry after an original in the Louvre, woven in Belgium on antique looms, 34" x 44" ($175).

A-7
AMERICAN HERITAGE PUBLISHING COMPANY, INC., Dept. CC
10 Rockefeller Plaza
New Yor'., NY 10020

American Heritage Catalogue, free, published annually, 16 pages, illustrated, color.

With the publication of their 1977–78 catalogue, the American Heritage Company launched itself into a new career: historic reproductions. Already established as publishers of fine Americana, the company introduced (in conjunction with museums around the world) some truly beautiful collectors' items: Amish doorstops; bracelets and pendants in 22 k. gold-on-silver based on designs in the British Museum; bootscrapers; mugs; pineapple sconces from the Hudson Valley; tinware; letter openers; furniture; bowls; glass and chinaware; clocks; tiles and more. Prices range from $17.50 for a daily reminder in tin from the kitchen of Washington Irving's "Sunnyside" to $550 for an Aaron Willard shelf clock from the Henry Ford Museum. Also listed in the catalogue are American Heritage publications and records, and back issues of *American Heritage, Horizon* and *Americana.*

"Quiet Pond with Mallards," a signed and numbered print by Maynard Reece. Mill Pond Press, M-19.

Turn-of-the-century circus poster. George J. Goodstadt, G-15.

A-8
AMERICAN INTERNATIONAL GALLERIES,
Dept. CC
1802 Kettering Street
Irvine, CA 92714

Automatic Musical Instruments, $3 per issue, $15 per 6-issue subscription, published two or three times a year, 112 pages, illustrated in monochrome.

Any collector of antique phonographs, music boxes, automata, player pianos and rolls; reproducing pianos, nickelodeon pianos with art glass fronts, orchestrions (automatic self-playing orchestras), postcards, circus organs and other automatic instruments from the past will find hours of delight in this informative, well-written magazine. American International Galleries is the U.S. division of Copenhagen's famed *Mekanisk Musik Museum* and the world's largest volume dealer in automatic musical instruments. They find, recondition and sell instruments to collectors, museums and dealers all over the world. Listings on individual pieces are often brief

essays stating explicit details on the condition of the instruments and any work that must be done. They also offer nineteenth- and twentieth-century postcards. In addition to the vast selection, there are articles, interviews and quizzes that make for fascinating and entertaining reading. Prices are competitive.

A-9
THE AMERICAN MUSEUM OF NATURAL HISTORY MUSEUM SHOP, Dept. CC
Central Park West at 79th Street
New York, NY 10024

Catalogue, free, published annually, 16 pages, illustrated, color.

At the time of writing, the Museum shop is in the process of preparing a catalogue, so we cannot give complete details, but we are informed it will offer many one-of-a-kind pieces, such as American Indian jewelry and pottery, jewelry from Mexico, China, Israel, the U.S. and crafts from the various cultures of the world—hangings, glass, wood, soapstone carvings and so on—also reproductions

---

THE CARE AND DISPLAY OF SMALL OBJECTS

An easy and attractive way to safeguard and show off very small objects, such as miniature silver, thimbles and spoons, is to line the drawer of a table with fine linen, silk or velvet, and arrange the objects so they show to best advantage. Among the pleasures of this method of housing a collection is that the little objects are easily seen and handled and the dusting reduced to a minimum, all without the barrier and relative inaccessibility of a glass or plastic case.

  More ways to show collections of small objects are: under glass or plastic on tables; in miniature vitrines; in shadow box frames (page 114); in typesetters' trays; freestanding on a shelf or table (pages 12, 144, 149); in a single niche in a bookcase or wall (pages 8, 180).

A graduated-tier table with revolving shelves is an ideal display piece for a collection of glass paperweights, allowing them to be examined without handling. Courtesy: Kittinger.

of various artifacts from the Museum's collection and a wide selection of books on natural history subjects.

A-10
AMERICAN REPRINTS CO., Dept. CC
111 West Dent Street
Ironton, MO 63650

Catalogue, $1, refundable with purchase, published annually, 40 pages, illustrated.

The bulk of this nicely produced catalogue is devoted to horology—books on clocks and watches—origins, designs, history, movements, catalogues, advertising, manuals, repair, clocks as furniture and much more. Frankly, we were surprised at the wealth of diverse material in print on the subject. The company also offers books on barometers, antique jewelry, antique wicker, foundry work, automatic musical instruments, music boxes and music box recordings, silver and gold hallmarks, cut glass, locks and keys, steins, early American primitives, knives and pocket knives, Depression glass, chronometers, guns and rifles, furniture, railroads, pottery and porcelain marks, lamps, old kitchenware, gold-leaf antiques, bottles and old books. Prices for books range from $2 to $40, plus postage and handling.

A-11
AMERICA'S HOBBY CENTER, INC., Dept. CC
146 West 22nd Street
New York, NY 10011

*Ships—Model Builder's Catalog, $1, 80 pages, illustrated, black and white. **HO and N Model Railroad Catalog,** $1.50, 144 pages, illustrated, black and white.*

The first catalogue has kits for every conceivable kind of sailing and power vessel, including submarines and hydroplanes, plus all the necessary tools, accessories, equipment, books on ship model-making and some rare early editions of *Jane's Fighting Ships* (from $14.95 to $40). There are also kits for cannons and field guns. The range of prices is wide.

The model railroad catalogue is even more extensive, with locomotives, passenger and freight cars, tracks, trackside buildings, signals, tunnels, bridges, trees, power packs, interior detailing kits, figures, materials, tools and books. There's an extensive selection of electric train sets by Bachmann and Arnold. Our only quarrel with these catalogues is that they are so crammed with tiny, blurred photographs and minuscule type on cheap paper that you need a magnifying glass to read them. Prices vary widely.

The Hobby Center also has a catalogue of model airplanes, boats and cars for $1.50 (which we were not sent) and a set of the three catalogues costs $3.50.

A-12
AMSTERDAM AIRPORT MAILORDER DEPARTMENT, Dept. CC
P. O. Box 7501 / Schiphol Airport
Amsterdam / The Netherlands

Amsterdam Airport Mailorder Department, *free, published annually, 32 pages, illustrated, color.*

A colorful catalogue offering some wares from the Netherlands. De Porceleyne Fles Royal Blue Delft heads the list with vases, bowls, plates and a candlestick. Cast-pewter figurines, 3″ to 4″ high, inspired by the seventeenth-century engravings of Johannes Luyken and made by contemporary Dutch artist Michael Warbroek, represent eighteen old professions and handicrafts—clog maker, cooper, glass blower, sheep shearer and so on. Clock collectors will be interested in the replicas of elaborate antique Dutch wall clocks made by Zurel Aalsmeer. All have 8-day movements. The largest, Friese Staartclock, 87 x 24 x 15 cm, comes in oak or walnut and has a lunar phase indicator, bell chime, brass weights and elaborate brass pendulum. There's a reproduction of the *Metamorphosis* poster by famous Dutch graphic artist M. C. Escher, printed in black plus two colors, and a brochure of other available Escher posters will be sent on request. Also available are English Coalport porcelain flower baskets, Wedgwood blue-and-white jasperware, Aynsley bone china and a few pieces of Waterford crystal. All prices in Dutch currency.

A-13
AMSTER RECORDER CO., Dept. CC
1624 Lavaca Street
Austin, TX 78701

Recorders, Recorder Music, *$1, refundable with purchase, published biannually with additional supplements, 56 pages, illustrated, black and white.*

Amster has a very large inventory of instruments —soprano, alto, tenor, sopranino and bass recorders, plastic recorders, wood recorders, Baroque recorders, Renaissance recorders, recorders made by the leading manufacturers. There are also guides to playing recordings of music for the recorder (including ones with "missing" parts for you to fill in) and a long list of sheet music for recorders. Prices range from 55¢ to $4,389.

ANTIQUARIAN BOOKSELLERS
[SEE PAGES 195—209 FOR COMPLETE LISTING]

The list of members of the Antiquarian Booksellers' Association of America, Inc., prepared by the Association, describes the specialties of each bookseller. Antiquarian booksellers constantly update their catalogues and price lists. They will supply these revised lists on request, usually without charge. Some of these same booksellers are also listed in the alphabetical text with their offerings described in detail. Antiquarian booksellers will also help you if you have individual books or libraries to be sold or professionally appraised, for which the Association gives these useful guidelines:

Although it may be very rare, or even unique, this alone does not make a book valuable. There are thousands of rare books which have little or no value to collectors, libraries, or dealers. A book's worth is governed by three factors operating together: intrinsic importance, collector's interest, and scarcity. Generally speaking, the books that are sought after are great works in literature, art, and science (including discovery in all fields), usually in their first editions. These are source books recording the development of man, which experienced professional book dealers can appraise or help owners sell at advantageous prices.

No reliable way has been found to tell you in a few paragraphs how to assess the value of books and manuscripts in your possession. Even if you can identify items with the help of your public or other library, factors such as condition, binding, inscriptions, former ownership, and many others may affect the value of your particular copies. Manuscript material, including letters and signatures of well known people, may be even more difficult to appraise realistically.

To determine the value of your books, consult an experienced antiquarian bookseller, such as one of the members of the Antiquarian Booksellers Association of America listed here. Antiquarian booksellers are persons who deal in old, rare, and valuable books and related materials. They are equipped to provide an appraisal of your books for insurance, tax or sale purposes. If you need an expert appraisal, remember that a bookseller's services, being professional, must be paid for; the fee will depend on the size or value of the collection, the time spent, and specialized knowledge required. If the books have little or no value, there may be no charge at all, and often the bookseller waives a fee if he is able to purchase the material involved. The professional bookseller has at his disposal many reference tools which enable him to evaluate correctly the material he examines. Since most booksellers today are specialists in particular fields, a reputable bookseller will refer you to a qualified colleague if he feels unable to evaluate specialized material.

The best way to dispose of valuable old books and manuscripts is most often through antiquarian booksellers. They are always willing to buy valuable materials for which there is a demand. Show or send a short description to a bookseller listing authors' names, titles, places and dates of publication (preferably from the title page), and any other details that may be helpful. The bookseller will let you know if the books or manuscripts are likely to have any value, will offer to view them for appraisal purposes or to buy them, and will ask to see them. Books can be sent safely by insured parcel post at the inexpensive book rate, or by UPS, and can be returned the same way. Most booksellers will travel to examine books numerous or important enough to justify the expense.

As a trade association of booksellers, the ABAA does not buy, sell or appraise literary property.

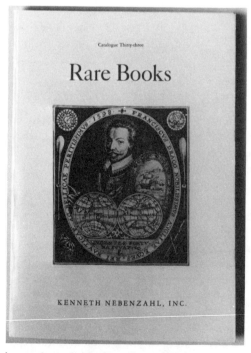

A catalogue of rare books from Kenneth Nebenzahl, page 203.

John Adams' signature on a 1799 marine document. Conway Barker, B-3.

Stamp collections from Kenmore, K-4.

One of the catalogues from The Book Chest, page 197.

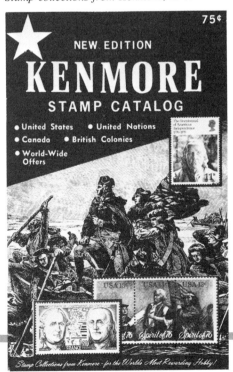

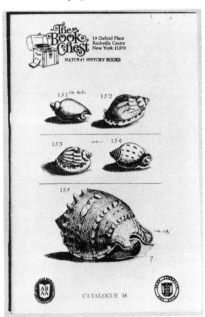

15

Irreplaceable paintings, sculptures and treasures such as these are fully protected against theft through a new international art registration service.

PROTECTION SERVICE FOR ART AND OTHER COLLECTIBLES

With the increase in art thefts, insurance is no longer sufficient to protect collectibles. World Art Services offers an invaluable service to serious collectors through an art registration system. Such things as rare books, antique firearms, chess sets, keepsakes and other impossible-to-replace items can be registered as well as works of art. Identification is established for each work being registered, and an individual identification number is issued for that work. A registration certificate attached to the work warns thieves that, if stolen, a report will be made to local and state law enforcement agencies, the Federal Bureau of Investigation, Interpol and a worldwide network of international art galleries. Although not in business to buy or sell art, World Art Services will also put buyers and sellers in touch through a buyers' finding service called ''Matchmaker.'' Registration for any single object, regardless of its value, is $15 for three years. Registration is transferable to a new owner at a nominal transfer fee, at his cost. Three-year renewal rates are one-half the original cost. For further information write to World Art Services, Inc., 701 Beacon Building, Tulsa, OK 74103.

A-15
ANTIQUE DOLL REPRODUCTIONS, Dept. CC
Box 103, Montevallo Route
Milo, MO 64767

Antique Doll Reproductions, 25¢ (or stamps), published periodically, 12 pages, illustrated, black and white.

While the selection of dolls sounds fascinating, unfortunately the only illustrations are two pages of rather blurred and small shots of dolls' heads and limbs, keyed to ten printed pages where each doll is named and described in detail—height, construction, prices of the different parts, with some dolls listed complete, at one price. To quote a typical description, "Blue Scarf doll is said to represent the Queen of Prussia, who had a goiter and wore the scarf to cover it. She is about 21″ tall and her head sells for $7.50. Her hands and feet are $4 for the set of four. Her china parts are mounted on a cotton-stuffed body, $20, and basic clothing is $10."

A-16
A&R PENNY SHOP, Dept. CC
Box 523
Wheeling, IL 60090

Price list, free, published periodically, 12 pages, black and white.

Pennies, in particular, are the stock-in-trade of the A&R Penny Shop, primarily a very extensive inventory of Lincoln cents from 1909 on, also Indian cents from 1857 to 1909, with 1900s circulated rolls at $21.50, 1800s circulated rolls at $24.50. In other coins, there are Jefferson nickels, buffalo nickels, Liberty nickels, Mercury dimes, Roosevelt dimes, barber dimes and quarters, Franklin halves and Washington quarters. Birth-year sets, from 1900, include 1-, 5-, 10-, 25- and 50-cent pieces mounted in a plastic mint-set holder and are priced from around $2.55 to $12. Whitman coin albums, 2-page, 3-page and 4-page, are also available. A&R Penny Shop is a member of the American Numismatic Association and will search for your requests if you send want lists for particular coins.

A-17
W. GRAHAM ARADER, III, Dept. CC
1000 Boxwood Court
King of Prussia, PA 19406

W. Graham Arader, III, Rare Maps, Books and Prints, $4 ($10 for three issues), refundable with purchase, published every six weeks, 44 pages, illustrated, black and white.

Browsing the Arader catalogue is a delightful experience because of its diversity, illustrations and bibliographic

Above, eighteenth-century American figure doll kits; Philadelphia Museum of Art, P-11. Below, Charlotte Weibull dolls from Sweden, W-7.

17

information. Historians and map collectors will enjoy seeing the various antique maps of America and literally watching the country grow. Print collectors will relish the Audubon quadrupeds priced from $250, Alexander Wilson's ornithological prints priced from $70, Selby ducks from $300 and a fascinating series of American Indian portraits by McKenny and Hall at $185 each. Atlases, instruments, books on travel, cartography, prints and antique maps of almost every part of the world predominate. Prices range from $7 for a copy of Edgar Breitenbach's 1975 collection of essays on *American Printmaking Before 1876* to a very fine Covens and Mortier 1745 edition of Guillaume Delisle's *Atlas Nouveau* for $12,000.

A-18
ARIEL COMPANY, Dept. CC
2894 Meadowbrook Boulevard
Cleveland, OH 44118

Birdmobile—Card Sculptures of Wild Birds in Flight, *free, illustrated, color.*

Utterly fascinating life-size "card sculpture" mobiles of a kingfisher, pigeon hawk, little owl and swallow designed by Malcolm Topp and authentic down to the last detail. Individual kits are priced from $3.95 to $5.95, the four for $17. By the time this appears there should also be available mobiles of a robin, nuthatch, woodpecker and wagtail.

A-19
ARM-ROY STEWART INC., Dept. CC
3376 Foothill Road
Carpinteria, CA 93013

Tradition and Experience bring you the Great Orchids from Armacost and Royston, *$1, refundable with purchase, published every two years, 20 pages, illustrated, color.*

Armacost and Royston, over fifty years in orchid culture, was acquired by Fred A. Stewart, Inc., in 1977, hence the change in name, although the company continues as Armacost's. Their catalogue reflects the experience and traditions of this fine old nursery and the glorious hybrids they have developed. In addition to their cattleyas, *Phalaenopsis* and Paphios, they offer anthuriums as easy-to-grow orchid companions. Armacost's also has a variety of plant-of-the-month plans, with which you get a thirteenth bonus plant free, and, of course, a list of orchid supplies. Prices range from $6 to $75.

A-20
ARROWHEAD PUBLISHING COMPANY,
Dept. CC
P.O. Box 1467
Garden Grove, CA 92642

Brochure, free.

The brochure gives details, with order form, of an important reference work written especially for archaeologists, students, collectors and laymen interested in the projectile points of early man in North America. *Arrowheads and Projectile Points* by G. E. Van Buren, 240 pages with inkline drawings and 50 photographs, costs $14.50 soft cover, $17.50 hard cover, which includes postage and handling within North America. The book introduces, for the first time, a classification system for projectile points. You can also order classification worksheets for projectile points, a projectile point classification coding handbook and wall chart complete with sketches of types of points and their primary characteristics used in the classification process.

A-21
ARS LIBRI, LTD., Dept. CC
711 Boylston Street
Boston, MA 02116

Photography 1839–1975, Catalogue No. 8, *free, published periodically by subject, 80 pages.*

Ars Libri is devoted to rare and out-of-print books, including those in languages other than English. They also sell nineteenth- and twentieth-century photographs, some original graphics and a small collection of autographs. Catalogue No. 8 lists nearly 400 books on photography, some illustrated with original photographs, along with a list of periodicals and original photographs by Alvin Langdon Coburn. The Coburns include photogravures from *The Novels and Tales of Henry James* (Scribner's 1907–1909) and from the magazine *Camera Work*. Among the splendid books are a signed, limited edition of Edward Steichen's 1936 *Walden* ($200), Gyorgy Kepes's 1944 *Language of Vision* ($35) and Arnold Genthe's *As I Remember,* published in 1936 ($50). Previous catalogues still in print deal with German art and architecture, *Art of the Book,* French illustrated books. Others are scheduled for the future. Shipping and handling charges are at cost.

A-22
ART GALLERY OF ONTARIO, Dept. CC
Grange Park
Toronto, Canada M5T 1G4

Gifts at the Gallery, *free, published annually, 40 pages, illustrated, black and white.*

The Art Gallery primarily offers books on the arts, catalogues, illustrated children's books, books on film, crafts, sculpture, photography, decorative arts, art history, individual artists, and works of scholarship, plus such things as calendars, postcards and slides. The Gallery houses the Henry Moore Sculpture Center and there's a three-color lithograph by Moore of *Four Standing Women,* 9″ x 15⅞″, in a limited, signed edition. Books cover such subjects as the photographer Charles Nègre (1820–1880), a limited-edition *Birds of the West Coast, Volume One,* a full-color *Canadian Wildflowers.* "Fotofolios" are sets of twelve loosely-bound postcards reproducing the work of major nineteenth- and twentieth-century photographers such as Muybridge, Cameron and Evans. Prices range from 20¢ to $700 for the Moore lithograph, and there is a small shipping and handling charge.

COMMEMORATIVE PLATES. Top, President John F. Kennedy by Norman Rockwell; Hickory House, H-17. Center, Rockwell Society Mother's Day, 1978, "Bed Time," third in series; Garnita's, G-6. Bottom, Knowles 1978 Americana Holidays, "Fourth of July"; Carol's Gift Shop, C-6.

A-23
ARTIQUES, Dept. CC
P. O. Box 399
Swormville, NY 14146

Authentic Pre-Columbian Reproductions, $1, refundable with purchase, published annually, 12 fold-out pages, illustrated, black and white. Authentic Pre-Columbian Jewelry Reproductions, $1, refundable with purchase, published annually, 8 pages, illustrated, color.

The pre-Columbian and pre-Hispanic reproductions sold by Artiques are made in the ceramic workshop of Mexico's great National Museum of Anthropology (INAH), using matrix imprints of the molds taken from the original figures in the Museum's collection. Each one is an exact reproduction, down to the patina reproducing the effect of centuries, with the INAH brand on the base, and comes with a certificate of reproduction explaining the original region, culture and general characteristics of the piece. The Artiques collection of some twenty-one pieces of pottery covers the Colima, Mayan (Jaina and Palenque), Teotihuacan, Central Veracruz, Monte Alban and Casa Grande regions. All are interesting examples and reasonably priced, from $5 for a ceramic medallion of an ornate crucifix from Veracruz, 2½″ x 2½″, to $70 for a Scribe of Cuilapan from the Monte Alban region, pre-classic period (300 B.C.), 13″ high. Included are figurines, heads, vessels in the form of animals and birds, and medallions.

The jewelry catalogue, which also has some wall plaques of Mayan figures in baked enamel on copper, mounted on ½″ board and ready for hanging ($15 to $40), comprises reproductions of the treasures in gold and precious stones found in the Monte Alban excavations, the Mixtec style around the end of the fifteenth century.

19

There's a descending eagle pendant ($70), Lord of Darkness pins, charm and earrings, a Chimali shield pin or pendant and a graceful Tarascan bell, the one non-Mixtec piece, for $44. The jewelry is made of 0.925 pure silver plated with 14k. gold. Artiques cautions that jewelry shipments take eight weeks to deliver. There's a $2 shipping and handling charge on each order.

A-24
SAM ASH MUSIC CORPORATION, Dept. CC
301 Peninsula Boulevard
Hempstead, NY 11550

Sam Ash Music Stores, *free, published annually, 62 pages, illustrated, black and white.*

The comprehensive catalogue of this chain of New York area music stores offers all kinds of band and orchestral instruments from a piccolo to a tuba, featuring every important brand name, plus such equipment as electronic keyboards and synthesizers, microphones, stands, amplifiers, professional audio systems, padded instrument bags. The Sam Ash stores also have an instrument

rental plan. The catalogue listings include special offers, one-of-a-kind closeouts and industry news. Prices seem very reasonable.

A-25
ASSOCIATED AMERICAN ARTISTS, Dept. CC
663 Fifth Avenue
New York, NY 10022

General Catalogue, *42 pages;* ***International Collection,*** *16 pages;* ***Master Print Collection,*** *12 pages; 50¢ for the three, published seasonally, illustrated, color and black and white.*

This long-established gallery sells signed, original etchings, woodcuts, serigraphs and lithographs by famous artists from all over the world. No more than 250 signed impressions are offered of any one print. Sonia Delaunay's *Rhythm in Color,* in an edition of 75, 26'' x 20¾'', is $325 plus $10 shipping, or $5 shipping if sent unmatted in a tube. A black-and-white lithograph by Thomas Hart Benson, 22'' x 26'', 150 unnumbered impressions, is $900 plus $8 shipping. One of David

Model of the famous "Cutty Sark," Scientific Models, S-8.

Antique ship's figurehead. John F. Rinaldi, R-14.

Stained-glass triptych. Glass Masters, G-13.

Hockney's etchings illustrating *Grimm's Fairy Tales,* 9½'' x 10¾'', in an edition of 200 is $425 plus $10 shipping. For Matisse collectors, there's a superb lithograph, *The Arab Blouse,* signed and numbered 4 of 10 artist's proofs (the edition numbered 50), 21¼'' x 17⅛'', framed, for $7,500 plus shipping.

A-26
AURA, INC., Dept. CC
P. O. Box 26625
Tucson, AZ 85726

> ***Catalog of Slides and Prints from Kitt Peak National Observatory and Cerro Tololo Inter-American Observatory,*** *$1, 42 pages, illustrated, color and black and white.*

AURA, the Association of Universities for Research in Astronomy, Inc., under contract with The National Science Foundation, is making available in this, their first catalogue, a spectacular selection of color and black-and-white slides, prints and posters from their two observatories showing galaxies, star clusters and nebula. This

is a catalogue for the knowledgeable collector and student of astronomy as well as the collector of kinetic art. Prices are reasonable; $2.75 for an 8'' x 10'' black-and-white glossy print ($6 in color), $6 for 4'' x 5'' color transparencies, $1 for a set of fourteen color postcards showing Kitt Peak scenes and astronomical subjects, $1 for borderless 16'' x 20'' color posters and $3.50 for a special, spectacular color poster, 22'' x 33'', of a lightning display over Kitt Peak.

A-27
AUTHENTIC SHIPMODELS AMSTERDAM, INC.,
Dept. CC
1 Bank Street
Stamford, CT 06901

> ***Authentic Shipmodels Amsterdam Portfolio,*** *$5, refundable with purchase, containing nineteen 4-color, one black-and-white descriptive folders, published annually.*

Perfection is also the model of this Amsterdam-based company of craftsmen as their portfolio testifies. Each folder features crisp, clear, detailed photographs of the completely handmade scale models along with a history of the particular ship. Sixteenth-century galleons, eighteenth-century xebecs, cutters, ketches, schooners, sloops—all classes of classic ships are represented in this fine collection. The models are all built of planks on timber and no plastic or synthetic resins are used. Every detail of the ships has been thoroughly researched and carefully handcrafted down to the brass armament, special rigging and color of paint. Prices range from $205 for a Halfmodel Cutter, man-of-war, to $5,850 for a Groninger Oostzeetjalk, to $11,300 for a magnificent reproduction of East India Man, Amsterdam 1749, which requires six months to a year for delivery. Other models take one to eight weeks for delivery, all are made in Amsterdam, shipped to the U.S. and priced f.o.b. Stamford. By the way, if you would like the Disaster of the Titanic miniaturized in a bottle, they have that, too, for only $240. (All specifications are listed in centimeters.)

A-28
AYNSLEY BONE CHINA, Dept. CC
225 Fifth Avenue
New York, NY 10010

Beauty, the Beasts & the Birds, *two free brochures, published annually, 32 pages and 12 pages, illustrated, color.*

Sculptured and hand-painted porcelain figurines of birds and beasts, charming and realistic, by Aynsley, the English potters of Stoke-on-Trent. A delightful group of birds, about 3″ high, includes a nuthatch ($28), pheasant, ptarmigan ($30) and owl. Animals like a winter stoat, otter, badger and seal are also quite captivating. "The Porcelain Jungle" can be ordered from Aynsley direct or through your favorite china store.

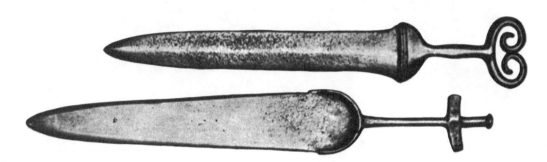

Miniature Late Bronze Age swords reproduced from originals in Nationalmuseets Forlag, N-6.

B-1
BALZEKAS MUSEUM OF LITHUANIAN CULTURE, Dept. CC
4012 S. Archer Avenue
Chicago, IL 60632

Lithuanian Museum Catalogue, free, 4 pages, black and white.

The ''catalogue'' we received is actually more of a newsletter about the museum and its members. On the last page is a listing of the gift shop merchandise—books on Lithuanian folk art, cookery, dictionaries and reference books (most of which seem to be in Lithuanian) and various items such as Lithuanian flags, Christmas straw ornaments, handmade Lithuanian dolls (10″ high, $14; 24″ high, $28.50), maps and stamps of Lithuania (a stamp sheet commemorating the Lituanica transatlantic flight in 1933 by Darius-Girenas is $2) and a Lithuanian stamp album with pictures of individual stamps ($8.75). For coin collectors, the bilingual *Encyclopedia of Lithuanian Numismatics* by Dr. A. M. Rackus, limited number only, costs $18. An annual membership to the museum is $10; a life membership, $150.

B-2
THE B & O RAILROAD MUSEUM, Dept. CC
Pratt & Poppleton Streets
Baltimore, MD 21223

Gifts with a Railroad Motif, free, published annually, 20 pages, illustrated, color and black and white.

The B & O is, of course, the Baltimore & Ohio Railroad, and the museum is packed with relics and re-creations of a century and a half of American railroading. The catalogue has a fascinating collection of things pertaining to the line, such as reproductions of the B & O's blue china, decorated with railroad scenes, first issued in 1927 for use on the colonial dining cars. A limited-edition commemorative service plate shows the laying of the first stone in 1828 ($20), and among the unusual pieces is a handled ice-cream shell ($9). Railroad memorabilia include a diesel headlight, oil hand lantern, regulation rear-end marker lantern, railroad spike that can be used as a paperweight, original spike maul, lapel and regulation hat emblems and cloth patches from the B & O and C & O (known as the Chessie), void ticket strips and a lithograph color poster of a painting by Howard Fogg showing the B & O's Ambassador, 16″ x 20″ ($3). The catalogue also has interesting books about railroading and recordings of railroad sounds.

B-3
CONWAY BARKER, AUTOGRAPH DEALER, Dept. CC
P. O. Box 30625 / Royal Lane Station
Dallas, TX 75230

Price list, free, 4 typewritten pages, published monthly.

Signatures of presidents on letters, documents, photographs, from John Adams ($1,650) and Thomas Jefferson (a letter written to a French diplomat while he was Minister to France, $2,200) to Kennedy and Nixon. On this list you will find a real John Hancock, when he was President of Congress ($475), and a lock of forty strands of George Washington's auburn hair ($750). These are among the more expensive. A Herbert Hoover signature on the flyleaf of a book is $48.50, and first ladies go for considerably less: $17.50 for Caroline Harrison, $20 for Frances Cleveland.

B-4
BARR ART STUDIO, Dept. CC
109 Ladder Hill Road
Weston, CT 06883

Horses in Wire, free, illustrated folder and order form, black and white.

Mary Ann Barr has an affinity for horses. Her matte finish black wire sculptures, which are 10″ to 12″ high and mounted on weathered wood bases, seem to come alive even in the not-too-sharp photos in the brochure. There are six models to choose from, ranging in price from about $125 to $150.

B-5

THE BARTLEY COLLECTION, LTD., Dept. CC
74 Oakwood Avenue
Lake Forest, IL 60045

Catalogue, $1, refundable with purchase, published annually, 24 pages, illustrated, color.

Reproductions of eighteenth-century furniture, available either in kit form, unassembled and ready to finish, with paste stain and varnish included, or assembled and hand-finished. Many are approved reproductions of pieces from the Henry Ford Museum furniture collection. Some of the choices are a Chippendale corner chair ($175 unassembled, $400 assembled); a Philadelphia Chippendale scrollwork mirror; a Queen Anne lowboy from a New England original, circa 1750; an eighteenth-century three-tier muffin stand that can be used to display part of a collection ($75 unassembled, $220 assembled); a candlestand, candle table and tray-top brandy stand tripod table. Most pieces are available in either mahogany or cherry. Shipping and handling extra.

B-6

BASKET BAZAAR AT VINTAGE 1870, Dept. CC
P. O. Box 2105
Yountville, CA 94599

Brochure, $1, published annually, 10 pages in folder, illustrated, black and white.

This small collection includes some perfectly delightful French country baskets of dark, unpeeled willow. One, to hang on the wall, could hold potted plants or a dried-flower arrangement and comes in large, medium and small sizes at prices from $8.95 for the large to $6.95 for the small. Grapevine baskets with side handles are great for logs or large plants and range from $32 for the 20½" wide by 18" deep size to $16 for the 15" wide by 14" deep basket. There's also a marvelous, rustic-looking baker's cooling rack for a loaf of bread, copied from an old French design, 12" in diameter, that would look stunning as part of a wall collection ($3.25). Shipping charges are extra.

B-7

BASKETS ETC., Dept. CC
P. O. Box 19976
Atlanta, GA 30325

Baskets etc., 50¢, published seasonally, 12 pages, illustrated, color.

A good selection of baskets and pieces of furniture in rattan and wicker. For collectors of the offbeat, an assortment of Chinese coolie hats at $11 would make an original wall grouping as would handmade fans of differ-

ent natural materials (an assortment of six, around $8). There are some amusing bamboo baskets with parrot or lion heads and lamps with various styles of basket base.

B-8

BAY COUNTRY WOODCRAFTS, Dept. CC
U. S. Route 13
Oak Hall, VA 23416

Bay Country Woodcrafts, 50¢, published annually, 16 pages, illustrated, color.

According to the copy in this handsome catalogue, the craft of decoy making is "the only form of folk art to originate in America." The Hornick family—Mary, who runs the business, and sons Leonard, who carves, and Raymond, who paints the finished decoys—is making sure the art stays alive. Each of the fine solid wood wildfowl carvings reflects painstaking care and attention to detail. Average price for a finished lifelike canvasback or mallard is $50. Kits of the same ducks are $14.95. There are fourteen species to choose from plus wildfowl books, accessories, trapunto pillows, weathervanes, clocks, potholders, bookends and woodcrafting tools. There is also a superb limited-edition carving of a Canada goose, 16" high by 24" long, hand signed and numbered, for $600.

B-9

BENJANE ARTS, Dept. CC
320 Hempstead Avenue
West Hempstead, NY 11552

Sea Shell Catalog, $2, refundable with purchase, published every two years, 36 pages, illustrated, black and white.

All kinds of sea shells, rare and common, various other forms of sea life such as coral, sea horses, sea urchins, starfish and also land snails, at prices ranging from a mere 10¢ to $450 to $750 for rare golden cowry shells. Minimum order is $10. The illustrations show only a small part of the complete stock, with a more complete listing in the price index at the back of the catalogue. For the collector, there are display stands and an unusual display idea, a typesetter's tray ($7.50, or with shells, glue and directions, $20 and $25). For shellcraft there are kits for mirrors, wreaths, boxes, mosaics and craft shells by the pound. There's also some attractive shell jewelry.

B-10

BENNINGTON MUSEUM, Dept. CC
West Main Street
Bennington, VT 05201

Bennington Museum Gift Catalog, free, published annually, 12 pages, illustrated, black and white.

A small, selective catalogue of items from the Bennington Museum, the Peter Matteson Tavern Museum and the Grandma Moses Schoolhouse Museum, including a variety of eighteenth- and nineteenth-century reproductions chosen for their unique design and utility. In art glass, there are delicate pitchers and vases from the Clevenger collection of South Jersey Reproduction Glass, hand-blown by traditional methods in varied shades of blue, green and amber. This glass is becoming scarce and will increase in value. A button-and-daisy bottle vase, 5″ tall, is just $6; a rose-in-snow pitcher, 8″ tall, $8.50. A reproduction of an original George Washington inaugural button of 1789, stamped "G. W." and "Long Live the President," in silver or copper color, is $3.50. Among the Peter Matteson Tavern selections are pure pewter spoons, a tin candle lantern, coffee pot and mug, and a limited edition print of the tavern, numbered and signed by artist James McKinney, $6. For playing-card collectors there's a pack of old-time, large-size cards, unusual because they have no numbers, $7.50, and for needlepointers, there's a design based on a trotting horse weathervane in the Museum's collection, $24.95 for the kit. From the Grandma Moses Museum there are books on the artist and her paintings, *The Night Before Christmas* with her color illustrations, $4.50, and a key chain with enameled replica of the U.S. commemorative stamp with her painting "July Fourth," issued in Grandma's honor in 1969, a great little gift at $4.

B-11
**BEREA COLLEGE STUDENT CRAFT
INDUSTRIES,** Dept. CC
CPO 2347
Berea, KY 40404

Berea College Student Craft Industries–Hand Crafts, 50¢, published annually, 28 pages, illustrated, black and white. Early American & Colonial Handcrafted Reproductions, $1, published annually, 22 pages, illustrated, black and white. Handex Country Furniture, free, published annually, 6 pages, illustrated, black and white.

The students at Berea College, eighty percent of whom come from 257 Appalachian counties of eight southern states, earn a part of their expenses by producing hand-crafted furniture and objects. Berea College Student Craft Industries is the central member of the Kentucky Guild of Artists and Craftsmen and the Southern Highland Handicraft Guild, and the quality of workmanship is high. The 50¢ handcraft catalogue shows a variety of the students' work in ceramics, needlecraft, woodcraft, weaving, wrought iron, jewelry, clothing. There are some delightful toys and traditional games such as a skittle game, complete with stand, in cherry or blond woods ($75 in

Mid-Victorian mahogany tall-case clock. Frank S. Schwarz & Sons, S-6.

cherry, $65 in blond woods), Chinese checkers, wooden tops and soft stuffed toys. A one-of-a-kind woven wool wall hanging in earth colors, 34″ x 48″, is $100; a boxed set of twelve Berea area fossils, identified and explained, is $2.75; and a set of six prints of Kentucky wildflowers, suitable for framing, 6″ x 8″, costs $12.

The catalogue of Early American and Colonial furniture shows a variety of pieces from spool beds to Sheraton-style tables and chairs, available in walnut, cherry and mahogany. No price list came with this catalogue, nor with the Handex brochure for simple, sturdy country furniture made of mountain (Appalachian) chestnut with a hand-rubbed oil finish and final coating of clear butcher's wax.

B-12
BERNARDO'S DOOR 26, Dept. CC
3131 Southwest Freeway
Houston, TX 77098

Brochure, free, published annually, illustrated, black and white.

Bernardo's Door 26 sells handmade silver jewelry created in Coban in the mountains of Guatemala. The designs are "as old and authentic as the ancient Mayan tribe of Quiche." A wedding necklace with 70″-long chain and earrings, silver-plated, are $23.60 and $10.80 respectively. They also have handmade dolls in traditional costume, no two alike, 9″ high, for $15.30 a pair. All prices are postpaid.

B-13
BILLARD'S OLD TELEPHONES, Dept. CC
21710 Regnart Road
Cupertino, CA 95014

Old Telephones & Parts Catalog, $1 (refundable with purchase), published annually, 12 pages, illustrated.

A fine source for collectors and restorers of old telephones. Four pages of sketches show 124 telephone models for which owner Gerry Billard can supply parts. He also has some 1920 coin-box phones ready to plug in for $98, a kit to convert any wood magneto set to practical use, $27, old mint-condition telephone directories and more. All prices include postage and handling charges.

B-14
ADELE BISHOP, INC., Dept. CC
Box 117
Dorset, VT 05251

Decorative Stencil Kits, $1, published annually, 16 pages, illustrated, color.

In the Adele Bishop catalogue are eleven complete stencil kits with the most comprehensive stenciling course ever offered. Most of the designs are Early American, except for one that has five Japanese designs. Seven of the eleven kits are designed for major home-decorating projects. Included in the kits will be new instant-drying Japan paints, stencils printed on frosted Mylar and specially manufactured super-size stencil brushes—the type used by professionals—that are designed to cover a surface area four times faster than the conventional artist's stencil brush sold in art supply stores. (One brush has a 1″-diameter bristle; the other, 1½″, is more practical for large projects such as floors and walls.) The range of kits contains materials that will stencil any possible stencil surface. *The Art of Decorative Stenciling,* the definitive work on the subject by Adele Bishop and Cile Lord, will be available in both hardcover and paperback. As the catalogue is currently being prepared, we cannot list prices.

B-15
BISHOP MUSEUM, VESTIBULE SHOP, Dept. CC
Dept. R / Box 6037
Honolulu, HI 96818

Bishop Museum, free, published annually, 14 pages, illustrated, black and white and color.

Reproductions of works in the Museum collection, craft items, jewelry, books, musical instruments and dolls relating to the Pacific area are offered by this important museum. There are a gourd rattle topped with brilliant feathers and waterworn beach or riverbed pebbles, both used in the traditional hula. A powerful hand-finished reproduction of a statue of a war god carried into battle by King Kamehameha the Great, 21¼″ high, is limited to an edition of 500. A game called Konane comes with a board of koa wood, playing pebbles of coral and lava, and complete playing instructions. Among the note cards are eight designs based on Hawaiian petroglyphs and eight designs of Hawaiian quilts. There are also delightful dolls in native costume and some fine reproductions of ancestral figures and gods. Prices range from 60¢ to $800, with a small handling and shipping charge.

B-16
BLUEJACKET SHIPCRAFTERS, Dept. CC
50 Water Street
South Norwalk, CT 06854

Scale Ship Models and Model Fittings, $1, refundable with purchase over $25, 64 pages, illustrated, black and white.

For over seventy years this firm has been offering scale

model kits and fittings for a wonderful range of ships—fishing schooners, brigs, frigates, steamboats, clippers, yawls, tea packets, sloops, tugs, destroyers and tankers. Their catalogue includes Henry Hudson's *Half Moon; Old Ironsides,* down to its brass bell and belaying pins; the America's Cup defender in 1885 (and winner) *Puritan;* the *Flying Cloud,* which set, and still holds, the record for fastest sailing from New York to San Francisco around the Horn. A splendid assortment of fittings, from blocks to cannons, is also available. Plans for most of the models can be bought separately as well. Prices range from 10¢ to $176, with a small charge for shipping and handling.

B-17
EDWARD MARSHALL BOEHM, INC., Dept. CC
    25 Fairfacts Street, P. O. Box 5051
    Trenton, NJ 08638

Boehm—Porcelain Objects of Art, *price of new catalogue to be determined, published periodically, 108 pages, illustrated, color.*

The Boehm Studios are famous for exquisite limited-edition collections of porcelain sculptures, plates and paintings. A new catalogue is currently being prepared and should be available by the time you read this. The one we received was published in 1976 and shows larks, owls, wrens and other birds amid their natural flora, sculpted in porcelain; animals; flowers from camellias and orchids to roses and iris; "paintings" of the seasons; floral bouquets; fruit still lifes. There are figures of opera stars, ornamental objects such as tureens and vases, and bone porcelain decorative art plates in series such as Birds of the World and Butterflies of the World. Special collections, such as the Tutankhamun and Ancient Egyptian Collection commissioned on the occasion of the special exhibition of The Treasures of Tutankhamun, include sculptures, commemorative plates, pendants and scarab and cartouche paperweights. The price list is very detailed, giving the hallmark, country of manufacture, year of issue, limited-edition goal and number so far completed, as well as the retail price. Prices range from under $50 for objects in open collections to over $9,000 for very small limited editions. Boehm sells only through appointed agents located across the country, who can also supply the catalogue.

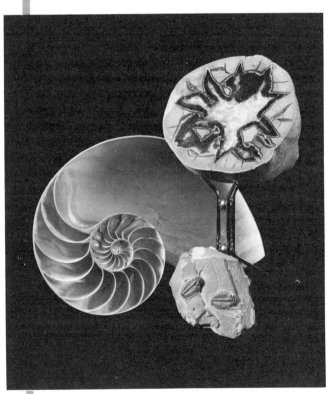

Chambered nautilus half, septarian concretion and fossil trilobite slab. Dover Scientific, D-14.

Venus comb shell from The Old Shell Game, O-5.

Above, crystal unicorn by William Burke, 6½'' tall; Paul McAfee & Friends, M-10. Below, Three-Sisters champagne glass from the American Decorative Arts collection at The Metropolitan Museum of Art, M-16.

B-18
BOSTON MUSEUM OF FINE ARTS, MUSEUM SHOP, Dept. CC
P. O. Box 3
Boston, MA 02112

Catalogue, 50¢, published seasonally, 48 pages, illustrated, color.

For collectors of silver there's a copy of a "Puritan" spoon by Jeremiah Dummer, America's first native-born goldsmith (1645–1710) found in the ruins of a building in Salem, Massachusetts ($21 in sterling, $7.75 in plate), or a five-piece coffee and tea service adapted from a design by Paul Revere II ($450 in silver plate). A peacock weather vane, reproduced in copper from a nineteenth-century American original, 5' tall including the shaft, costs $350. A clear glass copy, 3½'' in diameter, of an octagonal "portrait" cup plate dating from the mid-eighteen-hundreds with a bust of George Washington in profile is $3. A unique, hand-blown art-glass paperweight made by Steven V. Correia, signed and registered by the artist, is one of several priced from $40 to $65. There is also a wonderful "firing glass"—a stumpy drinking glass with a thick foot which derives from glasses used by nineteenth-century drinkers to express approval or appreciation by hammering their glasses vigorously on the table (4'' high, $15 each; $27.50 for two). The Museum also offers jewelry, sculpture, books, cards, decorative objects, furniture, needlepoint kits, jigsaw puzzles, playing cards, etc. From January through April and July through August items are available only at the Museum Shop, not by mail.

B-19
PATRICIA BOYD STUDIO, Dept. CC
Pitkin, CO 81241

Audubon Warbler, 24¢, folder, color.

Patricia Boyd is a craftsperson of sensitivity and skill. Her "Porcelains of Point Reyes Collection" started with the handsome polychrome porcelain "Audubon's Warbler on Red Alder" in a limited, signed edition of 500. The piece is 5½'' x 5¾'' x 6½'' and is also available in white. Since February 1978, the collection has been enlarged. Write for prices and further information.

B-20
THE BRADFORD EXCHANGE, Dept. CC
8700 Waukegan Road
Morton Grove, IL 60053

The Bradford Book of Collector's Plates, $8.95.

A directory of all the world's most actively traded limited-edition collector's plates that both experienced and novice collectors will find an invaluable reference and source book. The 1978 updated, expanded and revised edition, which is going to press as this is written, is printed for the first time in full color, with 961 four-color photographs of all the major collector's plates listed on the Bradford Exchange, and indexed to provide instant identification of country, manufacturer, series and issue, with information about the plate-maker's history, logos, trademarks and hallmarks. Information about each plate gives maker, material, artist, series and plate titles, hanging and numbering provisions, diameter, edition limit, issue date and issue price. This catalogue also includes a glossary of collector's plate and market terminology and a revised, expanded introduction with facts of interest to collectors. A twelve-page "Year in Review" recaps market activity for the previous year and offers a prognosis of future trends.

B-21
TURNER BRADSHAW & ASSOCIATES, Dept. CC
  10401 West Lincoln Avenue
  West Allis, WI 53227

Flyer, free, illustrated, color.

A full-color lithograph from a painting by Roger Lex of Tutankhamun's famous funerary mask measures 18″ x 24″ and is offered in a signed, numbered edition of 1,000, printed on 100 percent rag paper. It sells for $15 plus $1 shipping and handling charge.

B-22
M.E. BRASHER, Dept. CC
  Box 335
  Chickadee Valley
  Kent, CT 06757

A Catalogue of Original Wood Sculptures, $1, 24 pages, illustrated, black and white.

A bronze of fighting elk in an edition of fifty, signed and numbered (also available in walnut, painted), a snow owl and lively studies of horses are among the sculptures of M. E. Brasher. He usually works in walnut, although he also does a limited number of bronzes. Featured in the sculptor's catalogue are many illustrations of portraits commissioned by people of their pet dogs and cats or prized cattle. Prices of sculpture average between $60 and $1,000, with the commissioned portraits varying in price depending on size, pose and amount of detail; usually they are around $150 to $600. There is a shipping charge for air mail or special delivery.

Above, crystal elephant, 7″ tall, by William Burke; Paul McAfee & Friends, M-10. Below, "Cityscape," composition of five crystal columns by Lloyd Atkins. Steuben Glass, S-33.

29

Broadsides and posters from America's past. Buck Hill Associates, B-29.

B-23
BRENTANO'S—THE ROTEN COLLECTION,
Dept. CC
9645 Gerwig Lane
Columbia, MD 21046

Original Prints, $2, refundable with purchase, published annually, 4 pages, illustrated, color.

Original prints in signed, limited editions by a number of contemporary artists are listed by this company. Among those illustrated in the current brochure are Alexander Calder's lithograph *Eternity (Five Pyramids)* in an edition of 100; Ronald Searle's witty lithograph of a cat riding a bike—edition of 99; a decorative still life of leaves in a vase by Walter Cleveland—serigraph limited to 100; and a hand-colored etching of six musicians by Ira Moskowitz in an edition of 125. Other prints depict cats, views of the south of France, birds and trees. Prices range from $50 to $350 (unframed), and there is a small charge for postage and handling.

B-24
BREWSTER GALLERY, Dept. CC
1018 Madison Avenue
New York, NY 10021

Free lists of exhibition sale catalogues.

Brewster Gallery specializes in works of contemporary artists. Write to them to be put on their mailing list. The exhibition catalogue we received is of drawings and lithographs by the famed Costa Rican sculptor, Francisco Zuñiga, who lives and works in Mexico. His work, which he describes as a "continuous representation of femininity," portrays staunch and monumental females with Indian features, in repose, in groups, with children, or alone. The lithographs are in numbered, limited editions, the drawings all executed in pastel; the prices quoted range from $450 to $3,000. There is also a poster available for $30.

B-25
MARLIN BRINSER BOOKS ON MUSIC, Dept CC
643 Stuyvesant Avenue
Irvington, NJ 07111

Books on Music, price list, free, published annually.

Hardcover books on music from England and paperbound books from the U.S. constitute this amazing list of over 1,500 titles, making it, as the publisher claims, "the largest and most complete individual source of books on music." Subjects covered range from accompanying interpretation, dictionaries, operas, theory, harmony, composition and biography to vocal singing, musicals and much more. Prices are competitive and reasonable.

B-26
BRITISH-AMERICAN HISTORICAL ARTS, LTD.,
Dept. CC
10884 Santa Monica Blvd.
Los Angeles, CA 90025

Catalogue, free, published annually, 16 pages, illustrated, color.

This "assemblage of fine reproductions and antiques plus related accessories," as the catalogue is described on the cover, is pretty specialized and different from the usual run of catalogues of this kind. The current catalogue has a superb collection of mercury stick and banjo barometers, antiques and reproductions, at prices ranging from $125 for a very simple reproduction stick type to $1,050 for a late eighteenth-century classic antique. Handling, packing and shipping is included in the price. One captivating reproduction barometer in the Chinoiserie style, with a twisted stem, painted Chinese red with raised gold designs, handmade in England in limited quantities, is $700. Enameled boxes are another of the specialty items. Antique Battersea boxes run around $225; elegant gold-plated and enameled reproductions of eighteenth-century boxes by the English firm of Crummles & Company are $30 and $34. There's a glorious Regency inkstand with two glasses of ruby and white Bristol glass in a faceted design, and there's also an original Audubon hand-colored engraving and aquatint. Naturally, antiques are subject to prior sale.

B-27
BRITISH MUSEUM PUBLICATIONS LTD.,
Dept. CC
6 Bedford Square
London WC1B 3RA, England

British Museum Replicas, free, published annually, 40 pages, illustrated, black and white.

This great museum offers reproductions of works of sculpture, seals, ivories, reliefs and jewelry in its collections. Examples include an ivory chess set dating from the twelfth century (single pieces are also available); the Great Seal of Elizabeth I, showing the Queen on horseback; the head of a horse from the East Pediment of the Parthenon; an enchanting glazed hedgehog from Egypt dating from about 1850 B.C.; a bronze Egyptian cat sporting earrings, and an Assyrian bas relief of a king hunting lions, one of several subjects from the Palace of Ashwibanipal at Nineveh. Among the pieces of jewelry are a superb Roman pendant of Medusa and a portrait pendant of Elizabeth I designed by Nicholas Hilliard to commemorate the defeat of the Armada. The jewelry is reproduced in gilded base metal, sterling silver, gold on sterling silver, or 9k. gold. Prices, given in pounds sterling, range from as low as $5 to as high as $500 and depend on the current rate of exchange.

BROOKLYN MUSEUM GALLERY SHOP,
Dept. CC
188 Eastern Parkway
Brooklyn, NY 11238

The Brooklyn Museum Gallery Shop Mail Order Catalogue, *30¢, published annually, 32 pages, illustrated, color.*

The Gallery Shop of the Brooklyn Museum is noted for its excellent selection of crafts from different countries, and though the Christmas catalogue is a more gift-oriented sampling, with ties, aprons, tote bags, place mats, glassware and ceramics with design motifs adapted from objects in the Museum's collections, there are quite a few items of interest to collectors. One is a reproduction of an early American pewter footed baptismal bowl, 6⅝'' in diameter by 4¾'' high, from an original made in Philadelphia between 1838 and 1842 ($70); another is a pewter inkstand or writing box (which could be used for cigarettes), the original of which was made by Henry Will between 1761 and 1793 and is the only known example of an incised American inkstand of this type ($100). There's a stunningly beautiful twenty-eight-tile set of porcelain ''Egyptian'' dominoes with incised hieroglyphics symbolizing good fortune, made by Vista Alegre, Portugal. The set comes in a silk-screened canvas container and costs $60. For the art-minded there's a portfolio of sixteen reproductions of photographs by the distinguished American photographer, Lewis W. Hine, suitable for framing ($15). The greeting and note cards from the Gallery Shop are especially attractive.

BUCK HILL ASSOCIATES, Dept. CC
Garnet Lake Road
Johnsburg, NY 12843

Posters of the Past, *25¢, published from time to time, 20 pages, illustrated, black and white.*

This interesting little catalogue lists slightly under 1,000 posters, handbills, broadsides, prints and advertisements, authentic reproductions that trace the political and social history of America from the earliest times to the recent past. Most are printed in black ink on white paper, like the originals. Posters printed on colored paper or in full color are so described. Among the offerings are early maps; a 1767 playbill for *Romeo and Juliet;* a list of prices, in beaver skins, for goods bought by Indians; a 1768 lottery ticket signed G. Washington, sold to build a road across the Cumberland Mountains, blown up to 10'' x 4'' (45¢); song sheets; recruiting posters and Civil War Battle Portfolios, etched by Currier & Ives, containing six 15'' x 11'' prints, hand-colored silk-screen engravings at $3.95 a portfolio, $19.50 for a set of the eight portfolios. Posters are divided by category: American Colonies, Revolutionary War, George Washington, Slavery, Civil War, Lincoln, Later 1800s, Wild West, Guns, Medicine-Dentistry, Circus, Turn of the Century, Automobiles, Movies and Miscellaneous. Prices range from 25¢ to around $3 for individual posters, and there is a $3.95

The striking shapes and colors of primitive masks from many different cultures and other folk art provide lively decoration for a small dining area designed by Theresa Capuana. Photographer: Otto Maya.

minimum order, plus 50¢ postage and handling. Buck Hill also has reprints and facsimiles of old books on cookery, housekeeping and eighteenth- and nineteenth-century schoolbooks, such as McGuffey's *Pictorial Eclectic Primer* (facsimile reprint at $2.50).

B-30
BURGUES, Dept. CC
183 Spruce Street
Lakewood, NJ 08723

Nature in Porcelain, $3, folder of 40 color illustrations and small fold-out brochure, lists of edition limits and prices.

Although the limited-edition porcelain sculptures of birds, flowers, fish and animals by artist Burgues are available only through franchised representatives, you can study them at leisure in this large and lavishly illustrated sampling of his work, enjoying the incredibly lifelike detail of a Baltimore oriole perched among mock orange blossoms, a water lily, veiltail goldfish, a snowy owl or bighorn sheep. The lists give the size of each edition (some now closed) and the prices of those still available, which range from $75 for a cymbidium orchid in an edition of 200 to $10,000 for the American wild goat, an edition of only 10, which was commissioned by the state of Montana to commemorate the Bicentennial. Many of the Burgues porcelains are in museums and collections.

B-31
BUTEN MUSEUM OF WEDGWOOD, Dept. CC
246 North Bowman Avenue
Merion, PA 19066

Brochure and publications list, free.

Publications available from the Buten Museum include *Wedgwood Guide to Marks and Dating,* compiled by David Buten, $3.50; *Wedgwood Rarities* by Harry M. Buten, with large-size illustrations of 400 rare Wedgwood items, $12; and *Wedgwood Fairyland Lustre* by Daisy Makeig-Jones, the 1921 catalogue by the artist and designer of this highly sought-after Wedgwood ware, reprinted in a facsimile edition, $6. The Museum also publishes an annual merchandise catalogue, available to Museum members only. Annual membership is $20, and a membership form is part of the brochure. More than 10,000 examples of Wedgwood are available for examination at the Museum, which is open Tuesday, Wednesday and Thursday, 2 to 5 P.M. and on Saturdays from 10 A.M. to 1 P.M., closed July, August and September. The sales desk, which is open to visitors, offers Wedgwood special issues, remainders, grade II wares, books and slides.

Wa-Pel-La, chief of the Musquakees, color print, produced by McKenny & Hall, 1836. W. Graham Arader, III, A-17.

Sculptor Harry Jackson's "Chief Washekie." Trailside Galleries, T-6.

33

Left, "Pooff," a cork ball table game using jets of air. World Wide Games, W-20.

Below, tarot cards reproduced from the fifteenth-century Visconti Sforza tarocchi deck. U.S. Games Systems, U-8.

C-1
CAMPAIGN AMERICANA, Dept. CC
P. O. Box 275
Merrick, NY 11566

Political Americana—Campaign Americana, 50¢ a copy or $2 yearly subscription for six issues, 12 pages.

Everything pertaining to political America, from ribbons, buttons, bumperstrips, badges and stick pins to a Peanut Power T-shirt and Nixon-Agnew ceramic elephant mug ($7.50). It's truly amazing what devices have been dreamed up to publicize the candidate. For $10 you can get a 1957 inaugural ball invitation, for $20 an FDR glass paperweight surrounded by a wreath.

C-2
DOUGLAS CAMPBELL CO., Dept. CC
Mill Hill
Denmark, ME 04022
and
31 Bridge Street
Newport, RI 02840

Antique Furniture Copies, $2, published annually, 36 pages, illustrated, black and white.

Douglas Campbell, a small company specializing in custom-made copies of fine American antiques of the seventeeth and eighteenth centuries, has showrooms and workshops in Newport, Rhode Island, and Denmark, Maine. Judging by the photographed pieces in the catalogue, the quality is high, the craftsmanship skilled and sensitive and the detailing exceptional. The periods and styles range from William and Mary and Queen Anne to Chippendale, the Brewster armchair, Windsor chairs, a tavern table, porringer table, pencil-post bed, Sheraton turned bed and a simple hired man's bed. Prices range from a high of $5,375 for a superb Dunlap chest-on-chest-on-frame in maple with hand carved and hand dovetailed case and drawers to around $285 for a fan-back Windsor chair, maple with pine seat, stained or painted to order. There are a couple of lovely shell-carved demi-dome corner or flat cupboards, a shell-carved entrance ($2,695) and a stunning Connecticut Valley entrance in carved wood with seventeeth- and eighteenth-century ar-

chitectural parts and assemblies made to order ($3,115). A magnificent collection for lovers of traditional furniture. Pieces can be ordered in wood and size of your choice, and all prices include delivery.

C-3
CAPE COD CUPOLA, CO., INC., Dept. CC
78 State Road
North Dartmouth, MA 02747

Catalogue, 50¢, published annually, 48 pages, illustrated, black and white and one color.

In addition to making ready-built and fully assembled Cape Cod cupolas, this company sells a wide variety of weathervanes—animals, fish, birds and boats—some silhouette, some full-bodied, in both copper and cast aluminum with a black finish. Most amusing is a 34″ x 19″ copper pig ($360, or $540 with 23k. gold leaf), and there's also a hand-hammered copper grasshopper, designed after the one atop Faneuil Hall in Boston, 34″ long by 14″ high, $472.50 (around $709 in gold leaf). Some of the full-bodied copper weathervanes are handmade on molds over a hundred years old. They also have wall eagles, flagpole ornaments and other outdoor accessories.

C-4
CAPITAURUS MUSIC, Dept. CC
P. O. Box 153
5497 Highway 9, South
Felton, CA 95018

CapiTaurus Folk Music Catalog & Almanac, $2, published annually, 41 pages, illustrated, black and white. Price includes supplements such as Folk Musical Instrument Kits, Contemporary Dulcimer Collective and CapiTaurus Quarterly.

Here's a catalogue with two purposes: to provide "source information, features, listings and question/answer referral service in the tradition of an almanac, and to offer early, ethnic, custom and discount folk musical instruments and related items for sale or trade through the mail." It does both well. The collector and musician will find zithers, harps, lutes, various other stringed instruments, drums, other miscellaneous percussion, kazoos, flutes, horns and reeds, also supplies including books,

Cover from book of French eighteenth-century clocks in the J. Paul Getty Museum, G-9.

"The Clock Book" of kits from Craft Products, C-35.

plans and accessories for anyone wishing to repair or build a musical instrument. Kits, recordings and related reading matter are also available, as are sources for finding hurdy-gurdys, custom flute and lute makers, and much more. The *Quarterly,* which also contains the price list for the master catalogue, has feature articles on specific instruments as well as items additional to the catalogue. Prices are reasonable.

C-5
CAROLINA ART ASSOCIATION/GIBBES ART GALLERY, Dept. CC
135 Meeting Street
Charleston, SC 29401

Price list, free.

Books about Charleston and South Carolina, including a limited-edition three-volume set comprising *Art in South Carolina 1670–1970, Contemporary Artists of South Carolina* and *South Carolina Architecture, 1670–1970,* issued for the Tricentennial. These are paperbacks and cost $22.50 a set, $15 for members. At this time, there's also a brochure showing a limited edition of 984 numbered sets of eight prints depicting life on a Carolina rice plantation, after the original watercolors by Charleston artist Alice Ravenel Huger Smith (1876–1958), $125 for the portfolio of eight prints, plus $2 mailing charge. These may not be in stock when you write, but other books on Charleston are reprinted periodically.

C-6
CAROL'S GIFT SHOP, Dept CC
17601 S. Pioneer Boulevard
Artesia, CA 90262

Seasonal newsletters, free.

The newsletters cover the lines of collectibles carried by Carol's Gift Shop—collectors' plates, bells, dolls, thimbles, fine porcelains and limited-edition figurines. Also supplied are brochures from leading companies in the field.

C-7
CARROLL SOUND, INC., Dept. CC
351 West 41st Street
New York, NY 10036

Carroll Sound Catalog, *free, 16 pages, plus insertions and price list, published annually, illustrated, black and white.*

If you're a collector of sounds, musical instruments from exotic places or percussion specialties, you'll find them here. Want to create a wind storm? Carroll has a genuine wind and storm machine for $79.45. Or, for the same price, you can hear an army of men come marching through your home. How about wind chimes or an authentic Chinese bell tree, also a handsome display piece, for $98.50? Name your favorite sound effect and this catalogue probably has the instrument with which to re-create it. There is a large collection of instruments from China, Japan, India, Africa and the West Indies, plus bells, whistles and horns of all kinds. Prices range from $1.20 for a small brass hand bell to $1,500 for a complete set of twelve steel drums. The catalogue copy, which details each item as well as its history, makes for fascinating reading and some "So *that's* how they do it!" comments.

C-8
THE CARTOGRAPHER, Dept. CC
114 East 61st Street
New York, NY 10021

Catalogues, $3 each, published approximately four times a year, illustrated, black and white.

Fine maps, atlases, geographies, voyages, travels, prints, natural history and the history of cartography are the subjects of these handsome, well-produced catalogues. Each entry is clear, concise and informative, and prices range from a few dollars into the thousands. The maps in a current catalogue are all of the western hemisphere and date from the mid-1600s to the mid-1800s. A scarce copy of Berry's 1680 map of North America, dedicated to King Charles II, is $775; a 1795 map of the West Indies is $110. Henry Popple's famous 1733 map of North America lists at $6,500. Another catalogue, entitled *Maps and Prints from the Voyages of James Cook, 1768–1780,* is a fascinating record of his voyages. Prices are moderate, under $200, with many under $20, and some entries are documented with quotations from Cook's journals. If you live in Hawaii, you might be particularly interested in the 1779 chart of the Sandwich Islands (Hawaii, Maui, Oahu, Kauai) third voyage (1785), with an inset chart of Karakakooa Bay where Cook was killed, 11¼'' x 19'', $125.

C-9
CAULDRON PROMOTIONS, Dept. CC
47 Landseer Road
London N19 4JG
England

Poster (and Prints) Catalogue, *$1, published periodically, 24 pages (plus loose pages), illustrated, black and white and color.*

Take your pick of a poster of four Dalmatian puppies, a nostalgic Beatles poster from the '60s, one of several motor racing action images, a reminder of the Grateful

Bread dough Christmas figures. Gifts from the Andes, G-10.

Facsimile of Washington Irving's 1875 first edition of "Old Christmas." Sleepy Hollow Restorations, S-21.

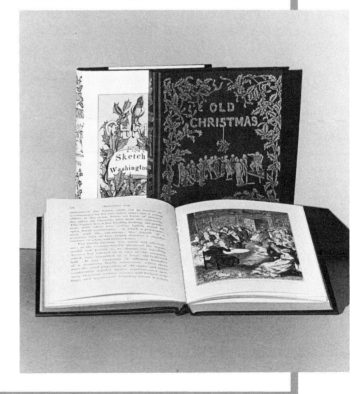

Dead or Jefferson Airplane rock concerts in San Francisco, an illustration from Beardsley's *Salome*, a fairy tale illustration. There are optic posters, tantra posters, psychedelic posters, surreal posters, posters for your sign of the zodiac and a variety of reproductions on parchment of old maps and documents. Prices range from about $1 to around $20 and in certain cases there are special rates, such as $8 for any twelve San Francisco posters. Postage and packing are extra.

C-10
THE CERAMIC BOOK COMPANY, Dept. CC
St. John's & Chepstow Roads
Newport, Gwent NPT 8GW
England

Price lists, free, published periodically.

The lists cover important books on all branches of antiques, new scarce and rare items, not only ceramics. Some of the more unusual on a current list were: *Chinese Art; The Minor Arts; Gold, Silver, Bronze, Cloisonné, Enamel, Lacquer, Wood,* a very scarce book with 202 illustrations, $90; *Oeuvres de Jean Pillement,* 101 engravings of Chinese figures and flowers of this distinguished French engraver, complete, 16'' x 12'', dated 1780, $90.50, which would be great for anyone interested in découpage. A fine source of reference for the serious collector.

C-11
NURHAN CEVAHIR, Dept. CC
Bekar Sokak 12/4
Beyoglu
Istanbul, Turkey

Nurpipe, free, published every three years, 24 pages, illustrated, black and white.

Turkey is the country of block meerschaum, and Mr. Cevahir specializes in handmade, hand-carved block meerschaum pipes, some plain, others so elaborately and finely carved as to be works of art. Among the head-style pipes are a laughing Bacchus ($18), a Viking, sultan, fisherman, Cleopatra, even Abraham Lincoln. Prices range according to size from around $5 to $22. Also shown and priced are some interesting cigarette and cigar holders, reasonable at $1 and $1.50, and a chess set (without board) for $50. Individual orders for pipes are sent by air parcel post, quantity orders by air cargo or surface freight (there's a ten percent discount for orders of more than 100 pipes). Mr. Cevahir informs us that pipes are free from duty in the U.S. but dutiable in Canada.

C-12
THE CHART HOUSE, Dept. CC
9255 Sunset Boulevard
Los Angeles, CA 90069

Flyers, free.

The Chart House offers a 20'' x 30'' full-color world map and a map of the U.S., framed in gold-trimmed walnut, with destination pins, line ruler and marking pen. Either map costs $16.95. Personalized versions are $18.95. In addition, the world map is available in a charted personalized version for $21.95. Maps are delivered ready to hang.

C-13
CHEROKEE STRIP LIVING MUSEUM, Dept. CC
Box 230
Arkansas City, KS 67005

No catalogue or brochure, but the Museum will supply on request sets of Cornish antique postcards, 1908–1910, $2.75 for large size, 95¢ for small; a book written by curator Herbert Marshall, *The History of the Cherokee Strip and The Cherokee Strip Museum,* 95¢; a Bicentennial cookbook by the Cher-O-Kan Gateway Association, $2.75; and note cards with black-and-white illustrations of Mr. Marshall's paintings of objects in the Museum, twelve for $1. Write for information on these and any other items available by mail.

C-14
CHESTERFIELD MUSIC SHOPS, INC., Dept. CC
12 Warren Street
New York, NY 10007

Brochure, free, issued three to four times a year.

Of interest to jazz buffs would be the jazz greats "Hall of Fame" recordings in the Chesterfield bulletins. Among those listed in the current bulletin are Red Nichols and his Five Pennies, Art Tatum and Mary Lou Williams, Duke Ellington and Earl "Fatha" Hines, sale priced at $2.49 each or three for $6.98.

C-15
CHESTNUT HILL STUDIO, LTD., Dept. CC
Box 907
Taylors, SC 29687

Chestnut Hill Studio, Ltd. Fine Miniatures, $3 (50¢ coupon good on first order), 44 pages, illustrated, black and white and color.

Handmade miniature furniture designed from examples of antiques in museums, reference books and private collections, all originals of the Chestnut Hill Studio and not sold

Above, American Indian pottery and jewelry from American Museum of Natural History, A-9. Below left, Mojave ''Cape'' design mosaic clock made by Senior Citizens Clock Factory; Colorado Indian Tribes Museum, C-29. Below right, Eskimo design needlepoint kit; Images North, I-2.

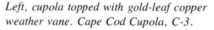
Pewter sundial after eighteenth-century original signed by Josiah Miller. Metropolitan Museum of Art, M-16.

Left, cupola topped with gold-leaf copper weather vane. Cape Cod Cupola, C-3.

Below, bronze sundial. Sundials & More, S-43.

elsewhere. The pieces are exactingly scaled (1'' to 1') and made in very limited quantities with meticulous attention to detail and craftsmanship—some have over 100 tiny individual pieces of wood, and many of the pine pieces are made from pine over 100 years old. In addition to miniature furniture, rugs, draperies, glassware, silverware, exquisite miniatures of Imari and blue-and-white, oil paintings, mirrors, chandeliers, lamps and a host of other accessories, there are rooms inspired by outstanding American interiors, carefully researched and accurate representations of the period. These rooms include a James River drawing room of the mid-eighteenth century, French Empire ballroom, Shaker room, ante-bellum bedroom, country pine kitchen and turn-of-the-century kitchen. Prices on these are broken down into individual furnishings and architectural details and range from about $1 for a pewter plate to almost $200 for the Oriental rug, 7'' x 11'', in the 1790 bedroom. You can special order small or large shadow-box rooms, on the same scale of 1'' to 1', to display your miniature collections, with interior painted or papered to your specification. And now you can even place a special order with Chestnut Hill to reproduce, in miniature, your own fine china. Sales are by mail order only. Satisfaction is guaranteed or your money refunded, provided the merchandise is returned within ten days in perfect condition and insured.

C-16
CHINACRAFT LTD., Dept. CC
130 Barlby Road
London W10 6BW / England

Chinacraft of London, *free, published biannually, 40 pages, illustrated, color.*

Chinacraft's catalogue has the finest English bone china, crystal, silver, collector's pieces and giftware by such famous firms as Wedgwood, Spode, Minton, Royal Doulton, Royal Crown Derby, Coalport, Aynsley, Crown Staffordshire, Royal Worcester and Waterford, each pattern or piece shown in color. In addition to china patterns, crystal, and silver place settings, there are Royal Doulton figurines, Coalport cottages, the Aynsley Animal Kingdom, Crown Staffordshire wall plates with reproductions of paintings by Renoir, Tenniel and Constable, sculptures in cold-cast bronze and limited-edition pieces by Royal Worcester and Hereford, such as the Duke of Marlborough on horseback, a Hereford barn owl or bull. With the catalogue comes a guide list of prices in U.S. dollars, but don't take them literally. Chinacraft, on receipt of your enquiry, will supply a detailed quotation based on the current exchange rate, shipping and insurance charges, together with an indication of the duty you would have to pay. Shipments are made by sea or air, as requested.

C-17
CHRISTIE'S CONTEMPORARY ART, Dept. CC
8 Dover Street
London W1 / England

Original Etchings, Lithographs, Etc., *free, published six times a year, 11 pages, illustrated, color.*

Christie's Contemporary Art is a subsidiary of the two-hundred-year-old auction house. Over eighty prints are reproduced in the catalogue. There are studies of the British coastline by John Brunsdon, moody landscapes by George Guest, a monochromatic study of lilies, views of places, figure compositions, studies of owls and other birds, a portrait of a lady in a hat. Some of the famous artists listed are Victor Pasmore, David Hockney, Barbara Hepworth, Pablo Picasso, William Scott and Henry Moore. Moore is represented by eleven lithographs including the *Helmet Head* series of 1974. All prints are in signed, limited, numbered editions. Prices are given for works unframed and framed and range from $80 to $5,200, which includes packing and delivery.

C-18
CHRISTIE'S SUBSCRIPTION DEPARTMENT,
Dept. CC
(Attention Mrs. D. Edwards)
White Brothers (Printers) Ltd.,
Offley Works / Prima Road
London SW9 0ND / England

Sale catalogues, by subscription. Illustrated, black and white and color.

The auction house of Christie, Manson & Woods International has been in business since 1766 and is known worldwide. Their catalogues are published regularly for sales in London and New York and can be subscribed to either by category (for instance, *Fine Eastern Rugs and Other Carpets,* $10, January to July) or in all categories, $2,301 for a year including post-sale price lists. An annual *Review* is also published at $35. Thousands of objects in every sort of category from great paintings to vintage cars are sold during each year, and while certain sales are in the stratospheric price range, as with all auction houses, many items can be bought for quite

reasonable prices. If you do not want to subscribe, but would like to buy one individual catalogue, you can write to Christie, Manson & Woods's U.S. office at 502 Park Avenue, New York, NY 10022.

C-19
CINCINNATI ART MUSEUM SHOP, Dept. CC
Eden Park
Cincinnati, OH 45202

Publications brochure, free.

The Museum Shop has no catalogue but will supply on request their publications brochure and accept orders, which should be placed directly with their Publications Clerk. Past and current publications, including those related to permanent collections and temporary exhibitions, are mostly paperback, with a few exceptions such as the *Sculpture Collection of the Cincinnati Art Museum, 1970,* $7.50. Among titles of interest to collectors are *Oriental Rugs in the Cincinnati Collections,* $5, a set of four books on exhibitions of twentieth-century Japanese prints from the Howard and Caroline Porter Collection, 75¢, and *Twentieth Century American Icons,* 25¢. Also available from the Publications Clerk are lists of color postcards of the Museum's major art works, 10¢ a card, and 35mm color slides, 50¢ each.

C-20
CJM ARMS
Division The Muller Co., Dept. CC
1801 S. Breton Place
Tucson, AZ 85710

Collectors Classics (Firearms), *24 pages, illustrated, color.* **The Americana Collection (Firearms),** *12 pages plus inserts, illustrated in monochrome.* **The Bicentennial Collection (Lanterns),** *8 pages, some color, illustrated, $2 for all three catalogues. Published annually.*

When is a gun not a gun? When it is one of the amazingly faithful non-firing reproductions from CJM Arms. In two of the catalogues, collectors will find precision-machined metal reproductions of historical firearms which can fool even the expert's eye. The guns and rifles are functional, for the most part, in every other respect. Costs are far below what the genuine firearm would sell for.

Collectors Classics features models and kits of flintlocks, Civil War guns, rifles, Derringers, Mausers, police guns, Revolutionary War grenadier swords, holsters, belt buckles, genuine issue German helmets, war flags and accessories. Framed replicas start at $49 for a handsomely mounted silver Derringer. The gun alone is about $23.95. Prices range up to around $240 for a reproduction of the 1777 Brown Bess musket.

The Americana Collection is devoted to meticulous reproductions of guns, rifles, wagon and pilot wheels and genuine powder flasks from America's past. There are also swords, pistol lamps and powder horns. Prices are very reasonable with the most expensive item an individually boxed 41″ samurai sword at $49.50.

Collectors of hand-wrought copper, brass and pewter lanterns will find a wide assortment in *The Bicentennial Collection*—whether it's a simple barn lantern ($43.50) or a lantern chandelier ($213). The collection is varied, attractive and moderately priced. The period represented is 1720–1820. All models are electrified.

C-21
CLASSIC CRAFTS, Dept. CC
P. O. Box 12
Point Clear, AL 36564

Mahogany Pieces by craftsman George DuBrock, *brochure, 25¢, illustrated, black and white.*

Small pieces of furniture of Honduras mahogany, designed along classic lines and available finished or in kit form (finishing materials are not included). Shown in the brochure are a footstool, fern or plant stands and a couple of good-looking collector's tables, regular and coffee-table height, to show off small collections under glass. The glass tops are hinged, fitted with lock and key, and the tray is lined with beige or black velvet (glass and velvet lining are not included with kits). No prices were listed on the brochure we received, so request a price list.

C-22
THE CLEVELAND MUSEUM OF ART SALES DESK, Dept. CC
11150 East Boulevard
Cleveland, OH 44106

Free lists of reproductions, exhibition catalogues, *books, slides.*

Among the exhibition catalogue subjects offered by the Cleveland Museum are Iranian art, twentieth-century design in the U.S., Van Gogh, Dutch drawings, Constable sketches, ancient Indian sculpture and lithography. Color reproductions include works by Burchfield, Cézanne, Degas, El Greco, Eakins, Gorky, Ingres, Monet, Picasso, Rembrandt, Renoir, Turner and Van Gogh, with Persian painting and sculpture, an Iranian relief, French missal illuminations and Chinese porcelain. Their list of books covers European painting before 1500, the Museum collection, French, English and American etching from 1850 to 1950, Rodin sculptures in the Museum collection, Japanese decorative arts and Fabergé and his contemporaries. Prices vary from 15¢ to $40, plus postage and handling.

C-23
CLEVELAND MUSEUM OF NATURAL HISTORY, Dept. CC
Wade Oval, University Circle
Cleveland, OH 44106

Christmas at the Ark in the Park, $1.25, published *annually, 8 pages, illustrated, black and white.*

Reproduction jewelry, plates decorated with dinosaurs, tote bags, posters, puzzles, boxes of silver and abalone shell from Mexico, pendants and necklaces from Teheran, one-of-a-kind American Indian jewelry, and delightful wooden napkin rings of six different dinosaurs are among the many items listed by the Museum of Natural History. Prices vary from $1.50 to $35, and there is a small additional charge for postage and handling.

C-24
COLBERT GALLERY, Dept. CC
8271 Melrose Avenue, Suite 101
Los Angeles, CA 90046

Original Graphics, 20th Century European Art *Posters, Turn-of-the-Century European Posters,* *loose pages in a portfolio, $2, published annually,* *illustrated, black and white and color.*

For the lover of nineteenth-century posters there are French examples advertising novels, operas, art exhibitions, aperitifs and casinos—all in the vivid, fluid style of the period and all in the original printings. From this century there are posters announcing exhibitions at museums and galleries of work by Erté, Beatrix Potter, Munch, Robert Delaunay, Cartier-Bresson, Chagall, Miró, Bonnard, Adami, Lichtenstein, Braque, Hockney. There are original graphics by Alechinsky, Matta, Lurçat and Tapiès and lesser known artists. Prices range from $5 to $450.

C-25
THE COLLECTOR'S CABINET, Dept. CC
153 East 57th Street
New York, NY 10022

Mother Earth Catalog, 50¢, 24 pages, illustrated, *color. Sea Shell Catalog, 50¢, 42 pages, no illustrations. A Collector's Guide to Sea Shells, by* *Jerome M. Eisenberg, $1, 26 pages, illustrated,* *black and white. Exotic Butterflies Catalog, 25¢,* *12 pages, no illustrations.*

The aim of Jerome Eisenberg, director and founder of The Collector's Cabinet, is to popularize the beauty of the earth's natural treasures and to encourage intelligent collecting. Branches of The Collector's Cabinet in six states sell thousands of items for the beginning collector and

Above, butterflies, beetles, shells and friends . . . and left, fossils and minerals, all from the vast collection at the Collector's Cabinet, C-25.

Rosettes of Oklahoma rose rock—clusters of barite crystals. Rose Rock Company of Oklahoma, R-20.

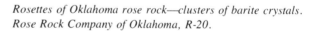

Life-size card sculpture of a bird in a mobile kit. Ariel, A-18.

Horus Falcon, Egyptian, 8'' high, original in the Louvre, Paris, reproduced in Alvastone. Museum Collections, M-28.

''The Robin'' porcelain plate by Boehm. Lenox China, L-7.

museum-quality objects in all price ranges from over 200 worldwide sources. Excellent color photographs in the Mother Earth Catalog show a carefully selected and tempting sampling of natural-history objects. Exotic butterflies in curved glass plaques, shadow boxes and frames, or pinned to cork disks in clear plastic specimen boxes are reasonably priced. Plaques run from $6 to $30 for an extra-large plaque with ten or more butterflies, framed butterflies from $6 to $60, shadow boxes from $8.50 to $50 and the plain plastic boxes from 50¢ for a mini-box to $15 for four or five exotic species from Mexico, Taiwan, Peru, Malaysia or Africa. There are wild flowers from Utah in metal or plastic frames, sea shells from the Pacific, sea life in frames and shadow boxes or mounted, mineral and stone eggs, slices and slabs of agate, fossil fish and ferns, paperweights of crystal-clear plastic enclosing a butterfly, sea horse, crab or scarab, priced from $5 to $10. Perhaps most fascinating of all are the ''scenes from Mother Earth''—serpentine jade that looks like a miniature mountain (6'' high, $15), Taiwan ''picture marble'' resembling trees on a snow-covered mountainside, a battery-operated clock made from scenic sandstone from Utah ($50 to $60, according to size). Exotica as beautiful as sculpture include deer antlers from Malaysia and Taiwan, on black Lucite or wood bases ($30); a gracefully curved, polished ox horn; a 16'' to 20'' sawfish beak edged with triangular teeth, mounted on a black Lucite base; and a milky-white ostrich egg shell from South Africa ($15). For postcard collectors, wildflowers, leaves, ferns and other botanical specimens, laminated on deckle-edged cards, are 50¢ each or $6 a boxed set of twelve. Among the display pieces sold by The Collector's Cabinet are well-designed, simple specimen holders in Lucite and brass, from 75¢ to $15 for an acrylic four-specimen holder, and Mexican glass-and-brass boxes and vitrines.

The *Sea Shell Catalog* lists and prices over 1,700 species of shells, various kinds of aquatic life (coral, sea urchins, barnacles, sponges, shark jaws and small stuffed sharks, even man-eating piranhas) and gives a selection of recommended books on the subject. Mr. Eisenberg's own booklet, *A Collector's Guide to Sea Shells,* illustrates 201 species of shells, the author's choice of a representative collection of more than 90,000 different species, with emphasis on the more colorful and exotic shells of the Indo-Pacific region. Each shell is shown in a black-and-white photograph, with a brief description of the shell and where it is to be found, average measurement and fair selling price.

Exotic Butterflies is a revised price list of butterflies and insects. All butterflies are fully spread and pinned to cork disks in clear polystyrene boxes.

C-26
COLLECTORS' GUILD, LTD., Dept. CC
185 Madison Avenue
New York, NY 10016

Collectors' Guild, $1, published quarterly, 35 pages, illustrated, color.

Lavishly illustrated catalogues of paintings, sculptures (both originals and reproductions), prints, jewelry, artificial flowers, porcelain, weavings, stained glass, beadwork, crystal and other items. The 1978 catalogue has lithographs signed on the stone by such notable artists as Joan Miró, Alexander Calder, Robert Indiana and Jasper Johns. The Indiana and Johns are $75 each, framed. A stone-signed Calder, *Autumn Harvest,* is $95; a pencil-signed Calder, *Pyramid,* in an edition of 100, $750; plate-signed etchings by Renoir, $115, and Dali, $65. Animal lovers will find a large selection of sculptures, paintings, prints and jewelry. There are rams' heads in sterling, signed and numbered by the artist, which can be worn as a belt buckle or a pendant ($311); a tiger painted in oil on a marble plaque in a limited edition of 250 signed by the artist ($65); a pewter cougar on a marble base ($50); a signed dove cast in Foundry-stone ($55). A

horse by Kaiko Moti, hand-cast and signed by the artist, 12″ high, sells for $195. Owl collectors will find owl sculptures, an owl bracelet, a "Wise Owl" in crystal ($40) and an owl ashtray. For collectors of paperweights, there's a Caithness crystal paperweight by Royal Worcester showing a yellow flower "in the rain" ($80). There are also some interesting Far West items and American Indian artifacts such as woodblock engravings by Frederick Remington, small sculptures of cowboys and buffalos, beaded belt buckles and a woven reproduction of a Navajo sand painting. Extra charges are given after price, and there are bonus gifts such as tote bags and art books.

C-27
THE COLONEL'S HOBBY, Dept. CC
8 Shawnee Trail
Harrison, NY 10528

The Miniature Silver of Guglielmo Cini, $1 and stamped self-addressed envelope, published periodically, 10 pages, black and white, illustrated.

The Colonel's hobby must be quite profitable, as you are asked to pay $1 (non-refundable with purchase) and send

Chinese dragon porcelain by Ispansky from Wakefield-Scearce Galleries, W-2.

a stamped envelope for a tiny 2¾″ x 4¼″ booklet with seven blurred black-and-white shots of a sweetmeat dish, round salver, fruit bowl, candelabra, candlestick, oblong tray, and sauceboat and tray, all miniatures by American silversmith Guglielmo Cini of antique silver museum pieces. Prices of the minatures make more sense, from $5 for the sweetmeat dish to $30 for a pair of candelabra.

C-28
COLONIAL WILLIAMSBURG FOUNDATION,
Dept. CC
Craft House
Williamsburg, VA 23185

Williamsburg Reproductions—Interior Designs for Today's Living, $4.95, published annually, 286 pages, illustrated, color. *A Selection of Gifts from Colonial Williamsburg,* free with the major catalogue, published for Christmas, 40 pages, illustrated, color.

Williamsburg Reproductions is a huge, beautiful, complete catalogue of all the Colonial Williamsburg reproductions—superb period furniture, wallpapers, fabrics, decorative hardware, candlesticks and lanterns, decorative pieces in brass, wood, porcelain, maps and prints, reproduction silver, pewter, glassware, china and pottery for the table. There's also a potpourri of good little gifts such as trivets, pins, needlepoint kits, record albums, games and puzzles, and books and publications relating to all aspects of Williamsburg. Of particular interest to the collector is the Bicentennial Collection—Royal Doulton porcelain figures of soldiers of the Revolution, a set of thirteen state seal commemorative plates made by Wedgwood and based on the rare original Virginia plate in the Colonial Williamsburg collection ($375 the set) and a copy of the Paul Revere sterling silver porringer ($500). Among the many other catalogue items that would appeal to collectors are Delftware, Chinese export porcelain, old maps, a limited edition of wildlife prints by John A. Ruthven, silver, glass wine rinsers in jewel tones of amethyst, aquamarine, amber and sapphire ($15.30 each) and the earthenware and saltglazed stoneware reproductions. The second catalogue has mostly gifts selected from the main collection—flower and fruit prints; reproductions of twelve hand-colored engravings by an eighteenth-century London horticulturist, each depicting a month of the year; fox hunt prints from originals by Robert Sayer of London ($24 each, $47 the pair); "character" Toby jugs of craftsmen made by Royal Doulton (from $14.80 to $31); stunning brass and wrought steel reproductions of antique kitchen utensils; the Wythe House clock, handrubbed mahogany with modern mechanisms, eight-day key-wound (nonstriking, $428, striking, $598); small gifts such as brass copies of pipe tampers in harlequin and lady's slipper shapes ($4.80 each) and a good assortment of Christmas cards, engagement calendars, note cards, place mats and tea towels.

C-29
COLORADO RIVER INDIAN TRIBES MUSEUM,
Dept. CC
Rte. 1, Box 23-B
Parker, AZ 85344

Price list, free.

The Colorado River Indian Tribes Museum is a repository for the arts and crafts of four tribes: Mojave, Chemehuevi, Navajo and Hopi. Clock collectors will find four unusual designs handmade by the Senior Citizens Clock Factory. Each design relates to the traditions of one of the tribes. Prices range from $24 to $75, depending on the size of the clock face. Pottery sculptures made by Elmer Gates of the Mojave tribe feature animals, effigies, jugs and dolls and are priced from $20. Rag dolls are available for less. Unfortunately there are no illustrations of Mr. Gates's work. The museum will also send you a brief history of each tribe and its cultural background.

C-30
COMMEMORATIVE IMPORTS, Dept. CC
Box D
Bayport, MN 55003

Commemorative Imports, free, published semiannually, 44 pages, illustrated, black and white.

A complete range of collectors' plates, from first editions of each series to current offerings, Anri to Wedgwood; bells, mugs and Christmas ornaments are also clearly presented and priced in this compact catalogue. Prices for plates range from $10 to $1,500 and include cost of packing, shipping and insurance. Commemorative Imports will buy or trade for plates they need (those they are especially interested in are marked "write"). They also have books for collectors, hardwood plate frames, plate stands and egg stands. Prices and details on request.

C-31
CONDOR ART, Dept. CC
P. O. Box 8054
Fountain Valley, CA 92708

Price list, $1, refundable with purchase, revised quarterly.

Condor specializes in wildlife and western collector prints in limited editions, priced from $40 to $225. Among artists represented are Charles Fracé, Peter Parnall, Arthur Singer, Frank McCarthy and James Bama.

C-32
CORCORAN SHOP, Dept. CC
  Corcoran Gallery of Art
  17th Street & New York Avenue, N.W.
  Washington, DC 20006

  List of current publications, free.

The Art Gallery shop offers exhibition catalogues, such as *The Nation's Capital in Photographs,* 1976, a series of eight 23-page booklets of black and white photographs by such distinguished photographers as Robert Cummings, Lee Friedlander and Lewis Baltz ($2.25 each), *Kenneth Noland—a Retrospective,* 1977, 160 pages, fifty-three black and white, seventy-one color ($9.95) and *Anamorphoses—Games of Perception and Illusion in Art,* 1977, black and white and color illustrations with a mylar sheet for viewing these fascinating distortions in art ($5.95). They also have postcards in black and white and color from the Corcoran collection (10¢ and 15¢), slides, a series of striking Graphicards with envelopes, ten to a package ($8) and reproductions of the Corcoran's paintings, prints of works by such artists as Degas, Boudin, Mary Cassatt, Edward Hopper and James Peale, ranging in price from 50¢ to $24. Their list of posters of past exhibitions varies in price. *Palladio in America,* 1976, offset, is $1.50; *Lowell Nesbitt,* 1973, lithograph, is $10 unsigned, $100 signed.

C-33
CORNER BOOK SHOP, Dept. CC
  102 Fourth Avenue
  New York, NY 10003

  Food & Drink, *$1, refundable with purchase, 20 pages.*

Most of the books relating to food and drink are rare, out-of-print or one-of-a-kind, so chances are that if you are looking for something special such as the Urbain-Dubois *Household Cookery-Book,* 1871, the first English translation (Chicago 1936) of the Apicius *Cookery and Dining in Imperial Rome,* early American cookbooks by Eliza Leslie, Lydia Child and Sarah Rorer, or André Simon's *History of the Wine Trade in England,* you will find it here.

C-34
COTTAGE CASTINGS, Dept. CC
  1580 Mossrock Place
  Boulder, CO 80302

  Cottage Castings, *$1, refundable with purchase, 17 pages, illustrated, black and white and color.*

A delightful catalogue illustrated with old steel engravings from German catalogues of 1919, showing the ¾ round lead-tin alloy figures in actual size. The castings are done one at a time from molds made in Germany just after World War I, and are entirely hand painted. Subjects include domestic and wild birds and animals, trees, cowboys and Indians, knights, athletes, soldiers and sailors. A nativity group of eleven pieces with a wonderful star (sold only as a set) costs $49.95. A palm tree or giraffe is $4.50, a sailing ship, $17.50, a Prussian soldier mounted on a horse, $9.95. Prices include shipping and handling.

C-35
CRAFT PRODUCTS, Dept. CC
  2200 Dean Street
  St. Charles, IL 60174

  Doll Houses and Furnishings, *48 pages,* **The Clock Book,** *100 pages and* **Home Ideas Book,** *104 pages, $1 for all three catalogues, published annually, illustrated, color and black and white.*

In the doll house catalogue there are doll houses of various types (town house, Williamsburg, Cape Cod, ranch, Victorian) in kit form, furnishings both ready-made and to make, every kind of imaginable accessory in miniature (even foods), doll-size toys and musical instruments, handmade doll families from Germany, one old-fashioned, the other up-to-date, and replicas of antique dolls made in Arkansas. Among the more interesting miniatures are black cast-iron stoves, $2.75 for a real old-time cook stove, $1.98 for a pot-bellied stove, and cast-iron cookware to match, all kinds of working light fixtures in kit form, miniature Williamsburg wallpapers and a miniature dappled hobby horse made of lead like the bygone toys. There are even the makings of a miniature English pub in this little catalogue. The clock book features, naturally, all kinds of clock kits, with different movements, chimes and dials shown separately. Grandfather clocks, shelf clocks, school clocks, steeple clocks, regulator clocks, they are all here, along with the necessary supplies, even professional sanders. Craft Products also offers finished clocks—a steeple clock is around $140, an Eli Terry clock around $248—and books on clock construction and collecting.

   The third catalogue is basically home-oriented. Some pieces, such as a spoon rack, corner shelf, what-not and curio cabinet, all designed to be made from patterns, could display collections.

C-36
CRANBROOK EDUCATIONAL COMMUNITY,
  Dept. CC
  500 Lone Pine Road
  Bloomfield Hills, MI 48013

  Cranbrook Institute of Science List of Publications, *free, published annually, 4 pages.*

Miniature Philadelphia ballroom in the French Empire style. Chestnut Hill Studio, C-15.

The books on the list of publications cover such subjects as anthropology, botany, geology and mineralogy, museology and zoology; they include *The Iroquois* by Frank G. Speck, a 95-page paperback by one of the country's great anthropologists ($2), a history of the founding of the Cranbrook Institute of Science and its first twenty-five years, and quite a few works on Michigan flora. Prices range from $1 to $9.

C-37
CRDO HANDICRAFTS, Dept. CC
    P. O. Box 5861
    Tsim Sha Tsui Post Office
    Kowloon, Hong Kong

    CRDO Handicrafts, $1, published annually, 12 pages, illustrated, black and white.

While most of the handicrafts shown in the pages of the slim CRDO (China Refugee Development Organization) catalogue are strictly of the souvenir-shop or gift type—brass and ivory paper knives, plain and engraved ivory chopsticks, teakwood salad bowls and pewter ashtrays—there are some bronze pieces that look more interesting, such as a set of ten ancient coins, a Ming-period type drinking vessel, 6'' high, and a door knocker in the shape of a Mandarin head, each one modestly priced at just over $6. Collectors of ship models will find a Chinese junk and a Hong Kong sampan in various sizes, ranging in price from an 8'' junk at around $2.40 to an 18'' model at around $7. Items are dutiable, and postage and insurance is billed upon receipt of order. Delivery takes three to four weeks.

C-38
CREATIVE NEEDLE, Dept. CC
    Box 8104
    Dallas, TX 75205

    Creative Needle, $2, published annually, 36 pages, illustrated, black and white.

Needlepoint designs of all kinds from Oriental to nature motifs to unusual combinations of quilt, ribbon and gingham designs. There are some intriguing mini-picture designs that can be displayed in Lucite picture stands, miniature rugs for doll houses, 5'' x 7'', and an amusing map of Texas with symbols of past and present traditions, 15'' square. Each design is keyed, presumably to a price list, but as this was not included with the catalogue we received, we can't give a price range for the kits.

C-39
CROSBY BOOKS, Dept. CC
P.O. Box 100
Fishguard, Wales 4B
Great Britain

New, Secondhand & Rare Books on Oriental Carpets, *free, published annually.*

A small but invaluable catalogue for the serious collector of books published in various countries on oriental carpets. The current catalogue lists 182 books, some out of print, each one carefully described, rated for condition from AA (new or as new) to FF (bad), and priced in pounds sterling. Crosby specializes in new, secondhand and rare books on oriental rugs, issues yearly catalogues and welcomes requests to be placed on the mailing list. They also have a special scheme for those who wish to sell out-of-print books. Rather than being bought outright for stock, they are sold at catalogue prices and the seller receives a percentage of the sale, starting at 80 percent of the catalogue price for books worth $20 to $400. One of the unusual books listed is *Turkoman Carpets* by Siawosch Azadi, based on his 1970 monograph and issued for the first time in English. Fifty-five rugs are shown in color, all specially photographed for the edition, which was published by The Crosby Press in hardcover, price around $50.

C-40
THE CURRENT COMPANY, Dept. CC
P.O. Box 46
Bristol, RI 02809

Pen & Pencil, *$1, 34 pages.*

For autograph collectors, more than 350 letters, manuscripts and autographs are documented in this slim volume. Prices range from $2 for the signature of Julian Huxley to $8,000 for a letter from Benjamin Franklin to his English friend and correspondent, David Hartley, to $18,500 for a letter from George Washington to Vice-President John Adams about Adams's son, John Quincy Adams, with a reference to the Jay Treaty. The Current Company, which is listed under Antiquarian Booksellers, also has catalogues on first editions and other rare books.

C-41
THE CURRIER GALLERY OF ART, Dept. CC
192 Orange Street
Manchester, NH 03104

British Pewter 1600-1850, *$2, 42 pages, illustrated, black and white.* ***19th Century American Painting from the Collection of Henry Melville Fuller,*** *$2.50, 94 pages, illustrated, black and white.*

These two exhibition catalogues are fine reference sources for collectors of pewter and nineteenth-century paintings. The pewter catalogue discusses flagons, tankards, ecclesiastical pieces, wine measures, baluster measures (named for their baluster shape), along with other types of measures, dishes, chargers, plates, bowls, salts, candlesticks, etc. The painting catalogue, with an introduction by William H. Gerdts, Jr., illustrates paintings by such artists as Albert Bierstadt, Frederic E. Church, Thomas Cole, Martin Johnson Heade and Eastman Johnson.

Nineteenth-century-style stoneware butter crock and jug with blue designs. Hale Farm and Village, H-2.

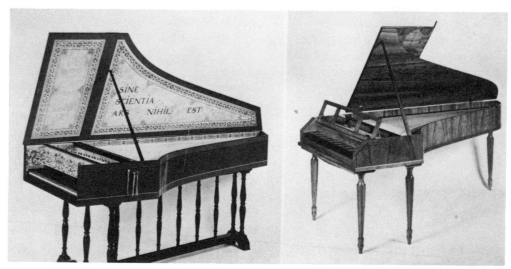

Harpsichord and fortepiano kits from Frank Hubbard, H-31.

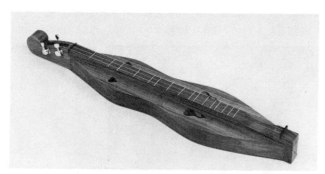

Banjo kit. Stewart-MacDonald, S-36.

Dulcimer kit. Woodcraft Collection, National Handcraft Institute, N-5.

Chinese tom-toms. Carroll Sound, C-7.

D-1
DAIRY SERVICES, INC., Dept. CC
P. O. Box 253
Bluffton, IN 46714

Price list, 25¢.

Anyone for milk cans and bottles? This company sells (both retail and wholesale) unpainted milk cans with lids in three-, five- and ten-gallon sizes, and a creamer that looks like a pitcher with a 4″ neck opening and loop handle. Price for any one of these is $11.95 in East and Central time zones, $12.95 in Mountain and Pacific time zones, ppd. There are various types, shapes and sizes of milk bottles, ranging in price from around $1.50 to $8.50 ppd. in Indiana and neighboring states, slightly higher in other zones. Bottles may be combined for a quantity discount of one dozen bottles at half price.

D-2
SALVADOR DALI MUSEUM, Dept. CC
24050 Commerce Park Road
Beachwood, OH 44122

Price list, 5¢, published three times a year.

This museum specializes in works by and about the famed Spanish painter, Salvador Dali, with a large number of books available only from the museum. A Fiftieth Anniversary issue of French *Vogue* with an original etching laid in, signed and numbered, is priced at $500, while reproductions can be bought for as little as 75¢. There are a number of lithographic posters listed, along with many original graphic works, both signed by the artist and plate signed, and a limited-edition wall tapestry after the famous painting, "Persistence of Memory" ($5,000). You can also buy greeting cards, photographs, slides, puzzles, limited-edition sculptures, neckties, plates and medallions, and postcards.

D-3
THE DANCE MART, Dept. CC
Box 48
Homecrest Station
Brooklyn, NY 11229

The Dance Mart, free, 12 pages, published twice a year, black and white.

A chockful book list covering all aspects of dance technique and studies: ballet, mime, folk and ethnic, modern dance, jazz dance, ballroom, tap, acrobatic and gymnastic and religious dance. There are also books on dance for children, anatomy for the dancer, dance therapy, as well as more general works. All are books in print and sold at publishers' list price.

D-4
DEBRETT'S PEERAGE, LTD., Dept. CC
67 Parchment Street
Winchester SO23 8AT / England

Debrett Ancestry Research, and Debrett Ancestry Research & Travel, $1, updated periodocially, each 12 pages.

The two booklets outline the services provided by Debrett, a name that is practically synonymous with genealogy, and has been ever since 1769, when John Debrett started delving into the subject. Once Debrett chronicled only British royalty and aristocracy, but now anyone may engage their services to research ancestry and family trees. The first booklet describes the process and tells what information is needed from you to start the research, which is handled in Britain and Europe by the Winchester office, in North America by Debrett Ancestry Research, Suite 303E, 200 Park Avenue, New York, NY 10017. There are also offices on the West Coast and in Canada. For those who would like to make a pilgrimage to the homes of their ancestors in the U.K. and study ancient family documents, Debrett has teamed with British Airways to provide ancestral tours, which are outlined on the back page of the second booklet. On the back page of the first booklet is a list of publications from Debrett, such as the famous reference work, *Debrett's Peerage and Baronetage* ($95) and *Debrett's Correct Form*, a guide to everything from drafting wedding invitations to addressing an Archbishop, and other niceties of social and professional etiquette ($12). In the U.S., these can be ordered from Arco Publishing Co. Inc., 219 Park Avenue South, New York, NY 10003.

This totally symmetrical cluster of art, figures, small objects and furniture by designers R&R Robinson is anchored by the large central painting. To work out the best possible arrangement, lay pictures flat on the floor and take measurements of the distances between them before hanging. Photographer: Grigsby.

HOW TO HANG AND DISPLAY PICTURES

Start with the basic equipment needed for picture hanging. First, a friend, preferably one with a good eye for placement, so you can take turns holding, adjusting and viewing. Next, inanimate objects: a hammer with claw (as you may need to remove a nail); picture hangers or nails, the size depending on the weight of the pictures; a measuring tape or yardstick to measure distances from ceiling to frame top and from wall to frame side, or from picture to picture; masking tape if your wall is likely to flake or crumble (stick a piece of masking tape where the nail will go and hammer nail rapidly, like a woodpecker); transparent nylon line to replace wire if this will be exposed, as you want to minimize it. For light pictures, you can buy packets of hooks on tape that stick to the wall, labeled with the weight they can support, but there is one drawback—the glue on the tape tends to dry out and the hook falls off the wall. A special picture hanger and nail is preferable.

If your picture is not already wired and ready to hang, measure the distance from the top of the frame and mark each side for the hole where the screw-eye will go, to make sure the holes line up. Make holes in the frame with a small awl, insert screw-eyes, then tighten them by placing a nail through the eye and turning it. Be sure not to use screw-eyes that are too long or large for the frame, or they may come through the front. The tightened screw-eyes should be at a diagonal, pointing toward the center top of the frame, where the pull of the wire or nylon line will be. Attach the wire or line and then hang the picture from your finger to make sure that the "give" won't expose the wire above the top of the frame when the picture is hung. For a protective touch, glue small circles of felt to the two back bottom corners of the frame, where they will touch the wall.

The next step is to consider the placement of the picture you want to hang in relation to the whole room. Place the picture on a chair or against the wall on which you'll hang it and do a 360 degree turn to see how it looks in relation to the rest of the room. Now leave the room, come back, and observe how the picture looks in relation to adjoining rooms. You can establish "prospects" for a picture in terms of viewing distance and color impact. A touch of yellow in a still-life, for instance, might echo a yellow wall or chair in an adjoining room.

The classic rule when hanging pictures is to place them at eye level, which means, roughly, that your eye will hit the center of the picture, but as people differ in height, a better rule-of-thumb is to hang the picture at a height harmonious with all the other objects in that part of the room. You should also consider whether the picture will normally be viewed from a standing or sitting position.

When it comes to choosing the best location, the eye is always the best judge. While symmetry may dictate that a painting be hung in the exact center of a wall, if there happens to be a door in the wall about three feet from one corner and a sofa or table in the center of the remaining unbroken expanse of wall, the painting would look ridiculous if it were hung as though the door weren't there. An exception would be if the nature and strength of the painting made it necessary to ignore the door and furniture in order to relate the painting to other elements on the wall. Rules can always be broken.

Take into account the relationship of the picture to the ceiling, floor, windows, furniture and other works of art when you align it. Again, your eye should be the judge, as a floor or ceiling can be out of plumb and the picture should appear straight to the eye and also reinforce the horizontal lines of other objects in the room, such as the top of a sofa or table or the top and hem of curtains.

When hanging a picture next to others, choose something to line it up with—either the vertical side or horizontal top or bottom of adjoining works, or the inner sides of a mat, if the works are matted. A group of pictures should anchor one another and not just dance about all over the wall. Before hanging a group of pictures, lay them flat on the floor in order to work out the best possible arrangement, and then group them that way on the wall.

As an alternative to hanging pictures on the wall (and to avoid the problem of nails and holes), consider building a shallow shelf with a slight lip in the front, like that of a school blackboard, along one wall of an otherwise pictureless room. The shelf can be made of wood, painted or papered to match the wall, or even of gleaming metal or transparent plexiglass. You might emulate the Japanese and display just one picture at a time, changing it periodically. Another nice way to display one painting at a time is on an easel. This switching around is the only way to display prints, watercolors or drawings, all of which tend to fade when exposed to strong light. They should be circulated and replaced every few weeks.

Asymmetrical or unbalanced arrangement of original prints in the conversation corner of a living room designed by Joseph Braswell, ASID, reinforces the horizontal line of the major seating piece. This is an effective way to draw attention to graphics of a spare, almost Oriental simplicity that might get lost in a larger wall grouping. Courtesy: Celanese House.

D-5
DELTA INTERNATIONAL, Dept. CC
Box 361
Lafayette, CA 94549

German World Wars I and II War Relics, *free, published seasonally, 20 pages, illustrated, black and white.*

Militaria, with emphasis on the Third Reich, is the theme of this grisly little catalogue, with such things as Waffen SS volunteer officer's collar tabs, epaulets, sleeve patches, panzer death's-head pins of silvered metal, storm trooper armbands, various badges, orders and medals. Almost all the entries are German, with the exception of a Japanese Imperial battle flag of the rising sun, Soviet Russian red star pins and old Ku Klux Klan member tokens. One item of real interest is a reproduction from the original dies of the famous Blue Max worn by the aces of Imperial Germany in World War I, in the correct shade of Prussian blue cloisonné, $14.50 with either neck ribbon or chain. For $245 (with one-week inspection privilege) you can get the *Deutschland Erwache* standard carried at the Nuremberg Party rallies by troopers of the SA and SS. The tone of this catalogue is best summed up in the copy for a $5.98 recording: "Sieg Heil! Songs of the Third Reich. Yes!! Now for the first time you can listen to the *original* spirit-stirring military music of the Third Reich in living *Stereophonic Sound!!* . . . such as Adolf Hitler's very own personal march 'From Finland to the Black Sea' . . . in total, 13 original songs in stereo just exactly as heard by the people and soldiers of Hitler's Germany!!''

D-6
JAMES DeNINNO & CO., Dept. CC
Suite 5—Pike Building
Viewmont Village
Scranton, PA 18508

Brochures, free.

The brochures are for U.S. coins, such as a Treasury collection of six obsolete silver coins minted early in this century.

D-7
THE DENVER ART MUSEUM, Dept. CC
100 West 14th Avenue Parkway
Denver, CO 80204

The Denver Art Museum, *brochure, free, 5 pages, illustrated, black and white.*

A list of exhibition catalogues and special publications including a *Guide to the Collection* with 8 color and 289 black-and-white illustrations, 216 pages, $4.95. *South Asian Sculpture* deals with the "impact of Indian art and culture on that of Nepal and Indonesia," 37 duotone illustrations, 48 pages, $4.50. *Quilts and Coverlets* discusses nineteenth- and twentieth-century examples from the Museum's collection, 8 color and 100 black-and-white illustrations, 144 pages, $6.50. A series of 119 leaflets dealing with the American Indian in North America is available at $14 or individually from 15¢ to 50¢. A small charge is made for postage and handling.

D-8
DESERT BOTANICAL GARDEN, Dept. CC
P.O. Box 5415
Phoenix, AZ 85010

Books, Seeds, Et Cetera, *free, published annually, 4 pages.*

On the price list from the Desert Botanical Garden Bookshop are books on Arizona, American Indians, the plants, flowers and wild life of the desert, gardening, uses of plants for food and dyes, and three local cookbooks; *Arizona Cookbook* ($3.25), *Cactus Cook Book* ($2.25) and *Western Mexican Cook Book* ($1.75). The bookshop can also supply fresh seeds packaged at the garden for cactus mixtures and wildflowers. For collectors of unusual prints and posters: the Agave (Century Plant) symbol in greens and red on a buff background, 22'' x 34'', $3.50 ppd.; a reproduction of John Miller's 1758 hand-colored engraving of *Agave americana* in bloom, limited and numbered edition, 18'' x 23'', $10.50 ppd.; and a portfolio, *Arizona Flora Suite,* of eight signed prints of Arizona plants by botanical artist Wendy Hodgson, edition limited to 100 numbered sets, 17'' x 14'', $100 ppd. and insured—available at the time of writing, but subject to prior sale.

D-9
DESPARD DESIGNS, Dept. CC
1150 Fifth Avenue
New York, NY 10028

Descriptive page, price list and color photos of clocks, $1.

Despard Designs offers three versions of an unusual modern wall clock, the "Giro," each 9'' in diameter, 2⅝'' deep, and operated by Seiko transistorized movements. The clock faces, each one highly imaginative and decorative, are: *Stars and Stripes,* with a large red star as the hour hand, a small blue star for minutes; *Yin-Yan Whales,* in red, yellow and blue with fins as time indicators; and *Moonstar,* a striking design with a black-as-midnight background, a gold sickle moon and silver stars as hands, gold moons and silver stars as numerals. The clocks, which weigh only 13 oz., are $29.95 each, with a small shipping and handling charge, and delivery is made UPS, unless otherwise requested.

D-10
DISCOVERY CORNER STORE, Dept. CC
Lawrence Hall of Science
University of California
Berkeley, CA 94720

***Discovery Corner. Gifts from the Lawrence Hall
of Science**, free, published annually, 28 pages,
illustrated, black and white.*

A handsomely designed and produced catalogue showing
some of the educational aids, posters, minerals and sea
shells, books and kits sold by the Discovery Corner Store.
For those interested in astronomy, there are books, kits, a
celestial sphere, sundial, astrolabe ($9) and sextant; as-
tronomy and constellation postcards ($1 a set of twelve);
posters, slides (including NASA slide sets of the earth and
moon) and a refracting telescope ($130). Also included
are books on field photography; a fascinating sunprint kit
that makes photographic-type images without chemicals,
only water and special paper ($1.80); Brazilian agate
bookends; and an unusual paperweight, "Accelerator
Forest," an acrylic cylinder charged with an electron
linear accelerator and then discharged, producing a pattern that looks like waving fronds ($8.95). Well worth
sending for.

D-11
DOLLSPART SUPPLY COMPANY, INC., Dept. CC
46-13 11th Street
Long Island City, NY 11101

***Dollspart Catalog**, free, published annually, 26
pages, illustrated, black and white.*

Everything for making and repairing dolls—wigs, eye-
lashes, eyes, limbs, bodies, shoes, stockings, hats, also
antique doll replicas from original molds, reproduction
kits, patterns for clothing of different styles and periods,
and repair accessories. One page has a column of helpful
hints about repairing and cleaning dolls. Another section
of the catalogue has authentic reproduction miniature
furniture kits for such pieces as a Hepplewhite three-piece
dining table ($8.95), Queen Anne fire screen ($2.95) and
a Chippendale wing chair ($5.95). At the back there's a
selection of doll books for hobbyists and collectors.

D-12
DOMINICA HANDCRAFTS COMPANY, Dept. CC
P. O. Box 22 / Hanover Street
Roseau
Dominica, West Indies

Brochure, free, 4 pages, illustrated.

The West Indian island of Dominica is known for its
beautiful handwoven straw mats, and the brochure shows
the different patterns by numbered illustration. These,
presumably, are the only handcrafts shipped, as an accompanying brochure of various other crafts (hats, bags,
place mats) has no identifications or prices. (The choice of
second color on the brochures, red, is unfortunate; the
designs would have shown up better in black and white.)
An F.O.B. price list for the mats gives prices for diame-
ters of circular mats, dimensions of oval mats, and price
per square foot. Rectangular and square mats can be made
up in desired sizes. Prices are quoted in E.C. (Eastern
Caribbean) dollars, currently less than half the U.S. dol-
lar. Mats, which are dutiable, can be shipped by air or sea.

D-13
DOVER PUBLICATIONS, INC., Dept. CC
180 Varick Street
New York, NY 10014

Catalogue of books, free, published annually.

Among Dover's listing of books in all areas are some on
art, antiques and collecting, and crafts. Special catalogues
are issued from time to time.

D-14
DOVER SCIENTIFIC CO., Dept. CC
Box 6011
Long Island City, NY 11106

***Shells, Fossils, Minerals, Indian Artifacts**, 50¢,
published annually, 44 pages, illustrated, black
and white. Portfolio of catalogue plus color photographs of selected shells and minerals, $2.*

The black-and-white catalogue contains a wide variety of
exotic and decorative shells, fossils, minerals, polished
and faceted gem stones, polished cabochons, mineral
eggs, gemrock ashtrays, with selected illustrations, in a
price range from 25¢ for nerite shells to $350 for an 18 x
13mm faceted green tourmaline. An Australian fossil
crab, over 60 million years old, 1½", is $15; a large
mammoth tooth from Pleistocene formation of Texas,
$100. The two pages of Indian artifacts show pieces of
thirteenth-century pueblo Indian polychrome and black-
and-white pottery, $10 a piece, flint ceremonial blades
and large fired clay sculptured figures made by Indians of
ancient Mexico, starting at $500. Dover also offers a wide
selection of books on nature, science, anthropology, archaeology, geology and general subjects, display stands
for minerals and fossils and handmade glass and brass
display cases, made in Mexico, from a small square
minibox at $3.50 to a rectangular three-shelf wall case,
11" high by 9" wide by 2¼" deep for $27.50. The color
photographs show some of the more colorful shells and
minerals, with keyed descriptions on the back related to
the price list in the catalogue.

D-15
DOWNS' COLLECTORS SHOWCASE, Dept. CC
1014 Davis Street
Evanston, IL 60204

Downs' Collectors Showcase, $1, 48 pages, published seasonally, illustrated, some color. Downs' Music Box Collection, 50¢, 16 pages, published seasonally, illustrated, color.

If you can see past the usual mail-order items that proliferate in the busy *Showcase* catalogue, there are a few worthwhile collectibles such as a kaleidoscope shaped like a mariner's telescope for $150, a millefiori Venetian glass carafe and drinking glass for $43.95; a set of twelve lacquered brass animal ornaments for $29.95. The Downs' music box collection offers a wide selection in all shapes and sizes, some animated, some not. A delightful player piano with bench is $10.95; an animated music-box clown is $45; and a lovely brocade box is $19.95. A handsome, simple walnut box that plays three tunes is $199; a Limoges two-tune musical mosque is $250; and an elegant rosewood music box with 144-note Reuge movement is $1,200.

D-16
DUNCRAFT, Dept. CC
25 South Main Street
Penacook, NH 03301

Duncraft Wild Bird Specialists, free, 32 pages, published annually, illustrated, color and black and white.

For ornithologists, Duncraft has a splendid collection of wild bird feeders and a series of twenty ceramic tiles showing in brilliant natural colors birds such as a scarlet tanager, towhee and rosebreasted grosbeak, 6'' x 6'', $2.95 per tile, or twenty for $52. The tiles can be installed around a sink or fireplace or wall-mounted by their back hooks, like pictures. There's also a good selection of books on wild birds and recordings of bird songs and the sounds of nature.

D-17
ELIZABETH F. DUNLAP, Dept. CC
6063 Westminster Place
St. Louis, MO 63112

Maps of North American Interest, 30¢ in stamps, 18-page mimeographed list, published semi-annually.

A good starting place for the novice collector looking for quality at low cost, as well as the seasoned cartographer seeking original and valuable maps, is offered by the Dunlap collection, which covers North America, the United States, states and cities, Canada and provinces, Mexico, Central America, the West Indies and the world with nearly 300 listings. Most of the maps are from the nineteenth century with some dating back to the late 1700s. The collection is extensive, the descriptions clear and concise, and the prices seem moderately low, with many maps offered for as little as $5 or $6. Few are in the over-$100 range. The most expensive is a map of "The United States of North America with the British Territories and Those of Spain, according to the Treaty of 1784," engraved by Wm. Faden, 1793 ($250).

Victorian gout footstool replica in hand-carved mahogany. Magnolia Hall, M-2.

E-1
EASTMAN KODAK COMPANY, PROFESSIONAL AND FINISHING MARKETS DIVISION,
Dept. CC
343 State Street
Rochester, NY 14650

Decorating with Photographic Art—An Idea Book, free, 20 pages, illustrated, color.

An interesting book for collectors of photographic art, showing ways to display photographs, framed or in shadow boxes, and photomurals in different settings, alone or in combination with other forms of art, with advice and tips on mounting, finishing and hanging.

E-2
EBELING & REUSS, Dept. CC
1041 West Valley Road
Devon, PA 19333

Cappé Porcelain Figures from Italy, free, 18 pages, illustrated, color. Kaiser Porcelains, free, 54 pages, illustrated, color.

Ebeling & Reuss are importers of and exclusive U.S. distributors for these European porcelains. The figures by Italian artist Giuseppi Cappé include humorous, cartoon-like studies of such subjects as a dentist, a sleeping fisherman, a pair of gossips, a junk peddler and two clubmen, and delicate, romantic depictions of lovers, a woman with a dove and a young man with a basket of fruit. No price list was included with this catalogue.

The Bavarian Kaiser porcelains are superb, finely detailed lifelike studies of wild birds and animals, horses, dogs, cats and character figures such as a goose girl or a man with falcon. Many of these are in limited editions, some are pure white, others full color. Prices range from $30 for small, simple white porcelain rabbits to $3,200 for a pheasant, 30'' x 16'', in a limited edition of 1,500. Sculptors for these porcelains are Gerhard Bochmann, Uwe Netzsch, Wolfgang Gawantka, Lowell Davis and Giuseppi Tagliariol.

E-3
EBERLING STAMP COMPANY, Dept. CC
105 Franklin Avenue
Staten Island, NY 10301

U.S. Postage Stamp Catalogue, free, published quarterly, 16 pages.

A listing of U.S. stamps—airmail, certified mail, commemoratives (mint and used), souvenir sheets and regular issues.

E-4
THE EDISON INSTITUTE, Dept. CC
20900 Oakwood Boulevard
Dearborn, MI 48121

Reproductions from the Collections of Greenfield Village and Henry Ford Museum, $2.50, 48 pages, illustrated, color and black and white.

A handsome catalogue of reproductions from the collections, comprising furniture, clocks, glassware, hooked rugs, lamps, mirrors, pewter, wallpaper and fabrics. A mahogany Aaron Willard banjo clock with reverse painted panels, 41½'' high by 11'' wide by 5'' deep, is around $1,400; a Federal girandole looking glass, from an original made in Philadelphia, is around $335; a man-sized pewter tankard copied from one made by Benjamin Day of Newport between 1725 and 1750, is around $38. There are also some handcrafted reproductions in glass, tin, pewter and pottery made by craftsmen in Greenfield Village. These include copies of nineteenth-century pitchers and bottles, some unusual glass paperweights, tin candle lanterns and pottery puzzle jugs.

E-5
EDITIONS LIMITED GALLERY INC., Dept. CC
919 Westfield Boulevard
Indianapolis, IN 46220

Brochure, $1, published seasonally, 4 pages, illustrated, color.

This gallery sells posters and prints, signed and unsigned, by contemporary artists such as Calder, LeRoy Neiman,

Peter Milton, Jurgen Peters and Will Barnet at prices ranging from $20 to $1,200.

E-6
EDUCATIONAL GRAPHICS, LTD., Dept. CC
43 Camden Passage
London N1
England

Leaflet, 50¢, published annually, illustrated, black and white and color.

Charmingly designed bookplates, 4″ x 3″, packed twenty-five of one design to a box for around $2 (plus postage and packing), art reproductions, animal posters, pictorial and relief maps, and charts originally published by the London *Sunday Times* (around $3.25) are among the offerings of this company, all of which are dutiable.

E-7
RUSS ELLIOTT STUDIO, Dept. CC
405 East 54th Street
New York, NY 10022

Prices on request.

The artist sells a series of lithographs, *Endangered Species,* dealing with animals and comprising six subjects. Prints measure 18″ x 22″. Also available on a custom basis are original paintings of animals, native market places and floral themes.

E-8
EMERSON BOOKS, INC., Dept. CC
Reynolds Lane
Buchanan, NY 10511

Book List, $1, refundable with purchase, 32 pages, illustrated, black and white.

Emerson lists books on a great number of subjects such as antiques, watches, music, how-to, arts and crafts, magic and games, antique jewelry, Staffordshire pottery figures, gem testing, etc. Prices range from $1.25 to $12.95. No extra handling charge on orders of three or more books.

E-9
THE ENCHANTED DOLL HOUSE, Dept. CC
Route 7
Manchester Center, VT 05255

The Enchanted Doll House, $2, published annually, 66 pages, illustrated, color.

A delightful catalogue of dolls and miniature furniture. Meticulously detailed doll houses in several styles, such as Federal, Victorian, Colonial town house, brownstone and Cape Cod mansion have appropriate furnishings and, in some cases, tiny doll inhabitants dressed in period costume. For the Victorian house there is Victorian Rococo furniture manufactured in Colombia, priced from $12.50 for a console mirror to $78 for a tête-à-tête; and an amusing set of eight Victorian dolls by Peggy Nisbet of family, household staff, lady and gentleman visitors ($30 each). All types and styles of miniature furniture are represented, including some charming wicker pieces, and just about everything that could go into furnishing a doll house is shown—tiny, hand-painted collectors' plates, pewter and china place settings and silver reproductions by Kirk on a scale of 1″ to 1′, fireplaces, musical instruments, kits for Oriental rugs. For building doll houses there are all the architectural components, hardware, wallpapers and floor coverings, lamps and fixtures, even an electrical wiring kit. Larger dolls include those of Madame Alexander, Effanbee, the British royal family in state robes by Peggy Nisbet, rag dolls, doll kits and some darling French country-cousin dolls with washable wigs and soft bodies, priced from $25 to $50. There's also a good selection of collectors' reference books and guides to doll houses and miniatures.

E-10
ESSEX COUNTY HISTORICAL SOCIETY,
Dept. CC
Box 428
Elizabethtown, NY 12932

Adirondack Center Museum Bookstore, 8-page brochure, $1, published annually.

A rather skimpy (for $1) list of Adirondack region books, maps, prints and notepaper available by mail from the museum shop. Listed are various books on local and regional history, architecture, bibliography, lore, biography, outdoor guides to trails, climbing and camping, including maps, local cookbooks and back issues of magazines such as *Reveille,* the Essex County Historical Society's quarterly. Among the maps there are a 1756 map of the province of New York ($1) and an 1874 map of the New York wilderness ($3), while the color prints include *Building a Smudge* by Winslow Homer and *Lake George* by Andrew Melrose ($1.95 each). An annual society membership costs $5, and members get a 10 percent discount on listed prices.

E-11
EUROPEAN PUBLISHERS REPRESENTATIVES,
INC., Dept. CC
11-03 46th Avenue
Long Island City, NY 11101

Brochures of magazines, periodicals, calendars, free.

Most of the brochures offer European papers and magazines on fashion, culture and art, architecture and interior design, sports and hobbies and so on; but there are also some excellent art calendars from Great Britain and Germany, such as Gardens of Britain, Artists' Wildlife Calendar, art and ballet calendars. A brochure of gifts from Poland includes cookbooks and books on culture, folklore and art; postcard sets of works by Polish artists (a mini art course of six Polish masters, fifty-four cards, is $3.95), and some interesting prints, such as *The Sunflower* by Karol Hiller, an abstract floral, mounted and framed in white, 12½″ x 10″, $8 ppd. and *A Lady with a Weasel,* the one work in Poland painted by Leonardo da Vinci.

The least expensive plate collection can be given importance by a clever display device such as designer Lee Bailey's arrangement of Japanese copies of the Meissen onion pattern on a deep blue dining room wall.
Courtesy: Eastman Chemical.

A massive but simple straight-lined breakfront at one end of Vincent Price's living room holds his priceless collection of American Indian pottery. The horizontal lines are balanced at the left by a tall window and at the right by a vertical grouping of art and objects. Photographer: Max Eckert.

F-1

STEPHEN FALLER (EXPORTS) LTD., Dept. CC
Mervue,
Galway,
Ireland

Fallers of Galway—Mail Order Catalogue, $1,
published annually, 88 pages, illustrated, color.

Fallers is a vintage Irish company, founded in 1879 and in the mail-order business for over twenty years. The catalogue has many attractive collectors' items—Lladro porcelain and Royal Doulton china figures, Galway crystal, Capo de Monte table bells, Wedgwood jasperware, Italian pewter tankards, Villeroy and Boch ceramic cachepots and vases, Aynsley bone china cachepots and vases, Blue Delft, Waterford crystal, fireside animals and some utterly enchanting Beatrix Potter figures by Beswick. Royal Doulton character jugs of Henry VIII and Falstaff are presently priced at around $28, although the price will no doubt have risen by the time you read this, as the new edition of the catalogue is currently being prepared. The Beatrix Potter figures are currently $27 for a set of any three single figures, $52 for a set of six, and $100 for a set of twelve. Fallers also sells china and earthenware place settings, clothes, Irish pure wool blankets and other export items. All prices listed include insurance and surface mailing, and Fallers points out that even with import duty (4 percent for figurines, 17½ percent for tableware, 10 percent for glassware) and shipping costs, their prices show considerable savings over U.S. store prices, as much as 40 percent lower in many cases. Purchases may be charged to American Express, VISA or Mastercharge.

F-2

FEDERAL SMALLWARES CORPORATION,
Dept. CC
85 Fifth Avenue
New York, NY 10003

Collector Miniatures, $1, published seasonally,
148 pages, illustrated, black and white.

Every sort of miniature imaginable—furniture, tele-phones and desk accessories, musical instruments, clocks, mirrors, glassware, pillows and mats, baskets, bicycles, sewing-machines, old-fashioned bathroom sets, Franklin and Shaker stoves, tea services, books and magazines, kitchen appliances, even wood clothespins just ⅜″ long. Prices are reasonable—a rolltop Sheraton desk, 3½″ high by 3¼″ wide is $12.50; a Tiffany-style chandelier, $7; little throw pillows, $2 a set of six; an antique canopy bed, $12; a metal mailbox, $4.50; a tiny clay flowerpot, ½″ high, 75¢. The offerings include a handmade leaded glass hothouse, 8″ x 7¼″ x 7¼″ ($25), that would make an unusual terrarium; general-store miniatures such as a platform scale; post office counter with cubbyholes ($9); a cast metal ceiling fan ($4). There are also doll house families, doll kits and a collection of doll replicas, in period costume, of museum and collector originals from Europe and America. These are larger, ranging from 2¼″ to an antique bisque doll in Victorian costume, 20″ tall ($35). The doll house decorator can find miniature antique hardware, leaded-glass window panels, wallpaper, bricks and ceramic tiles in this miniature-world catalogue. Fun to browse through. A separate 120-page doll house catalogue is also available for $1, refundable with order.

F-3

THE FENTON ART GLASS COMPANY, Dept. CC
Williamstown, WV 26187

Catalogue, $2, published every two years, 70
pages, illustrated, color.

The various kinds of art glass shown in the catalogue are sold only through Fenton dealers, not by mail, and include decorative items from cake plates to lamps. Of more interest to collectors is the limited edition glass collector's society established by Fenton. A current brochure offers a limited edition of four vases by Fenton's artist in residence, glassblower Robert Barber, whose work is represented in a number of museum collections. There are two vases with hanging-heart pattern, one bittersweet, one iridescent turquoise, two feather vases, in hyacinth and blue, ranging in price from $85 to $175, each a beautiful work of art.

F-4
FIESTA ARTS, INC., Dept. CC
Greenvale, NY 11548

Ricordi Poster Collection, *brochure, 50¢ (refundable with purchase), published annually, 4 pages, illustrated, color.*

Fiesta offers full-color print-posters, 19½'' x 27½'', printed from the stone matrixes of the originals in ''limited editions'' (no numbers are given). The style of the posters is that of the Belle Epoque and Art Nouveau. There are marvelous bold designs advertising motorcars like the Isotta Fraschini and Mercedes; coffee and candy; Campari and Strega; motorcycles and bicycles; as well as a series of La Scala posters for such operas as *Turandot, Parsifal* and *Tosca,* each $4. The company also has Metropolitan ''First Performance'' posters—the grand opening with Gounod's *Faust* in 1883, the 1901 *Tosca,* etc., 12'' x 16'' for $1.25. You can also order an authentic 18½'' x 33'' peanut sack from Jimmy Carter's farm or one of several reproduction Victorian footstools.

F-5
THE FIFE AND DRUM, Dept. CC
P.O. Box 6
Valley Forge, PA 19841

Here are the Men who Made it all Possible, *brochure, free, mailed on request.*

Rare, colorful and authentic military costume prints of the men of Washington's Army from original paintings by Raymond Desvarreux Larpenteur, official artist of the *Ministère de Guerre* and *Musée de l'Armée (Invalides),* Paris. Lithographs were made in a limited edition of 500 copies on parchment paper at $5 each (many of these are no longer available), and an unlimited edition at $3.50 each, and measure 16'' x 10½'', with ample margins for framing, which is not supplied by The Fife and Drum. Four series of prints include soldiers from regiments and battalions of the different states and Washington's Guard. A Foreign Series set of four prints shows soldiers of famous French and British regiments, Soissonais, Royal Deux-Ponts, Royal Welch Fusiliers and the Black Watch, same editions and prices as the Washington's Army series. The Fife and Drum also sells thirteen-star and fifty-star American flags, at $12 for the Betsy Ross thirteen-star and $12.50 for the standard fifty-star, and reproductions of eight famous documents in American history, such as the Gettysburg Address in Lincoln's handwriting and the Declaration of Independence, all full-size copies of the originals, the set of eight for $4.25. Postage and packing are extra, and you can return any items for a cash refund within ten days if not fully satisfied.

F-6
FLINT INSTITUTE OF ARTS, Dept. CC
1120 East Kearsley Street
Flint, MI 48503

The American Indian/The American Flag, *$9, 148 pages, illustrated, black and white and color.*

This exhibition catalogue from the Flint Institute's shop provides a fascinating picture of the use of the image of the American flag by Indians. Articles of clothing such as shirts and trousers and moccasins, plaques, pouches, rugs, quilts, cradles, baskets, rattles, and even a tepee, are wonderfully decorated with the stars and stripes, including work with dyed porcupine quills, beadwork and wicker.

F-7
THE FLYING COLORS COLLECTION, Dept. CC
221 Park Avenue South
New York, NY 10003

Mailers, free, illustrated, color.

Series of lithographs created by the sculptor Alexander Calder, including several designs originally executed for a Braniff jet plane, are available in signed numbered editions from $650 to $1,700. There are also six plate-signed designs, 20'' x 26'', in an unlimited edition and framed for $65 each. Price includes shipping and handling and insurance.

F-8
FOCKE & MELTZER AMSTERDAM B.V.,
Dept. CC
Kalverstraat 152
Amsterdam, The Netherlands

Christmas Folder *and* ***Étagère,*** *$1, refundable with purchase, illustrated, color.*

This Dutch company specializes in commemorative plates, mugs, bells and figurines by Royal Copenhagen, Orrefors, De Porceleyne Fles Delftware, Wedgwood, Bing & Grondahl, Makkum, Hutschenreuther and other companies, and in addition to the current editions can supply older editions from stock. They offer a bonus of one specially priced plate for every $10 value of the order—for instance, with an order you could get a 1969 Wedgwood Apollo plate for $12. These, and pewter figures from the Old Handcrafts collection, are shown in the blue-on-white six-page Christmas folder in English with prices in U.S. dollars. *Étagère,* a monthly newsletter in four-color has write-ups of exhibitions and news about decorative porcelain and crystal, with biographies of the designers (Dali, Vasarely, Wiinblad), but as it is written in Dutch, you won't get much out of it unless you can read the language.

Above left, Tutankhamun mask in miniature reproduced in vermeil or solid gold; Replicas of Antiquity, R-10. Right, falcon head pendant adapted from the terminal of an Egyptian broad-collar necklace; Brooklyn Museum Gallery Shop, B-28. Below, Egyptian footed bowl, reproduced from the original; Metropolitan Museum of Art, M-16.

Instead of a painting, a family mural of photographs in the simplest of slip-on aluminum frames fills the end wall of a living room. Courtesy: Family Circle.

F-9
FOGELSONG STUDIOS, Dept. CC
11 Peabody Terrace, Suite 1901
Cambridge, MA 02138

Brochure, free, published annually, illustrated, color.

Artist Jill Fogelsong's signed and numbered limited edition prints are of wildlife—in the current offering, an African leopard, lion and cheetah and a Bengal tiger. All are head studies, life-size, and through Mrs. Fogelsong's special and painstaking drybrush watercolor technique, in which as many as seven layers of different colors are applied in minute brush strokes, incredibly lifelike. Each print comes with an affidavit of registration and titled nameplate and costs $45, packaging and shipping extra. Plates are destroyed after the edition is printed, but new subjects are always available if the edition is sold out.

F-10
FRAME HOUSE GALLERY, Dept. CC
110 West Market Street
Louisville, KY 40202

Frame House Gallery Limited Edition Collector Prints, $2.50, 64 pages, published annually, illustrated, color.

Wildlife and nature are the themes in the Frame House catalogue. All of the artists are ornithologists, biologists or botanists in their own right. Twenty-one of the gallery's regular artists are represented with color and black-and-white reproductions of their work, biographical data, specific details about each lithograph, along with price and collector's value. In addition the catalogue lists nine guest artists and a collection of books and portfolios. New collectors will find the catalogue particularly helpful for its information on ''collector prints''—what they are, how they are made, their worth as an investment and general hints on collecting and caring for fine lithographs.

F-11
FRANCISCA'S SHOPPE, Dept. CC
P. O. Box 335
Ogunquit, ME 03907

Handmade Weathervanes, brochure, 50¢, 16 pages, illustrated, black and white.

A grasshopper (34'' long), a feather (from 18'' to 60'' long), a Gabriel (18'' or 32'' long), a fish, a clipper ship, a whale, a pig, an eagle, are among the many handsome reproduction weathervanes this shop sells. Most come in a variety of sizes and are finished either in 23k. gold leaf, natural copper or antique verdigris patina that simulates natural weathering. Prices vary from $25 to $750, and those finished in gold leaf are subject to current costs. Also offered are weathervane parts; lanterns; flagpole ornaments; ceramics; pinecone wreaths; and driftwood flowers.

F-12
THE FRANKLIN INSTITUTE SCIENCE MUSEUM, Dept. CC
Benjamin Franklin Parkway at 20th Street
Philadelphia, PA 19103

Ben's Gift Shop, 25¢, published annually, 14 pages, illustrated, sepia and black and white.

Not unexpectedly, this catalogue has attractive educational objects. There is a kit for an authentic replica of Cousteau's *Calypso*, 13'' long, that includes a helicopter, Galeazzi diving chamber, inflatable boat and two mini-subs; model ships of paper include a whaler, a Viking ship and the *Santa Maria* that float if their bottoms are shellacked. Books on solar energy and the stars; telescopes and microscopes; a 4'' sundial; an 8-oz. pewter Jefferson goblet and a set of two pewter Jefferson cups, 2½'' high; and necklaces in silver and gold with pendant stars or suns or a lightning bolt are also included. Prices vary from 25¢ to $195, and there is a small shipping and handling charge.

F-13
FRANLEY STUDIOS, Dept. CC
5 Main Street
Cold Spring Harbor, NY 11724

Franley Studios Needlepoint, $2, refundable with purchase, published periodically, 14 pages, two tones of blue on white.

This catalogue has some delightful needlepoint designs—flora and fauna, paisley, Persian patterns taken from Near Eastern rugs and fabrics, adaptations of classic medieval tapestries, heraldic crests, scenics, and classic designs such as Botticelli's *Primavera* and a Versailles rug. The only pity is that they are not shown in color. The designs lose a great deal in the blue-on-white format. Prices start at $18 a kit. A particular favorite of ours is the *Unicorn in Captivity,* from the medieval tapestry series, with millefleurs in various colors on a navy background, 10½'' x 17'', $65.

F-14

FREER GALLERY OF ART, Dept. CC
12th and Jefferson Drive, S.W.
Washington, DC 20560

Freer Gallery of Art Sales Catalogue, $1, published annually, 60 pages, illustrated, black and white.

The great oriental collection of the Freer is reproduced in various forms—notepaper, color reproductions, needlepoint kits, desk accessories, playing cards and billfolds. The museum also sells slides, postcards and publications. A Hokusai *Boy and Mount Fuji* reproduction, 13¼'' x 9½'' including border, is $2. A 3½'' x 12¹/₁₆'' reproduction of a work in ink on paper dating from the fourteenth century in Japan, mounted on cream paper, 10¼'' x 14¼'', costs 50¢. *Chrysanthemums,* a needlepoint image taken from a Japanese fan painting of the late seventeenth century, measures 12'' x 12'' and costs $25. Sterling or gold-filled charms are $6 and $7, a Byzantine medallion necklace in gold-washed metal is $17.50. Full-color reproductions of the superb Whistler paintings in the museum's collection cost as little as 25¢ for *Nocturne,* 6¾'' x 10½''. There's a $1 charge for postage and handling.

F-15

FRIENDS OF THE FREE LIBRARY GIFT SHOP,
Dept. CC
Logan Square
Philadelphia, PA 19103

Friends of the Free Library of Philadelphia Gift Shop, free, published annually, 16 pages, illustrated, black and white.

The Library sells various items based on its collections. For instance, needlepoint designs of Pennsylvania German *fraktur* (described as a "marriage of decorative lettering and colorful folk motifs") include such things as bookmarks ($6), brick covers ($35) and an 1815 birth and baptismal certificate for which the artist will fill in initials or dates on request ($42.50). Persian wool yarn and needle are included. A book of thirty-two picture postcards of Old Philadelphia, ready to tear out and mail, is $2. From the Rare Book Collection and print and picture collections there are reproductions of work by famous illustrators such as Kate Greenaway, Arthur Rackham and Thomas Nast on greeting cards and notepaper (average prices are $1.50 to $3 for ten).

F-16

FULTON COUNTY HISTORICAL SOCIETY,
Dept. CC
7th and Pontiac Streets
Rochester, IN 46975

Book and publication list, free, 1 page.

A number of paperback booklets and four hard-cover books on Indiana and Fulton County. Books include an *1883 Atlas of Fulton County* by A. L. Kingman, $12, and *Home Folks,* stories by old settlers of Fulton County, in two volumes, 1909 and 1911, by Marguerite Miller, $10. For collectors of glass insulators from telephone poles, the Society has both clear and green glass in different shapes and sizes, for 25¢ each—somewhat of a bargain these days.

Reproduction of Amish cast-iron bookends from the American Heritage collection, A-7.

G-1
GALLERY OF AMSTERDAM, Dept. CC
Wallins Corner Road
Amsterdam, NY 12010

The Gallery of Amsterdam, free, published quarterly, 64 pages, illustrated, color.

Primarily a gift catalogue, this has some items of interest to collectors. There's a model of the Thomas Flyer, the classic car that won the New York to Paris race in 1908, available in kit form for around $15; there are also English-made models of nineteenth-century steam vehicles, fully operating, that raise live steam, run forward and in reverse and even haul loads, $60 for a steam tractor, $80 for a steam wagon. Operating models of steam engines range from $18 to $55, and other classic car kits are priced from around $11 to $26. A kit of a blue water ketch is around $18. Framed collections of great American Presidents commemorative coins sell for $10.

G-2
GALLERY OF PREHISTORIC ART, Dept. CC
20 East 12th Street
New York, NY 10003

Collector Editions of Prehistoric Paintings, $3, published annually, 12 pages, illustrated, color.

The gallery offers in this current catalogue fifty serigraphs hand-screened by David Mazonowicz after cave and rock art in France, Spain, the Central Sahara Desert and by early American Indians, and a number of works taken from art in Etruscan tombs in Tarquinia, Italy. All are in limited editions of 75 (except for two of 1,000), signed and numbered. An Etruscan panel, 35'' x 144'', is $3,000; a yellow horse from Lascaux, $2,000; an elephant from El Castillo, $80. Prints are mailed rolled or can be ordered mounted for an additional charge of $5 per square foot.

G-3
GARDEN ACCENTS, Dept. CC
5205 Ashbrook Street
Houston, TX 77081

Garden Accents for Home, Garden and Country Estate, free, updated periodically, 12 pages, illustrated, black and white.

The rather grandiloquent title of the catalogue is not really a very apt description for this collection of delightful, fanciful silhouette sculptures in designs taken from primitive weather vanes in museums and on public display, many the designs of Connecticut weather-vane authority Kenneth Lynch. The steel sculptures, which come with stands and may be used as vanes, mailbox decorations or pieces of free-standing sculpture indoors or out, are finished with a special rust-culturing process protected by a clear urethane coating. All are handmade and hand finished by craftsmen in a small German settlement in Texas, and custom work is invited (send photographs or sketch for quotation). Subjects include mermaids, deer, angels, ships, archers, arrows, birds and beasts, fish, and horseback riders, and the cost is $55 in rust finish or $97 in hand-painted finish with a choice of four types of stand: garden, floor, table or roof. Price includes packaging, shipping and insurance.

G-4
ISABELLA STEWART GARDNER MUSEUM,
Dept. CC
2 Palace Road
Boston, MA 02115

Publications list, free.

The publications cover the European and American paintings and drawings and the oriental and Islamic art in the museum, a museum guide and various other things, such as a biography of the famous and formidable Isabella (whose plunging-neckline portrait by Sargent was considered by her husband too daring to be shown). If you are going to be in Boston, a good way to bone up.

G-5
GARGOYLES LTD., Dept. CC
512 South Third Street
Philadelphia, PA 19147

Gargoyles Ltd. Architectural Antiques and Reproductions, $4, published about every 2 years, 32 pages, illustrated, color.

Gargoyles has made a reputation as the general store for designers, architects, restaurateurs and collectors because of their fantastic and constantly growing inventory of architectural antiques, priceless objects from buildings of the past that they save from the wrecker, here and abroad. Lately, because they cannot always locate an item that fits a specific need, they have launched into the world of reproductions, which they skillfully blend with the old. Their list of acquisitions and offerings is impressive: antiques, architectural embellishments, bars, balusters, benches, brackets, brassware, tin ceilings, ceiling fans, doors, entryways, fretwork, lampposts, lighting, mantels, mirrors, newels, furniture for indoors and out, terra cotta, soda fountains, wall decor, nautical gear, advertising memorabilia, paneling, stairways, chandeliers, cupolas, brilliant cut glass, pub signs and mirrors, railroad relics, stained glass, statuary, even shop fittings, country stores and complete chemists' shops. Browsing through their catalogue is like visiting a vanished age. Their antique pub mirrors are especially fine, their ornamental ironwork and fretwork "gingerbread" from the nineteenth century a delight to the eye. We especially like the terra cotta and stone sculptures that once embellished European and American buildings and the fanciful period lighting fixtures. They will also make stained-glass windows to your specifications. The only price lists we received with the catalogue were for the reproductions —groundstone sculptures and advertising mirrors. The mirrors range in price from $34 to $110. Of course, as so many of the items in the catalogue are one-of-a-kind, inventory and prices are constantly changing.

G-6
GARNITA'S PLATE COLLECTIONS, Dept. CC
Box 534
Solvang, CA 93463

Collector's Plates, $1, published twice a year (Spring and Christmas), with 3 special mailings per year.

The catalogues offered for $1 are actually a complete price index for most collector's plates on the market with information on new editions, special offerings, tips on

investment and accessories for plates such as stands and hangers. Once you are on the mailing list, you will get the catalogue without charge. The 1977 Christmas catalogue shows a few examples of current plates, but lists hundreds, with year and price—the Bing & Grondahl Christmas plate of 1895 is $3,300; the 1977 plate, $29.50, which gives some idea of the investment value of plates. The list starts with American Aviation and continues through such familiar names as Arabia, Bareuther, Delft, Gorham, Lenox, Rockwell Society, Rosenthal, Royal Copenhagen and Royal Worcester to Wedgwood. Special mailings included with the catalogue we received were "The Navigators," a 1977 Heritage plate by Bing & Grondahl; Paul Detlefsen's "American Memories" series; "The Flower Girl" in the Children series by Southwestern artist De Grazia; and a color brochure of The Kern Collectibles, fifteen different limited-edition plates. This company pays shipping and insurance costs on all orders, which are sent UPS.

G-7
GARTH'S AUCTIONS, INC., Dept. CC
2690 Stratford Road, P. O. Box 315
Delaware, OH 43015

Auction catalogues (approximately 20 a year), $25.

The catalogues advertise Garth's auctions of Early American antiques, with all items listed and many pictured. Absentee bids may be made by mail or telephone for competitive bidding at the auctions. Items bought are then shipped by Garth's. They guarantee a refund if the item is not as described.

G-8
GENTRY-LUCAS TAPESTRY WORKS, Dept. CC
4530 Nakoma, P. O. Box 252
Okemos, MI 48864

Tufted Tapestry (TM), flyer, free, published periodically, illustrated, color.

Gentry-Lucas makes a specialty of transforming your family coat-of-arms into a wool or acrylic tapestry measuring 3' x 5', with pile height from ⅜'' to 1'' deep. They will also work from symbols, logos, portraits, artworks or original designs. Prices range from around $200 to $575 depending on size and material. A small sample will be sent for $5, refunded when the sample is returned.

G-9
THE J. PAUL GETTY MUSEUM, Dept. CC
17985 Pacific Coast Highway
Malibu, CA 90265

List of publications, free.

Alma Tedema's Spring, $1.75, 28 pages, illustrated, black and white and color and *A Greek Prayer,* $1.50, 24 pages, illustrated, sepia and color are two examples of exhibition catalogues from the Getty Museum, which publishes works that "apply to the art collection." The *Tedema* deals with a painting of a Roman celebration complete with young women garlanded with flowers. The *Prayer* catalogue is a translation and history of a short burial prayer engraved on a tiny sheet of gold and found among the ashes of a Greek cinerary urn. Other titles include a guidebook to the museum; *Clocks—French Eighteenth-Century Clocks in the J. Paul Getty Museum; Royal Decorative Arts; The Ardabil Carpets; The Bronze Statue of a Youth,* etc. Postcards and a calendar are also available. Prices range from 30¢ to $9.95.

G-10
GIFTS FROM THE ANDES, Dept. CC
P. O. Box 7524
Oakland, CA 94601

Special Christmas Collection, brochure, $1, refundable with first order, published seasonally, 4 pages, illustrated, two colors. **Special Collection of Handmade Miniatures from South America,** *brochure, $1, refundable with purchase, published annually, illustrated, black and white.*

The Christmas collection brochure shows straw figures handmade by artisans of Southern Ecuador and Colombian miniature straw ornaments. Ecuadorian straw finger puppets, 2¼" to 3½", are three for $2.75. The miniature collection catalogue, currently in preparation, will feature fifty different miniatures of folk art from South America, and the company also plans to sell Ecuadorian bread-dough ornaments. Meanwhile, you can order for $2 a four-page booklet of recipes, pictures and directions for making your own bread-dough figures from baker's clay—a fun project for the family.

G-11
GILCREASE GIFT SHOP, Dept. CC
Route 6
Tulsa, OK 74127

Thomas Gilcrease Institute of American History and Art, Gift Shop Catalogue, *free, 8 pages, illustrated, black and white.*

Reproduction prints, postcards, note cards, slides and books from the Gilcrease Institute's collection, primarily of Western subjects. There are prints of works by C. M. Russell, Frederic Remington, Thomas Moran, George

Durrie and Albert Bierstadt; full-color reproductions of twenty-four watercolors from Olaf C. Seltzer's *Character Scenes* of Indians and Westerners; a portfolio of five Kiowa paintings, each 11" x 14", for $12.50; a Catlin portfolio of four Indian portraits, 11" x 14", for $6.95; 35mm slides of works by Russell, Remington and other artists; and books on *The Art of the Old West,* The Gilcrease Collection and American Indian painters. You can also order volumes of *American Scene Magazine,* published quarterly by the Institute.

G-12
GIRARD NURSERIES, Dept. CC
Box 428
Geneva, OH 44041

Catalogue, free, published annually, 36 pages, illustrated, color.

For the horticultural hobbyist, Girard has bonsai trees, evergreens, some rare and unusual pines, flowering shrubs and ornamental and shade trees. All the baby bonsai are two and three years old, root-pruned and potted in 2" and 3" pots and cost $1.50 each. There's also a bonsai starter collection of sixteen trees for $17.50.

G-13
GLASS MASTERS, INC., Dept. CC
154 West 18th Street
New York, NY 10001

The Glassmasters Collection, *$1, refundable with purchase, 8 pages, illustrated, color.*

The Glassmasters Collection has some stunning stained-glass ornaments and panels derived from different countries and centuries. The Collection includes a unicorn panel, 11⅝" x 16"; a circular unicorn and oak leaves in the medieval manner, 7½" in diameter; a Birds of America series, approximately 8½" in diameter (each design is $26); charming miniatures of European fifteenth- to seventeenth-century beasts—unicorn, lion rampant and cat, each $8.50; an American Wildflower series; heavenly bodies such as a sun face and sun, moon and stars; a sixteenth-century Dutch ship; and an absolutely entrancing tidal pool with shells and a fish, 8½" diameter, $22.50. Also available are stands, pewter finish chains and suction cups for display. For collectors of stained glass, this is a gem of a catalogue. There's a minimum purchase of $5, and with the catalogue you get a coupon worth $1 that may be applied to the order. Glass Masters also has the *Glass Masters Guild Supply Catalog,* which you may order for $1.

G-14

EDWARD GOLEMBERSKI, Dept. CC
93 Whitemoor Road
Nottingham NG6 OHJ
England

Antique & Curio Catalogue, $4 for subscription to six consecutive catalogues per year, airmailed, 28 pages, not illustrated.

This slim, all-print catalogue lists current offerings in the fields of pottery and porcelain; glass; books and prints; clocks and watches; things appertaining to dining and drinking such as corkscrews, tankards, teapots, flatware, toast racks, pans; and, under "miscellany and curios," a mixed bag of military relics, medals and badges, Australian and British coins (the latter pre-decimal), jewelry, traveling letter boxes, horse brasses, old tins, Nottingham lace and candlesticks. Prices seem very reasonable. In the November 1977 catalogue, a Masons ironstone decorated jug is around $10; an 1882 Minton earthenware display plate with transfer landscape print about the same price; a commemorative earthenware beaker for Queen Victoria's Diamond Jubilee about $17; and various decorative nineteenth-century tiles are around $1.50 to $2. In glassware, a rare and perfect Georgian cut-glass decanter is under $60; a Georgian solitaire, or wine-glass cooler, around $16; a pair of old colored glass menu holders shaped like fish around $6; and various examples of nineteenth-century leaded glass are around $7 to $16. Other things of interest selected at random are 1875 Chapman and Hall editions of Dickens; sugar tongs; a silver-plated fish knife and fork serving set; a late nineteenth-century clockwork brass roasting spit by Salter (in perfect working order), around $35; and a matching pair of silver-plated Art Nouveau candlesticks by James Dixon, around $20. While antiques are not dutiable, duty on more recent items varies according to type. Shipping and insurance charges are not included and must be prepaid. For your convenience, there's a conversion table for U.S. dollars with each catalogue, and your purchase is payable by the rate given in the table, not the floating exchange rate of pounds sterling. A good source for the collector of unusual items.

G-15

GEORGE J. GOODSTADT, INC., Dept. CC
225 Park Avenue South, Room 816
New York, NY 10003

Brochures, free, illustrated, black and white and color.

Turn-of-the-century lithographed posters from $75. Toulouse-Lautrec posters, authorized by the Musée Toulouse-Lautrec in Albi, France, in an edition of 2,000 are $75 each. Calder lithographs, signed and numbered in editions of 75 to 100 are $850 to $1,700. There are also charming and witty lithographs and etchings by Sandra Calder Davidson, $60 to $100, and Audubon's lithographs of *Birds of America,* approved by the American Museum of Natural History, $65 to $125. For theater buffs there are signed lithographs in full color of Kabuki actors by Al Hirschfeld and black-and-white etchings of famous performers like Judy Garland and Fred Astaire, also by Hirschfeld, in editions of 25 and 150 at $75 to $90.

G-16

VIRGINIA GOODWIN, Dept. CC
P. O. Box 3603
Charlotte, NC 28203

Brochure of leaflets, 25¢, illustrated, black and white.

The Goodwin family have been weavers since 1812, first in England, then in America. The current branch of the family lives in the North Carolina mountains, where they ply the traditional art of the family guild, using authentic antique patterns and antique looms to produce beautiful bedspreads (woven in one piece), a fishnet canopy, afghan, tablecloth, place mats, napkins and runner. Especially interesting to collectors are the spread patterns: "Honeycomb" in 100 percent cotton, "Whig Rose" (first woven in Tennessee to commemorate the formation of the Whig Party under Andrew Jackson's administration), "Lover's Knot," and "Morning Star," a favorite colonial pattern; all these in virgin wool and cotton. Prices of spreads range from just over $100 to around $132.

G-17

A. GOTO, Dept. CC
1-23-9 Higashi Shibuya Ku
Tokyo
Japan

Price list on request.

This company specializes in objects mostly forty to one hundred years old. Collectors of netsuke, the little sash ornaments depicting animals, birds, family seals, etc., can find examples made from such materials as gold, jade, mother-of-pearl, amber and lacquer. Prices vary from as little as $1.50 to $100. Snuff bottles are also available in a wide range of types. There are Mongolian silver bottles inlaid with coral or turquoise ($80 to $100) and cloisonné animals—a frog 5" x 4" x 2" costs $100, a deer 6½" x 3" x 5½", $220. Burmese jade buttons are $3 to $8 each. Old, large buttons begin at $15. There is a minimum order of $30. Orders are shipped by sea (minimum shipping charge $5) unless otherwise requested. For mail ship-

Above, Frederic Remington's ''Coming Thru the Rye'' bronze; Remington Art Memorial Museum, R-8. Below, ''Peace Riders,'' porcelain sculpture by Ispansky. Wakefield-Scearce Galleries, W-2.

Porcelain reproductions of Egyptian XI and XVIII Dynasty wall carvings. Brooklyn Museum Gallery Shop, B-28.

ments add 10 percent of the value of the order. No duty in U.S. on items over one hundred years old.

G-18
GRAND RAPIDS MUSEUM ASSOCIATION,
Dept. CC
54 Jefferson SE
Grand Rapids, MI 49502

Beads: Their Use by Upper Great Lakes Indians, *$6.95, 84 pages, 121 illustrations, 8 color pages.* *Spirits in Ebony: Woodcarving of the African Makonde, $1.50, 35 pages, 40 black-and-white illustrations.*

Collectors of beads and African woodcarvings will find much to enjoy in these exhibition catalogues. Aside from photographs of the exhibits, *Beads* contains four essays on the production and care of beadwork and *Spirits in Ebony* has one essay on the African Makonde craft.

G-19
GRAPHIS LARISSA, Dept. CC
Box 899-CC
Columbia, MD 21044

Authentic John James Audubon Prints of American Birds and Animals, $1, 20 pages.

Graphis Larissa specializes in antique prints of natural history. Their Audubon prints are those hand-colored lithographs from the original royal octavo edition of 1840–1844 published by the artist himself. The exact edition is not known, but 1,750 is suggested, and as most have entered museums and other collections, they are now fairly rare. The lithographic image averages 8'' x 5''. Prices range from $65 to $175 and you can buy one of the less popular birds for as little as $45 if you let the dealer make the choice. All prints are returnable for full refund within fifteen days of date of shipment provided you prepay and return the prints insured in the box they were shipped in. Shipping and insurance is $2 on orders under $100.

G-20
GREAT LAKES ORCHIDS, Dept. CC
P. O. Box 1114
Monroe, MI 48161

Orchid Species, free, published seasonally, 8 pages.

There is no illustration in this eight-page alphabetical listing of just descriptions and prices, but the descriptions are quite detailed.

G-21
GREEK ISLAND, LTD., Dept. CC
215 East 49th Street
New York, NY 10017

Greek Island Ltd., free, published annually, 36 pages, illustrated, black and white.

While the emphasis in this catalogue is on clothes, unusual jewelry and Greek handcrafts, there are a few items that might interest collectors. Examples in the current catalogue are line-for-line copies, hand-carved in white alabaster, of prehistoric Cycladic idol figures, one a Brancusi-like egghead, 4'' high ($75), the other a small eyeless contemplator, 3½'' high ($55); ikon reproductions from the gift shop of the Benaki Museum in Athens ($15), and terra-cotta roofline tiles from old torn-down buildings in the late-nineteenth-century neo-classic style of decoration in Greek architecture ($25).

G-22
RICHARD GREEN, Dept. CC
44 Dover Street
London W1X 4JO
England

Christmas Catalogue, $2, refundable with purchase, 48 pages, illustrated, black and white.

Richard Green's catalogue of Victorian paintings and watercolors includes all the usual subjects—views of towns and villages, seascapes, portraits of pets, landscapes, still lifes, daily dramas and views of Venice. The 1977 catalogue offers an elegant study of carnations by Sir George Clausen, 12½'' x 10½'', for around $3,300; a beguiling canvas of two pugs with a kitten, signed by Horatio Henry Couldery; a watercolor of the Bay of Naples by Myles Birket Foster; Theodore Hines' *The Thames Near Streatley* and *Whitchurch on Thames,* each 10'' x 14'', just over $4,000 the pair. A watercolor of a little girl with her pets, signed Briton Riviere, is around $550. All paintings listed are subject to prior sale. There is no duty on these works of art.

G-23
THE GREEN TIGER PRESS, Dept. CC
7458 La Jolla Boulevard
La Jolla, CA 92037

The Dream Pedlar Unpacks His Wares, 90¢ (in stamps), published twice a year, 20 pages, illustrated, black and white and color.

Green Tiger Press has enchanting reproductions of illustrations from children's books in the form of postcards, note cards, gift enclosures, matted prints, posters, stationery, seals and stickers, bookplates and bookmarks, wrapping paper and several books dealing with children's book illustration. All the great names are here—Tenniel, Greenaway, Rackham, Parrish, Wyeth, Dulac, Potter Heath Robinson, Nielson and so on. A full-color poster of one of Rackham's illustrations for *The Wind in the Willows* is $5 (minimum order two of ten subjects). Prints (average size 8'' x 10'') range from $1.50 to $4. Bookplates are sold in packages of twenty-five of the same design, full color $2.50, one color $1.50. Postcards cost from 15¢ to 30¢, note cards from 35¢ to 55¢, and can be ordered in boxes or packets of various quantities at prices ranging from $2.75 to $5.70. Six colored note cards with wonderful quotations suitable for valentines are 65¢ each. An introductory package with examples of stationery, postcards, prints, seals, bookplates, etc., is $10. There is a small charge for postage and handling.

G-24
GREGOIRE HARPSICHORD SHOP, Dept. CC
10551 Victory Lane, N.E.
Seattle, WA 98125

Sassman Harpsichords, *$1, refunded with purchase, published periodically (with model changes), 30 pages, illustrated, black and white.*

Gregoire Harpsichord Shop, with dealer-agencies throughout the U.S., is the exclusive distributor of the fine German-made Sassman harpsichords and spinets, relatively unknown in this country due to the limited number of instruments that have been available for export until now. Sassman has recently enlarged its facilities and can assure an ample supply of the nineteen standard models. While not exact copies of early instruments, they do not

Left, oversized pewter tankard after Benjamin Day of Newport, Rhode Island, in Collections of Greenfield Village and the Henry Ford Museum; Edison Institute, E-4. Below, footed pewter baptismal bowl reproduced from the Brooklyn Museum Collection, B-28.

deviate from historical models in any way that will cause any fundamental change in the quality of tone. The twelve models shown in the catalogue, which is printed in German, but has detailed descriptions in English, range in price from around $2,600 to over $10,000. Models other than those shown in the catalogue (prices on request) include authentic copies of Ruckers, Taskin and Zell harpsichords made by Sassman's skilled craftsmen, a clavichord and virginal, and Sassman invites orders to customers' individual requirements. Standard harpsichords are delivered in three to four months, special orders in six to eight months. Prices, computed from the Deutschmark, are subject to rate of exchange F.O.B. Boston.

G-25
GUILD OF SHAKER CRAFTS, Dept. CC
401 West Savidge Street
Spring Lake, MI 49456

Guild of Shaker Crafts, Crafters and Distributors of Authentic Shaker Replicas, *$2.50, published annually, 28 pages, illustrated, color and black and white.*

The Guild is noted for meticulous reproductions of the spare, simple Shaker furniture. The copies, made by local craftsmen from originals in various Shaker communities, include furniture (chairs, tables, benches, chests, cupboards, desks, beds, rockers) and other objects from community life such as a wood box, pegboard with thonged hangers, candlesticks and sconces, a cast-iron stove, yarn measure, mirror and rack, framed crewel "Tree of Life" wall hanging and "spirit paintings," Shaker doll, trays and boxes. The Guild supplies Shaker

colors in paint and stain and chair tapes by the yard in authentic Shaker colors and patterns. Collectors of Shaker furniture will be interested to know that the Guild has a special service for repairing and restoring original Shaker pieces. The price list and order form customarily sent with the catalogue were missing from ours, but we know from previous experience that prices are relatively modest for such fine work. If you are not happy with your order, merchandise will be accepted for refund if returned within ten days of receipt.

G-26
GUMP'S, Dept. CC
250 Post Street
San Francisco, CA 94108

Gump's Gift Book, *$1, published annually, 80 pages, illustrated, black and white and color.*

This famous San Francisco store sells by mail a wide range of items of interest to collectors. Illustrated in their current catalogue are flowering trees handcarved in jade and rose quartz, animals and gods carved from semiprecious stones by artisans of Kofu, Japan (exclusively for Gump's), antique porcelain, small sculptures, lacquerware, crystal, antique silver, pewter and jewelry. An eighteenth-century silver kettle and burner stand made in London by Benjamin J. Godfrey, 10" high, is priced at $6,000; a Baccarat crystal owl on a teakwood stand, 5⅛" high, is $47.50. Porcelain chopstick rests in the shape of birds, fish and people range in price from $15 to $28. A rose quartz rabbit on a polished persimmon wood stand, 3" high, sells for $95, and a rare octagonal Imari plate, circa 1820, one of only nine, is listed at $700. Shipping charges are extra.

Hand-wrought steel and brass utensils reproduced from the Colonial Williamsburg Collection, C-28.

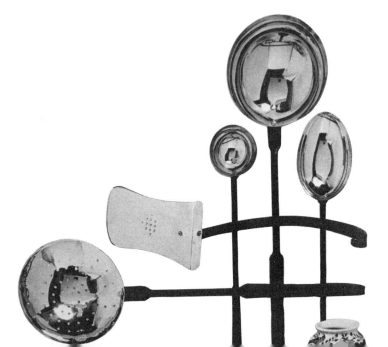

Above, cast-iron hansom cab, replica of a nineteenth-century toy; Museum of the City of New York, M-32. Below, a hand-painted mechanical toy bank. Gallery of Amsterdam, G-1.

H-1
HAGLEY MUSEUM STORE, Dept. CC
Barley Mill Road
P. O. Box 3630
Greenville, DE 19807

Hagley Museum Store, *free, published periodically, 6 pages, illustrated, color.*

The Hagley Museum Store specializes in items having to do with the du Pont powder mills and the Brandywine Valley. There are handmade copies of animal weather vanes in black metal, averaging 40″ high; color prints of old Brandywine recipes; hand-carved and painted wooden local birds by James Stewart—each one of a kind; a color print of a nineteenth-century advertisement, *Du Pont's Gun Powder;* a hand-molded replica of a nineteenth-century powder can; a metal mortar eprouvette paperweight, originally used to test gunpowder. A selection of books on nineteenth-century industry, technology, American history and decorative arts is also available. Prices range from 75¢ to $125.

H-2
HALE FARM AND VILLAGE, Dept. CC
Box 256
Bath, OH 44210

Authentic Crafts from Hale Farm and Village, *free brochure, published annually (Christmas), 6 pages, illustrated, black and white.*

The Hale Farm and Village, a department of the Western Reserve Historical Society, is a museum village of original old buildings and exhibits depicting the life of the pioneer settlers of the Western Reserve. The brochure shows a few simple crafts made by hand in the village workshops, such as a stoneware butter crock and jug with blue designs in the nineteenth-century style ($10 for the crock, $16 for the jug, shipping inclusive) and reproductions of a glass sugar bowl and a footed bowl with ribbed pattern. For the collector of paperweights, there is one of clear glass embedded with shards from the 1824 Franklin Glassworks ($10). The brochure also offers memberships in the Western Reserve Historical Society.

H-3
CHARLES HAMILTON GALLERIES, INC.,
Dept. CC
25 East 77th Street
New York, NY 10021

Autographs at Auction, *$35, published ten times a year (individual catalogues $2), 60 pages, illustrated, black and white.*

Charles Hamilton Galleries are experts in autographed materials such as letters and documents. Among the fascinating items offered are a letter by the black composer Samuel Coleridge-Taylor; a portion of a program for *Elektra* at the Metropolitan Opera signed by Richard Strauss; a signed portrait postcard of Lord Alfred Douglas; No. 444 of 650 copies of Robert Frost's *Aforesaid,* signed; several lots of Nazi memorabilia including items signed by Hitler; and a score of *La Bohème* inscribed by Puccini. Over 250 items are listed in this one catalogue. Prices range from around $75 to $850 and there are additional charges for shipping. A brochure, *How to Sell Your Autographs,* is available free on request.

H-4
THE HAMILTON MINT, Dept. CC
40 East University Drive
Arlington Heights, IL 60004

A Collector's Christmas from the Hamilton Collection, *free, published seasonally, 24 pages, illustrated, color.*

The catalogue covers a comprehensive and unusual collection of items selected both for beauty and for investment value—limited-edition plates, porcelain sculptures and engravings, reproductions of fine art pieces, antique Chinese porcelains and Limoges boxes—garnered from many sources. In the current catalogue, there are adaptations from Boehm, Haviland-Parlon and Arthur Court of some of the treasures of Tutankhamun, such as a lovely blue faience cup, 3″ high and 4″ in diameter ($35), a limited-edition plate from Haviland-Parlon with a jewelry design of winged birds and scarabs, and a scarab paperweight by Boehm of hand-painted porcelain in gold and blue, reproduced from Tutankhamun's lapis lazuli and gold scarab bracelet. The catalogue also lists a sleek green Lalique crystal lizard ($95), and a Blue Canton reproduction platter from the Historic Charleston collection ($125). A Villeroy & Boch stein from Mettlach, West Germany, in a limited production of just 3,000, is decorated with castles and churches and the Mettlach-trademark Old Tower on the lid ($200). Then there's the "lost" series of twelve Delft plates depicting the months of the year in the Dutch countryside, originally designed between 1890 and 1895 by Adolph le Compte, but never produced until now (of the 6,000 sets made, The Hamilton Collection was allocated 2,500, all of which have undoubtedly already been sold). Among other treasures are a beautifully hand-painted "Anna" decanter by Orrefors with matching bell, a Lalique crystal "leaf" paperweight ($75) and some enchanting examples of oriental kite art, hand-screened, signed and numbered miniature kites, 14″ square with mat and frame ($30 each).

H-5
HANSEN PLANETARIUM, Dept. CC
15 S. State Street
Salt Lake City, UT 84111

Hansen Planetarium Publications, free, 10 pages, illustrated, black and white.

The Hansen Planetarium offers a collection of slides and maps at very reasonable prices. Twenty superslides of the planets, comets and meteors cost $6 a set or 35¢ apiece; Celestron International slides are 35¢; a collection of NASA color slides, $1.50 per set of five. An 18″ x 37″ extremely accurate chart of the heavens costs 60¢. New moon maps from Rand McNally sell for $1 and $1.95 depending on size. There are also constellation postcards, a solar system chart and several posters relating to space travel and astronomy.

H-6
HAPPY THINGS, Dept. CC
73 Spring Street
Eureka Springs, AR 72632

Happy Things, 35¢, 6 pages, published annually, illustrated, one color.

This old-fashioned toy shop in the Victorian hill town of Eureka Springs specializes in Victorian doll houses and furnishings. The kit for a Country Victorian doll house, 32″ wide, 31″ high, 21″ deep, comes with prepunched gingerbread trim, requires only hand tools to assemble

and costs $79.75 plus $4 shipping. A ten-light wiring kit is available for an additional $18. The miniature Victorian furnishings for every room, scale 1″ to 1′, are sumptuous. For the library and music room, a carved walnut grand piano is $25, the Queen Anne English chaise longue covered in cranberry fabric, $32. A beautiful, thick, 100 percent wool oriental rug is $20. The Victorian bathroom includes a three-piece porcelain set—bathtub, basin and toilet with high tank, $5.95; His & Hers towel set, $1.25; soap dish, $1.10; and standing mirror, $2.50. A complete country store interior, with pattern and materials ($12.40) includes everything from a sunbonnet ($1.50) to a peanut machine by Chrysnbon ($3.95), with stock for the shelves. Also available are shadow box rooms of kitchens, nurseries and parlors. Write for such specific items mentioned, but not shown, as mechanical banks from John Wright Co., Madame Alexander dolls, Kewpie dolls and dolls with china heads.

H-7
H. R. HARMER, INC., Dept. CC
6 West 48th Street
New York, NY 10036

Rare Postage Stamps, $1, approximately 128 pages, published bimonthly, September to July, illustrated, black and white.

With branches in London, Sydney and San Francisco, Harmers of New York, Inc., is one of the more prestigious stamp auction houses. Over 25,000 lots are offered annually, and the well-documented catalogue of auctions comes with a bidding envelope and specific instructions for placing bids as well as information on viewing the collections.

H-8
HARMER ROOKE NUMISMATISTS, LTD.,
Dept. CC
3 East 57th Street
New York, NY 10022

Harmer Rooke Coin Sale, $2.50, 25 pages, illustrated, black and white. Alpha Sale of Pre-Columbian and Ancient Antiquities, $10, 100 pages, illustrated, color.

Besides specializing in every kind of numismatic item—ancient, modern, domestic, foreign, in numerous metals—this noted auction house also deals in ancient artifacts and antiques. Auctions are held a number of times throughout the year and for a fee of $1 you will be put on their mailing list.

H-9

HARRAH'S AUTOMOBILE COLLECTION,
Dept. CC
P. O. Box 10
Reno, NV 89504

***Harrah's Automobile Collection Special Edition
Roster,*** *$10.90 (includes postage and handling),
illustrated, color.*

The catalogue contains 180 color photographs of the
Fords, Franklins, Packards, Duesenbergs and Bugattis
that are part of Harrah's extraordinary collection of 1,500
classic automobiles. Color slides and postcards of shop
areas (the automobiles are constantly being worked on)
and cars are also available. Prices range from 10¢ to $10,
with a small charge for postage and handling.

H-10

H.E. HARRIS & CO., INC., Dept. CC
645 Summer Street
Boston, MA 02210

*Harris Reference Catalog of Postage Stamp Prices
of the United States, United Nations, Canada &
Provinces, $1.95, 218 pages, published twice a
year, illustrated, black and white.*

Founded in 1916, Harris is the world's largest stamp firm
and the only major catalogue publisher to buy and sell
stamps, so the individual market prices listed represent
their actual mail-order selling prices. Their very comprehensive catalogue, edited by professional stamp
buyers, covers every stamp of the U.S., U.S. posses-
sions, Canada and the United Nations, with the exception
of great rarities. Advanced collectors and specialists interested in rarities, covers and special items not listed are
invited to write specifying their requirements. One con-
venience is that if you have such credit cards as American
Express or Master Charge, you can open a charge account
with Harris. In addition to the detailed price list, with
black-and-white pictures of the stamps, there's a stamp
identifying guide that tells you how to distinguish between rare and common U.S. stamps that look alike, and
lists of books, accessories and supplies for the collector.
A most useful reference, well worth the money.

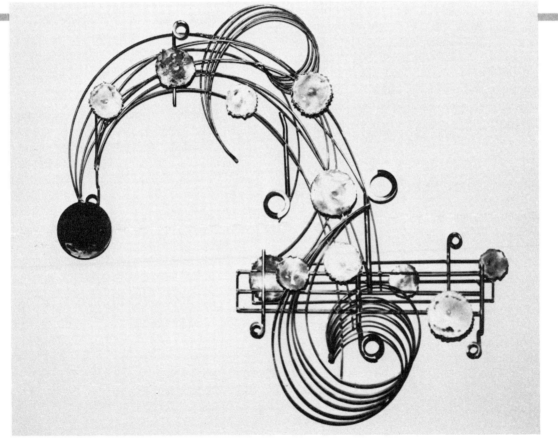

"Staff" sculpture in copper, brass and steel. Addison Greene, A-1.

H-11
JOHN HATHAWAY, Dept. CC
410 West 6th Street (Box 1287)
San Pedro, CA 90731

The Card Model, *free, published annually, 24 pages, illustrated, black and white.*

Though a relatively new hobby in this country, paper modeling (finely detailed scale models built of paper) is one of the oldest crafts, dating back to ancient Egypt. Popular in Europe as a challenging hobby requiring great skill, patience and attention to detail, the designs are truly beautiful and highly collectible. Some date back to eighteenth-century France. Whole towns and cities in scale serve as backgrounds for model railroads. Historical cathedrals, castles and houses become living history lessons. Model aircraft, automobiles, boats and ships in exciting three-dimension and accurate detail are surprisingly strong when finished. For bird lovers there are paper sculptures, which Mr. Hathaway rightly describes as "taxidermy in paper." They are life-size, life-like, full color and make marvelous mobiles. John Hathaway has collected what he considers the best of the card models manufactured in England, France, Germany and Holland. Prices are low. The "Fairy Tale" palace of Ludwig II (copied for Disneyland), 12'' x 18'' in 1:120 scale, is $7.35. An 18'' x 25'' German village is $4.85. A model of Canyon City (41'' x 22'') costs $7.95. The birds start at $2.20 for a swallow with 11½'' wing span. The *U.S.S. Pensacola* can be had for $2.25, and a Fokker DR-1 is $2.85. Assembly requires a matte knife, white glue and a straight edge.

H-12
THE HAWAIIAN SHOPPER, Dept. CC
P. O. Box 8886
Honolulu, HI 96815

The Hawaiian Shopper, *free, published seasonally, 32 pages, illustrated, color.*

The most interesting items in this gift catalogue of things from the Hawaiian Islands are tropical plants, such as white ginger, torch ginger, plumeria, orchids and tree ferns, available as rooted seedlings or in 2'' or 4'' pots with blooms. A sprouted coconut palm tree, 12'' tall, is $12.50 plus $1.50 postage and handling; fragrant white ginger in a 4'' pot, $3.50 each or three for $9.50, $1.25 postage and handling; a graceful Hawaiian tree fern, $6.75, $1.50 postage and handling. Cattleya and Dendrobium orchid seedlings are $4.95 each, a ti plant in 4'' pot, $3.50. There's also a Hawaiian chess set, with black pieces made of lava, brown of hapa-wood, each chessman symbolizing Hawaiian legends or ancestry (a booklet describes each piece) for $135, $2.50 postage and handling;

coral and ivory jewelry and, of course, all the usual gift items and foods. Orders may be called in to a toll-free number and charged to major credit cards.

H-13
HAYES-LEGER, LTD., Dept. CC
P. O. Box 14143
Atlanta, GA 30324

Catalogue, free, 9 loose pages, illustrated, color and black and white.

A mini catalogue consisting of separate sheets, packaged envelope fashion, with a small selection of gifts from around the world, pleasant but not unusual. In the current mailing piece, there's a handcrafted sterling silver angel tree ornament from Mexico, 7¼'' high, $25; Chinese handwoven split bamboo baskets in various shapes and sizes; a 12'' reproduction Imari chop plate with stand ($25); and a reproduction in handwrought iron and brass of an antique French baker's rack, 39'' wide, 18'' deep and 86'' high, that would make an elegant display piece for china, $525.

H-14
HEATHER HILL CRAFTS, Dept. CC
4312 West 178th Street
Torrance, CA 90504

Heather Hill Crafts, *50¢, published annually, 20 pages, illustrated, sepia sketches.*

There are many delightful handcrafted things in this cheerful little catalogue—toys, pillow kits, reproductions of Pennsylvania Dutch *fraktur* (wedding and birth certificates) on antiqued plaques that can be ordered personalized with your own names and dates for an extra $2 added to the $12.50 price of the plaque. Mirrors with stained-glass panels are $24 and stained-glass windows can be designed and made to order. They also have miniature furniture, dollhouses and various kinds of dolls, both in kits and ready made. One group of museum-quality dolls in period costume, authentic down to the last detail, is made in a limited number of 100 of each design. The artist will make any doll to order, number it and give a certificate of authenticity.

H-15
G. HENSON STUDIO, Dept. CC
328 Rockledge Lane
Manitou Springs, CO 80829

G. Henson Bronzes, *$3, 16 loose pages in folder, illustrated, black and white and color.*

Mr. Henson sculpts chiefly Western subjects—a mustang rearing dramatically (11¼'' high); a buffalo attacking an

Indian brave and his pony (9″ high); cowboys at their jobs; mustangs on the run; gulls skimming the waves. Works are available in various patinas and some are painted. Prices on request.

H-16
HERE, INC., Dept. CC
29 S. E. Main Street
Minneapolis, MN 55414

Here, Inc., free, 5 pages, illustrated, black and white.

Here, Inc., specializes in mountain dulcimers, hammered dulcimers, mountain banjos, psaltery and thumb pianos in final, unfinished or kit forms. They also carry books, records and hardware. Kits come complete with everything but glue. Dulcimer kits start at $21, banjos at $57.75. Prices are expected to rise in the near future.

H-17
HICKORY HOUSE COLLECTOR, Dept. CC
108 E. Main
Ottumwa, IA 52501

Hickory House Collector, $1, 24 pages, published twice yearly, illustrated, black and white.

Christmas collectibles, limited-edition collector plates, bells, eggs, figurines, tankards, thimbles, dolls and holiday items make up this busy little catalogue. Prices range from around $4 for a wildlife Christmas ornament to $150 for a set of four 8½″ diameter Bing & Grondahl "Carl Larson" porcelain plates.

H-18
HIRSCHEL & ADLER GALLERIES, Dept. CC
21 East 70th Street
New York, NY 10021

A Gallery Collects, $5, 84 pages, illustrated, black and white and color. American Folk Art, $4.50, 44 pages, illustrated, black and white and color.

Two of the exhibition catalogues this noted gallery publishes four to six times a year. *A Gallery Collects* contains illustrations of a number of superb paintings by world famous artists such as Corot, Bonnard, Picasso, Modigliani, Derain, Whistler, Sargent, Homer, Cassatt, Demuth, Audubon, etc. Some of the pictures shown: a wonderful atmospheric study of a *Girl at the Window* by Eastman Johnson; a brilliant, sun-drenched picture of girls resting from croquet by Winslow Homer; a fool-the-eye painting of a horseshoe and a newspaper clipping mounted on a door by William Harnett; Maurice Prendergast's watercolor of *St. Mark's Venice*; studies of flowers and fruit by Charles Demuth; one of Charles

Burchfield's uncanny watercolors of an *Insect Chorus in September*. *American Folk Art* illustrates typical semi-naive portraits of parents and children, commemorative allegories, views of villages and homes, sea battles, weather vanes and a quilt. There is a beautiful still life of citrus fruit and a portrait of a young man holding a bird by the "Beardsley Limner." Prices on request.

H-19
HISPANIC SOCIETY OF AMERICA, Dept. CC
613 West 155th Street
New York, NY 10032

List of publications, library subjects, free, 10 pages. List of publications, museum subjects, free, 14 pages.

Publications listed under museum subjects cover the Hispanic Society itself, archeology, architecture, biography, ceramics, costume, glass, jewelry, lace, numismatics, art, sculpture and textiles. Library subjects include bibliography, biography, bookbinding, history, language, literature, manuscripts and music. Recordings and rental films in Spanish are also listed. Prices range from 25¢ to $35 for a book on *Juan Martinez Montañés, Sevillian Sculptor*. A good source for those interested in Hispanic culture.

H-20
HISTORICAL TECHNOLOGY, INC., Dept. CC
6 Mugford Street
Marblehead, MA 01945

Historical Technology, $4 for two issues a year, 66 pages, illustrated, black and white.

A fine, authoritative and often amusing catalogue for collectors of rare books on marine navigation, first editions of the most important books in the history of American navigation, rare handwritten navigation notebooks and a vast collection of rare instruments. The well-documented descriptions are chattily written and the editorial comments on items or their designers are informative and frequently witty. To quote from the publisher's "Condition of Instruments": "All the instruments in this catalog are intended for display purposes only. However, they are generally functioning although almost certainly not to their original accuracy. (When they are, please do not worry. We will be the first to let you know.) . . . None are offered in 'as is' condition. Descriptions of conditions may even tend to be slightly pessimistic."

Microscopes, maps, spy glasses, globes, chronometers, prospect glasses, quadrants, sextants, circumferentors, cameras can all be found here. Prices range from approximately $30 for a first edition of Edward Bausch's *Manipulations of the Microscope* (1885) to $4,895 for a

Battersea and Chelsea reproduction enamel boxes. Horchow Collection, H-25.

mid-eighteenth-century American Davis quadrant. How nice to find a technical catalogue that is written with care and love and in a style that holds the attention.

H-21
HISTORICAL T-SHIRTS, Dept. CC
Box 220
Cambridge, MA 02138

Historical T-Shirts, *free.*

This company sells by mail white cotton T-shirts with such illustrious faces and names as Virginia Woolf, Jung, Freud, Marx, Mao, Nijinsky, Bach and Mahler. Sizes are small, medium, large and extra-large, and at the time of writing the ppd. price was $6.

H-22
HISTORIC CHARLESTON REPRODUCTIONS,
Dept. CC
105 Broad Street
Charleston, SC 29401

Historic Charleston Reproductions, *$4, refundable with purchase of $25 or more, published annually, 32 pages, illustrated, black and white and color.*

This beautifully illustrated catalogue shows a wide range of items reproduced from historic artifacts in Charleston private and public collections. All copies are authorized by the Historic Charleston Foundation and include furniture, silver, porcelain, crystal, pewter, brass, fabrics, wallpaper and needlework. Some examples are a small mahogany handkerchief table in Queen Anne style, 28″ high; an octagonal mahogany stand, 18″ high, with a blue-and-white nineteenth-century Canton platter; a Queen Anne stand, 20″ high, with an eighteenth-century plate—platter and plate reproduced by Vista Alegre in Portugal; a lovely black lacquer spider-leg tea table with chinoiserie decoration, from an eighteenth-century original, 11½″ wide by 28″ deep by 27¼″ high; an elegant painted Sheraton settee in black, gold and terra-cotta with cane seat. Other offerings are pewter plates, bowls and candlesticks copied from early American examples, silver cups and spoons along with a Chippendale footed salver, sets of blue-and-white Canton china, China Trade porcelain, Gorham's "King Charles" silver and crystal and a number of lovely candlesticks reproduced in solid cast brass. Prices range from $5 to $3,774. There is a small charge for postage and insurance for furniture, which is shipped freight and insurance collect.

H-23
HOLLY CITY BOTTLE, Dept. CC
Box 344
Millville, NJ 08332

Price lists, free, illustrated, black and white.

Holly City Bottle makes glass decanters decorated with designs commemorating such occasions as Queen Elizabeth II's Silver Jubilee and the 1976 Tall Ships review in New York Harbor. A hand-numbered bottle honoring Jimmy Carter is priced at $30 first run, $10 second run; the Queen Elizabeth decanter is $30 first run; the Tall Ships $15 first run. Prices range from $10 to $150, and there are bonuses for each $30 ordered. Also offered are a series of commemorative paperweights and plates, and a Noritake bone china Easter egg, $15, and Christmas bell, $17.50.

H-24
HONOLULU ACADEMY OF ARTS ACADEMY
SHOP, Dept. CC
900 South Beretania Street
Honolulu, HI 96814

No catalogue.

The Academy Shop offers one item by mail, *Hawaiian Quilts* by Stella Jones at $4.50.

H-25
THE HORCHOW COLLECTION, Dept. CC
P. O. Box 34257
Dallas, TX 75234

The Horchow Collection Catalogue, $1 for six issues a year, illustrated, color.

This elegant, expensive gift catalogue always has some very special items of interest to collectors. Examples, from a 1977 issue, are simple, beautiful 300-year-old carved wood Himalayan rice bowls, ranging in size from 7″ to 13″ in diameter, 4½″ to 7″ tall, each $45; antique (circa 1850) English carriage lamps, restored but not wired, 17″ tall, at $350 a pair; *Jungle Garden* by Fleur Cowles, an original screen print from a limited edition of 100, signed, titled and numbered by the artist, $175. Other treasures that caught our eye are stunning antique Chinese leather chests, dating from the nineteenth century, lacquered in red or black and hand painted in gold, with lacquered or leather interiors, approximately 32″ x 14″ x 22″, $650 each, and some small antique porcelains from the Ch'ing Dynasty—bowls, teapots, paint boxes—ranging in price from $35 for a blue-and-white or *famille rose* paint box to $95 for a handsome blue-and-white traditional goldfish bowl, 8″ tall, 10″ in diameter, that would make a gorgeous cachepot. Then there were a stunning Baccarat crystal vase in a classic shape, Baccarat *objets d'art* like an obelisk and an Egyptian cat, a Tiffany sterling silver dish handcrafted to look like a lily pad ($88) and pairs of rare old cloisonné birds and animals from Peking—parrots, pandas, rams, horses—at prices ranging from $1,200 to $2,200.

H-26
HOTCHKISS HOUSE, INC., Dept. CC
18 Hearthstone Road
Pittsford, NY 14534

A Complete Catalogue of Books on Antiques & Collectibles, free, with spring and fall supplements, 12 pages, black and white.

A great reference source for the collector. The 1977 Hotchkiss catalogue lists over 1,400 selected titles of books in stock and sold by mail, divided and indexed into sixty categories of antiques, arts, hobbies and collecting. Each book is listed by title and author with a brief resumé of contents. Among the subjects covered in the table of contents are Americana, arms and armor, art and artists, art glass, barbed wire, books and autographs, bottles, buttons and thimbles, china and ceramics, clocks and watches, coins and currency, decoys, Depression glass, dolls, early advertising, furniture, games and postcards, ironware, kitchenware, maps and posters, marbles, musical instruments, netsuke, needlework and quilts, Old West, paperweights, pewter, railroads, sea shells, silver and silverplate, stamps, tinware and toleware, toys and banks, woodenware and carving, plus general antique and reference books. There are some useful price guides in different categories and a small, 192-page book by John F. Hotchkiss, *Limited Edition Collectibles,* about acquiring limited-edition art works and commemorative items, with hundreds listed, illustrated, named, dated and priced ($5.95). Orders are shipped the day they are received, unless the book is temporarily out of stock. There's a 10 percent discount for libraries, museums, dealers, and clubs and associations sending cash orders for at least five books shipped to the same destination.

H-27
MARTHA M. HOUSE, Dept. CC
1022 South Decatur Street
Montgomery, AL 36104

Southern Heirlooms from Martha M. House, $1, refundable with purchase, published annually, 40 pages, illustrated, black and white and color.

Reproductions of Victorian furniture originally made for Southern mansions, with illustrations and detailed specifications. There are copies of the Seignorette dining chairs and table from the old Jefferson Davis home in Montgomery, the original White House of the Confederacy; the Lincoln rocker in mahogany (around $340); lyre-base tables and console tables; sofas, side chairs and armchairs; chests, commodes and bedroom suites; and a charming little armless folding rocker (about $140). Samples of upholstery fabrics (velvets, brocades and tapestries) are sent for your selection.

H-28
HOUSE OF ALBI—GREAT CREATIONS, Dept. CC
1801 Midvale Court
Bakersfield, CA 93309

Santiago de Santiago: A Small Selection of His Art, $2, published periodically, 28 pages, illustrated, black and white and color.

Great Creations is the exclusive U.S. representative of the sculptor, de Santiago, who works in all the sculptural media from marble to clay. Among the works illustrated in the catalogue are portrait heads of children, a monumental nude (39' high), and nude allegories (of the seven elements, of the seven starry moments). Prices on request.

H-29
HOUSE OF MARTIAL KNIVES, Dept. CC
800 Kersey Road
Silver Spring, MD 20902

Authentic Reproductions, $2, refundable with purchase, revised as new items are added, 22 pages, illustrated, black and white.

Knives, swords and battle axes are the specialty of this company, and nineteen are illustrated, described in detail and priced in the current catalogue. There are some fascinating items like the Arkansas toothpick—a reproduction of one of America's most famous fighting knives, carried in a cowboy's boot to deal with rattlers, rustlers and other foes—a blade long sought after by collectors ($35, $6 for the sheath). Another is the dog-faced kriss, with a wavy 11'' blade and butt like the head of a dog with open mouth showing two canine teeth, a most unusual knife with handle of carved bone ($20 with sheath). Additional offerings include a Rajput combat dagger, an Arab khanjar, the khukri of the Ghurka soldiers, the classic tomahawk, double-headed battle axe, mace and the flail, or morningstar, a fourteenth-century devilish invention to be used only on horseback, 30'' long with a massive spiked steel ball on a chain that could be used to crush an opponent's armor, tear his sword from his hand or overshoot his shield ($29).

H-30
HOWARD CLOCK PRODUCTS, INC., Dept. CC
256 Charles Street
Waltham, MA 02154

Information sheet, free, illustrated.

From time to time, E. Howard & Co., ''the nation's timekeepers since 1842,'' re-issues limited editions of some of their famous clocks of the past, each recreated with the care and detail of the original. The purchaser is furnished with a signed certificate giving serial number and date of manufacture. Among the re-issues available at this writing were a Model #5, circa 1842; ''Figure Eight'' clock, circa 1860, and the ''Vienna'' style clock from around 1878. Prices start at over $600.

H-31
FRANK HUBBARD HARPSICHORDS, INC.,
Dept. CC
185A Lyman Street
Waltham, MA 02154

Keyboard Instruments from Frank Hubbard, free, published annually, 22 pages, illustrated, black and white.

Beautiful, classic harpsichords, either custom built or in kit form, are sold by this company, which was started twenty-five years ago by Frank Hubbard in his loft workshop in Boston. Today, the harpsichords are built by skilled craftsmen in a reconditioned eighteenth-century carriage house on the grounds of the historic Lyman Estate in Waltham. The custom-made instruments, accurate reproductions of those made by the great sixteenth-, seventeenth- and eighteenth-century instrument builders, Ruckers, Taskin, Moermans, Hemsch and others, range in price from around $4,000 for an Italian single-manual harpsichord based on seventeenth-century prototypes to $8,000 for an eighteenth-century French double-manual harpsichord after Hemsch. Kits for harpsichords, spinets and fortepianos start at under $1,000 for an English bentside spinet. Packing charges are extra. This is a fascinating, well-written and informative catalogue.

To display an offbeat collection of shears, scissors, spearheads and tools, designer Barbara D'Arcy created a counterpoint of the strong, simple shapes against an intricately patterned wallpaper. Courtesy: Bloomingdale's.

Famous British artist Roger Bacon contrasts the classicism of his collection of Greek and Roman heads and an eighteenth-century gilt-and-marble console with his own contemporary portraits. Photographer: John Vaughan.

H-32

HUGHES DULCIMER COMPANY, Dept. CC
8665 W. 13th Avenue—64
Denver, CO 80215

Catalogue, free, 8 pages, illustrated, black and white.

For musical hobbyists and collectors, Hughes offers stringed instruments that you can buy complete, or in kit form to assemble yourself at a considerable saving. For example, a trapezoidal guitar is $85 complete, $13.95 in kit form, and can be assembled in thirty to forty hours as the shape is much easier to build than the traditional guitar. (The shape does not affect the sound.) A simpler instrument like the hourglass dulcimer, which takes only eight to twelve hours to assemble, costs about $40 less if bought as a kit. The highest kit price for this dulcimer is $27.95, the lowest $17.95, according to size and wood. Completed instruments and kits range from dulcimers, including the hammered dulcimer (also known as a psaltery when it is plucked with the fingers, rather than hammered) to banjos, guitars, a mandolin, lyre, balalaika, Bardic, Celtic and Irish folk harps (smaller than the concert type) and the African kalimba, a rhythm instrument played by plucking metal reeds. Only common hand tools are needed for assembly. The catalogue also has a list of instructional books, records, supplies such as glue, spray stains and finishes, fret saw, and various accessories like string sets, pitchpipes, bags and cases. Packing and mailing extra.

Below, pre-Columbian warrior, Colima region, reproduction from Artiques, A-23. Right, Pierrot terra-cotta sculpture by Peggy Mach. Museum Collections, M-28.

Left, a poster advertising Mercedes Daimler; Fiesta Arts, F-4. Below, hood ornaments/radiator caps, called "mascots," from vintage automobiles; Harrah's Automobile Collection, H-9.

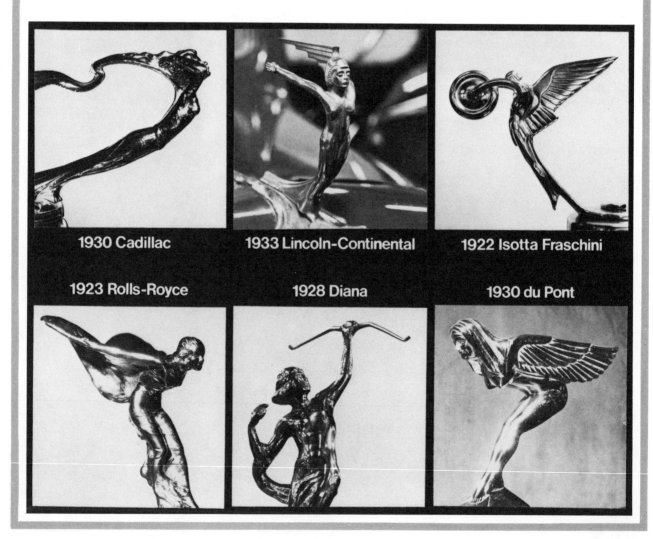

1930 Cadillac   1933 Lincoln-Continental   1922 Isotta Fraschini

1923 Rolls-Royce   1928 Diana   1930 du Pont

I

I-1
THE ICART VENDOR, Dept. CC
3146 Purdue Avenue
Los Angeles, CA 90066

Inventory list, 50¢ and stamped self-addressed envelope.

Original etchings by Louis Icart and reproductions of his work are the specialty of The Icart Vendor. Original etchings are in the $500 to $800 price range. There are also some intriguing turn-of-the-century French posters, Art Deco and Art Nouveau posters, among them reproductions of Maxfield Parrish and A. Mucha.

I-2
IMAGES NORTH, Dept. CC
P. O. Box 1275
Fairbanks, AK 99707

The Alaska Needlepoint Collection, 50¢, published annually, 20 pages, illustrated, sepia.

An unusual collection of needlepoint designs adapted from rare museum pieces—woven baskets, ivory and soapstone carvings, wooden masks, blankets and beadwork—artifacts which represent centuries in the art history of the Northern peoples. Each design, available as a kit with yarn, or with the printed canvas only, includes a legend card giving the history and origin. Examples are a shaman's mask, Tlingit killer whale, arrow basket pattern, Haida frog and Thunderbird. Prices range from $8.95 for the Aleut geometric kit, graph and canvas, no yarn, to $39.95 for the Thunderbird kit. Postage and handling for each kit is $2.50. There's also an Eskimo doll called Pani, created by Jacqueline Butler, president of Images North, to introduce young people to the art of needlepoint ($15.95 for the kit). Any of the designs in the catalogue can be adapted to your special size requirements and Images North will also custom design to order from a photograph of the design you wish to have adapted to needlepoint, particularly Alaskan or other native American designs.

I-3
IMPRESSIONS WORKSHOP AND GALLERY,
Dept. CC
29 Stanhope Street
Boston, MA 02116

Impressions Quarterly, I and II, $1 each, published as new print editions become available, loose sheets in folders, illustrated, black and white.

Colored lithographs, etchings and wood engravings by contemporary artists in signed, limited editions are offered by this Boston workshop/gallery. There are abstractions, surrealist fantasies and figurative images, landscapes, still-life studies, scenes of people at play—for example, the subtle abstractions of Adja Yunkers, the Proustian images of Peter Milton, Herb Jackson's semiabstractions of seasons and elements. Prices range from $80 to $800.

I-4
INDIAN HOUSE, Dept. CC
Box 472
Taos, NM 87571

Indian House Record and Tape Catalogue, free, 6 pages, illustrated, black and white.

An unusual and fascinating catalogue featuring Indian songs recorded on LPs, eight-track tapes and cassettes (each $6) that range from peyote morning songs to Navajo corn-grinding and shoe game songs to dance songs of the Taos and San Juan pueblos to recordings made live at the Zuni Fair and Forty-eighth Inter-Tribal Indian Ceremonial at Gallup, New Mexico. There are also recordings by The Badlands Singers, Ashland Singers and Old Agency Singers of the Blood Reserve. Worth sending for if you are into American Indian music and rituals.

I-5
INDUSTRIAS AKIOS, Dept. CC
P. O. Box 219
Quito, Ecuador

Artesanias Akios Handcrafts," $2, *published
every two years, 60 pages, illustrated, black and
white.*

The handcrafts and tourist center of Quito has put together a bilingual catalogue that, although primitive, is worth browsing. Original oil paintings by "competent Ecuadorian artists of reputation" may be had for as little as $2. Typical Indian native dolls with hand-carved features are a steal at $2.50 for a 7″ pair. Musical instruments include flutes, maracas and drums. Among the Indian trophies are blow guns with darts and quivers, bows, arrows and imitation shrunken heads. More decorative items include gourd *chicha* bottles, tapestries made of *llanchama* treebark, jibaro uniforms, feather crowns, beads, earrings, boxes, purses and even a bellows. Carved wood and stone figures, some based on Incan designs, are good buys and unusual pieces. There is a handsome chess set hand carved in cedarwood in which the chess pieces are Incan idols, $10 without box, $15 with. A similar set is carved from ivory nut. Woven

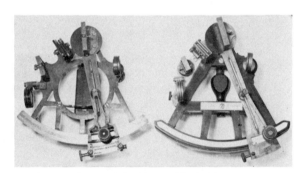

Antique quadrants. John F. Rinaldi, R-14.

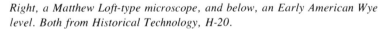

*Right, a Matthew Loft-type microscope, and below, an Early American Wye
level. Both from Historical Technology, H-20.*

blankets, tapestries, handmade wool rugs, toys, masks, bread-dough Christmas ornaments, bread-dough mirrors, accessories and clothes fill out the catalogue.

While many of the items are "touristy," some seem quite unusual. Keep in mind that all orders are dutiable and sent on a pro forma basis. Customers should allow up to eight weeks for delivery after payment has reached Quito.

I-6
INTERNATIONAL CENTER OF PHOTOGRAPHY, Dept. CC
1130 Fifth Avenue
New York, NY 10028

Museum Shop Catalogue/Holiday Supplement, *$1, published seasonally, 48-page catalogue with 16-page supplement, illustrated, black and white.*

The catalogue is ring-bound so that future supplements may be added and contains a wide and impressive range of books, cards, posters, catalogues, calendars and periodicals pertaining to photography and the leading photographers. A super source. The material is carefully selected, comprehensive and outstanding in quality. In the holiday supplement for 1977: a special limited-edition portfolio, *The Earth and the Fullness Thereof,* ten color prints, mounted, matted and ready for framing, by noted photographer-journalist Gail Rubin (around $1,250) and four portfolios of the work of Andreas Feininger, each with twelve original prints signed and numbered by the photographer in a limited edition of 100 for each series ($1,750 a portfolio). The general catalogue also lists a selection of audio visuals (slides in a carousel tray with tape cassette soundtrack and illustrated booklet of transcripts, biographies and texts) on fascinating subjects. One is the *Images of Man* series with photographs and text by nine photographers, another *The Decisive Moment: the photographer as artist* by Henri Cartier-Bresson ($75). A $25 membership to ICP would be well worthwhile, even if you couldn't attend the exhibits, films, special events and previews in New York, as members get a 15 percent discount on orders.

I-7
INTERNATIONAL FINE ARTS LTD., Dept. CC
3601 N.W. 19th Street
Lauderdale Lakes, FL 33311

Original Contemporary Graphics, *$12.50 (refundable with purchase), published annually, 104 pages, illustrated, black and white.*

The best of modern prints, all guaranteed original, hand-signed works. The catalogue lists only a small portion of the inventory. Most of the great names are included —Picasso, Moore, Tamayo, Vasarely, Dali, Miró, Chagall along with top Americans like Baskin, Krushenick, Indiana, Lindner and Tobey. Baskin's etching *Iris for Lisa,* 22″ x 30″, signed edition of 130, costs $300. One of an edition of 200, Chagall's 1975 *Song of Songs,* a colored lithograph, 18″ x 24″, is $5,000. One of the many Dali prints is an illustration for the *Divine Comedy,* 7″ x 10″ plus margins, dated 1970, in an edition of 60, costing $250. *Watermelon* by Tamayo, a 1972 lithograph in an edition of 100, 36″ x 24½″, is priced at $1,000. *The Family,* an etching by Romare Bearden, 19½″ x 26″, costs $400 (pre-publication) in an edition of 175.

I-8
INTERNATIONAL IMPORTS, Dept. CC
Box 2010
Toluca Lake, CA 91620

Occult Digest, *$1, refundable with purchase, 128 pages, published annually, illustrated, black and white.*

International Imports is one of the three largest suppliers of occult products in the United States. On this mystical shopping tour you will find almost everything occult in the way of books, candles, potions, conjure bags, crystal balls, herbs and herb jewelry, incense, oils and powders, prints and posters, records, gnostic seals, talismans, planetary seals, hex signs, power squares, voodoo veves, stones, tarot cards, astrology charts and symbolic jewelry . . . all sold as curios, of course. Prices seem down-to-earth reasonable.

I-9
IROQRAFTS, LTD., Dept. CC
RR #2
Ohsweken, Ontario NOA IMO
Canada

Arts and Crafts, *$1, refundable with purchase, 40 pages, published periodically, illustrated, black and white and color.*

A large selection of traditional and ceremonial Iroquois crafts and arts from the Six Nations reservation. Among them are Iroquois watercolors and baskets, and Mohawk paintings, pottery and ceremonial jewelry. Iroqrafts also carries Eskimo art, stone sculptures, masks and musical instruments and various arts and crafts representing the Cree, Ojibwa and North West Coast tribes. Masks, sculptures and original art enter the U.S. duty-free. Books, graphics and craft supplies are also available. Prices range from 10¢ to hundreds of dollars.

Above, one of "Set of Six Restauration Style Chairs," circa 1845 from Frank S. Schwarz & Sons, S-6. Right, Shaker writing desk kit; National Handcraft Institute, N-5. Below, "Breakfast table," reproduced from a mid-eighteenth-century Pembroke table; Historic Charleston Reproductions, H-22.

Long Island Kas, American, circa 1730. Frank S. Schwarz & Sons, S-6.

J-1

CHARLES W. JACOBSEN, INC., Dept. CC
401 South Salina Street
Syracuse, NY 13201

Brochures and descriptive lists, free, some illustrated in color.

Jacobsen has a wide selection of handwoven oriental rugs imported from such countries as Iran, India, Pakistan, Turkey and Rumania. There are handsome new designs and designs in antique patterns and colors. Savonnerie and Chinese-style rugs woven in India are also listed. Sizes vary from 2' x 3' to 13' x 19' and prices run from $59 to $11,800 depending on size, type and quality. A limited number of antique and semi-antique (from ten to fifty years old) rugs are also offered. Two books by Charles W. Jacobsen are available, *Check Points on How to Buy Oriental Rugs* ($11.50) and *Oriental Rugs, A Complete Guide* ($22.50). If you buy a rug for $300 or more, the price of the books will be credited against your purchase. Kodachrome slides of rugs will be sent on receipt of their listed number and the rugs themselves sent on approval, shipping charges paid both ways, within a radius of 2,000 miles from Syracuse.

J-2

JAVO DISTRIBUTING CO., Dept. CC
P. O. Box 13288
Tampa, FL 33681

Price lists of shells and shell reference books, free, 5 pages, published annually, with several price revision reprints.

This company sells sea shells from all over the world priced from 25¢ to $25, with many under $1. They do not have cut shells or shellcraft supplies. For beginners, there's a small paperback, *Sea Shells of the World,* by R. Tucker Abbot, 160 pages with 790 color illustrations, for around $2. The price list is the order form; you merely circle the price of the shells you want, total your order, then mail the list back with your check. Shipping is free for orders of $10 or more. The one-page book list offers books Javo believes would be most helpful to their clients, ranging in price from $4.50 for paperbacks on Caribbean and North American sea shells to $41.50 for *Living Cowries of the World* by C.M. Burgess, a hardbound book with 389 pages and 44 color plates.

J-3

JEFFERSON STAMP COMPANY, INC., Dept. CC
44 Pondfield Road
Bronxville, NY 10708

JSC–United States Stamps. 19th and Early 20th Century Classic, free, published semi-annually, 24 pages.

Jefferson has two catalogues, for different grades of United States stamps. The white cover lists those that are extremely fine and very fine; the blue cover, fine and fine average, both mint and used. The minimum order is $15 with a 5 percent discount on purchases over $500, 10 percent on purchases over $1,000. There's also a convenient 24-hour, 7-days-a-week telephone-order service.

J-4

THE JEWISH MUSEUM, Dept. CC
1109 Fifth Avenue
New York, NY 10028

Judaica Reproductions, 50¢, published annually, color photographs in silver presentation envelope.

The Jewish Museum offers an attractive collection of reproductions from their collection. Each color photograph is backed with a description of the original piece's history. Size and price are listed on the order form. There are amulets, kiddush cups, a menorah (Hanukkah lamp), mezuzahs, hamsas, Purim and Passover plates, a swivel ring and a wedding ring. Pieces are available in pewter or silver at prices ranging from $5 for the pewter wedding ring ($20 in silver) to $75 for the 13''-diameter pewter Seder plate. The museum also offers a beautifully illuminated marriage contract on parchment paper and embroidery and needlepoint kits based on Jewish themes.

J-5
JONES & SCULLY, INC., Dept. CC
2200 N.W. 33rd Avenue
Miami, FL 33142

Recommendations, *$4, published annually, 158 pages, illustrated, color.*

A very complete and lavishly illustrated catalogue that emphasizes hybrids (mature and seedling sizes) and collected species of merit for the orchidist. The genera are listed alphabetically, and each is introduced under a magenta heading. Mature plants are shown first, followed by seedlings of the genus and mericlones, each differentiated by a panel or page of color. Flowering seasons for the northern hemisphere are shown for each listing. There are also sections on books for an orchid reference library and other horticultural subjects, and supplies for the orchidist, including a kit for an orchid house that ranges in price from $460 for a house 7′ x 10′ x 8′ without cover to over $1,000 for a 9′ x 20′ x 8′ size with cover. Prices range widely, from $4 up to $1,500 for very special clones.

J-6
JOY'S LIMITED EDITIONS, Dept. CC
851 Seton Court
Wheeling, IL 60090

The Limited Edition Collector, *free, published seasonally, 24 pages, illustrated, color.*

The Christmas catalogue has a pleasant selection of limited-edition collector's plates, including Haviland-Parlon tapestry plates (a series started in 1976), an Art Nouveau "Lily" plate by Tiziano, the annual Hamilton Mint pewter Christmas plate and many others, some of which are listed at $5 to $10 off the printed price. The catalogue also has a Goebel porcelain crèche, hand-painted ($110) or classic white ($63.50), with wood manger; Christmas bells such as the Currier & Ives bell by Gorham ($9.95) and various figurines and Christmas tree ornaments (the Gorham crystal snowflake is especially beautiful). A printed newsletter in the center of the catalogue gives chatty details about the offerings. Order form and price list included. There's a $2 charge for postage and handling on orders under $30.

William the Conqueror's boat, adapted from the Bayeux tapestry in a crewel-work kit. Jane Whitmire, W-12.

Above left, Early American wooden dancing doll from World Wide Games, W-20. Right, whimsical stuffed animals; Berea College Student Craft Industries, B-2. Below, a hand-carved rocking horse from a Vermont original, circa 1850; Edison Institute, E-4.

K-1
KALEIDOSCOPE, Dept. CC
2201 Faulkner Road N.E.
Atlanta, GA 30324

Kaleidoscope, *free, published eight times a year, 38 pages, illustrated, color.*

A mail-order catalogue with a number of delightful things of interest to collectors, among them a signed and registered paperweight (one of several) in amethyst art glass with silver overlay of the moon and the sea, a hand crafted window pendant of stained glass depicting shells and sea creatures, a "Gertrude Stein" ceramic stein, a stuffed unicorn in satin and corduroy, a hand-painted Kutani porcelain cat and a Ming Dynasty design of a blue-and-white cat that takes a candle inside. Perhaps the most spectacular offerings are the hand-carved cypress-wood boxes with Noh theatrical masks, reproduced from the classic Japanese originals, servings as lids. Prices range from $6 to $535, with a small additional charge for postage and handling.

K-2
KEELEY'S MUSEUM SHOP, Dept. CC
P. O. Box 409
Cody, WY 82414

Keeley's Museum Shop, Buffalo Bill Historical Center, *price list, free, published annually.* ***The Schmid Collection of Donald Polland's American West,*** *free, 16 pages, color, published annually.* ***Donald Polland, Sculptor. Western Bronze Miniatures,*** *free, sepia-tone flyers in folder, photographs.*

The *Keeley's Museum Shop* price list features quality reproductions in color of Remington, Charles Russell and other Western artists, lithographs on paper and artists' canvas board, priced from $1.75 to $18.50, Buffalo Bill

Circus posters, books and slides on the Old West, cookbooks, etc.

The *Schmid Collection* catalogue shows Polland's pewter sculptures (in limited editions) of western scenes. Each piece, cast by Lance of New England, bears the sculptor's signature, the Lance touchmark and registration number. Prices range from $175 to $300, depending on size of edition.

The folder of photographs is devoted to limited-edition Polland miniature bronzes of action in the Old West. Prices range from $450 for a 5¼" x 3¼" *War Chief Plaque* in an edition of sixty, to a 12" x 32" x 46" *Ambush at Rock Canyon* in an edition of five for $25,000. Unfortunately, the sepia-tone photographs are not sharp enough for the artist's work to be fully appreciated.

K-3
THOMAS F. KELLETT, Dept. CC
P. O. Box 91
Lombard, IL 60148

Mint United States Stamps, *price lists, 35¢, published as market requires.*

The price lists are also the order form; you circle the price of the desired item, total each column and page and return the marked pages with remittance. All stamps are fine or better. Kellett will also buy or trade mint U.S. material.

K-4
KENMORE STAMP COMPANY, Dept. CC
Milford, NH 03055

Kenmore Stamp Catalog, *free with $2.95 purchase of 1,000 all-different U.S.A. and foreign stamps, published semiannually, 80 pages, illustrated, black and white.*

H.E. Harris, owner of Kenmore Stamps, claims that the 1,000 stamp offer is worth over $30 at standard catalogue

Above, Cappé porcelain figures from Italy; Ebeling & Reuss, E-2. Below, Wedgwood's Cutlers vase in three-color jasper; John Sinclair, S-20.

prices and has been so successful that he has not had a single request to date for a "money-back guarantee" refund. *You cannot get the catalogue unless you order the stamps.* The catalogue is fairly basic, mostly U.S. singles, sets and commemoratives. However, Kenmore offers complete mail-order service and welcomes the chance to search stamps and buy collections. Every purchase is backed by a ten-day money-back guarantee.

K-5
KENNEDY GALLERIES, INC., Dept. CC
40 West 57th Street
New York, NY 10019

Unique Art Objects, $5, 16 pages. The City as Source, $9, 62 pages. The Kennedy Galleries Collection of Fine Graphics, $5, 48 pages. All illustrated, black and white and color.

Exhibition catalogues and a general print catalogue from a top New York gallery primarily devoted to figurative art by Americans offer a fascinating number of choices for the collector. In *The City as Source* there are major works by major artists—a 1934 John Marin watercolor; street scenes by Charles Burchfield; watercolors of theater folk by Charles Demuth; a drawing of Central Park by Marsden Hartley; works by Hopper, Guy Pène Du Bois, Feininger, Levine, Luks, Sheeler, Marsh. The *Objects* catalogue shows such things as whimsical silver sculptures by Earl Krentzin depicting looney bird-monsters, an ostrich egg being launched; sculptures by Eskimos from the village of Shishmareff in Alaska made from ivory, bone, sandstone, etc.; paintings of wildlife; small bronzes; assorted watercolors and drawings. Prices range from $150 to $2,000. The graphics collection catalogue shows limited, signed editions by a number of distinguished artists, important posters, lithographs by Currier & Ives, prints of Americana (such as early New York). Prices are generally available only on request.

K-6
JOSEPH H. KILLIAN, Dept. CC
39 Glen Byron Avenue
South Nyack, NY 10960

Antique Silver and Old Sheffield Plate, $2, refundable with purchase, 10 pages, published three times a year.

An impressive and wide-ranging list that starts with one 18k. gold item, an 1849 snuffbox made for the Earl of Belfast ($8,000) and goes on to various silver pieces by Paul Storr—such as a very rare 1836 tumbler cup ($6,500)—Hester Bateman, Irish silver, English silver and old Sheffield plate. Silver prices range from $25 for a single fiddle-pattern dessert spoon to $14,000 for a massive tea tray (1814) by Paul Storr. There are many small pieces under $100, such as sugar nippers, egg spoons, a cream ladle and pairs of salt spoons. Mid-eighteenth-century silver marrow scoops by Thomas Mann and Isaac Callard are $175 each. Each piece is fully described, with date, maker, measurements and marks. Everything on the list is, of course, one-of-a-kind and subject to prior sale, but a substitute is usually possible.

K-7
KING GEORGE AUTOGRAPHS, Dept. CC
86 King George Road
Poughkeepsie, NY 12603

King George Autographs, free, published 6 times a year, 24 pages.

The subject matter sets this company apart. These, say owners Michael and Patricia Karet, are ''autographs for the discriminating collector'' and almost half the items listed are signed by famous theatrical personalities such as Sir Henry Irving, Ellen Terry, Charles Kean, Charlotte Cushman, Edwin Booth, Dion Boucicault and William C. Macready, with a collection of thirteen theatrical broadsides or playbills, such as a Royal Lyceum Theatre playbill for June 13, 14 and 16, 1879, with Irving playing Richelieu ($20). There's also a series of liability release forms from a well-known New York newspaper signed by various show-biz personalities from June Allyson to Teresa Wright, among them Paul Newman, Marlene Dietrich and Ava Gardner, priced from $15 to $20. Apart from members of the acting fraternity, there are autographed documents and letters from John Philip Sousa ($100), Theodore Roosevelt ($400), Lord Nelson, Abraham Lincoln, Charles Dickens and William F. Cody, signed both W. F. Cody and Buffalo Bill ($115). Other unusual items in the catalogue are an Imperial Airways ticket for a Paris to London flight in October 1925 (Imperial was the world's first commercial passenger airline) and three deeds to the Salt Lake City property on which Brigham Young built his Bee-Hive ($450).

K-8
KOCH RECORDERS, Dept. CC
Haverhill, NH 03765

Koch Recorders, pamphlet, free, illustrated, black and white.

Since 1934 the Koch family has been turning out fine handcrafted recorders. Tuned to A440 pitch and with English (Baroque) fingering, there are four models (soprano, alto, tenor, bass) available in a choice of finishes. Prices start at $24 for a black cherry or maple soprano instrument. Repair service and replacement parts are also available.

K-9
KULICKE FRAMES INC., Dept. CC
636 Broadway
New York, NY 10012

Kulicke, $1, six loose sheets in folder, illustrated, black and white and color.

This widely known framer offers clear plastic wrap-around frames ready to hang or stand vertically or horizontally; metal section frames in different depths to take thin photographs or canvas stretchers; trap frames—two sheets of clear acrylic held together by aluminum slide-on edges; solid aluminum frames; a clear plastic frame made from a single piece of clear acrylic with frosted sides, designed at the request of the Museum of Modern Art in New York; welded aluminum and brass frames with polished tops and satin sides; a free-standing frame designed in collaboration with Andy Warhol which allows two-side visibility; and a number of other frames including traditional classics. Prices for the standard items range from $3.75 to $245 (for 480 feet of gold aluminum lineal elements). There is a small charge for shipping and handling.

Pug rag toy kit from the Museum of the City of New York, M-32.

The kind of family memorabilia normally relegated to a photo album can be given new life and purpose when enhanced by the decorative shapes and materials of a collection of old frames. Here, the grouping should be made with an eye for scale and balance.

Parlor from Victorian doll house kit. Craft Products, C-35.

Country kitchen in miniature. Scientific Models, S-8.

L-1

G. LAMBOR, Dept. CC
    5 Ventnor Lodge
    Ventnor Villas
    Hove, Sussex, BN3 3DD
    England

Brochure, $1 for four, published bimonthly, 4 pages, illustrated, black and white.

Mr. Lambor lists Egyptian, Mesopotamian, Anatolian, Greek, Etruscan, Roman and Islamic antiquities. Then, ranging beyond the Mediterranean, he adds Paleolithic, Celtic, Indian, Chinese, Aztec and Inca artifacts. The current brochure has a Syrian terra-cotta figurine of the goddess Astarte dating from 1,000 B.C.; a Ptolemaic inscribed papyrus fragment from Egypt; a third century B.C. pair of gold Greek earrings with bulls' head terminals; a black Etruscan cup; a Saxon glass bowl; a pre-Columbian Chimu blackware decorated pot from the eleventh century A.D.; and an English silver penny of William the Conqueror. Translations of ancient authors and numerous reference books are also available. Prices vary from around $1.50 to $500 and are subject to current exchange rates.

L-2

THE LANDFALL COLLECTION (Division of Carroll Reed, Inc.), Dept. CC
    9 State Street
    Marblehead, MA 01945

The Landfall Collection, free, published spring and fall, 32 pages, illustrated, color.

A catalogue of most attractive gifts with several special items related to the water and outdoors that would interest collectors. In the winter 1977 issue there is the first of an exclusive series of hand-carved and painted New England shorebirds by Cape Cod artist Reid Higgins. Gull or tern chicks, 3½'' long, are $22 each; the sanderling, 5½'' long, $120. Among other exclusives are one-of-a-kind chart tables made from oak timbers salvaged from shipwrecks in the Great Lakes, with a plaque identifying the wreck, 36'' x 24'' x 16'' high, with chart of your choice,

$520; an engraved handmade pewter plate commemorating the U.S. contenders in the 1977 America's Cup race, 11'' in diameter, in limited quantity, $48; and mineral sculptures on clear Lucite bases, the creations of Arthur Court, each stone related to an astrological sign, $16. A Lucite display shelf for the minerals, 18'' x 18'', is $100. For ship collectors there is a model kit of the famous clipper *Flying Cloud,* 37'' long, with carved wooden hull, fittings, plans and instructions, $81.50. Unusual and charming Christmas tree ornaments made from trochus and star turban sea shells are $18 a dozen.

L-3

LANE'S REPOSITORY, Dept. CC
    1187 Dakota Road
    North Brunswick, NJ 08902

Old Maps and Prints (1600's through 1900), free, 12 pages, published periodically.

Larry and Florence Lane specialize in Americana, specifically a straightforward, unillustrated, documented listing of early, original regional maps of America, including some French editions; coastal charts; and engravings and lithographs covering a wide range of subjects, with several Civil War scenes, cityscapes and portraits. Prices range from $8.50 for an 1897 map of Virginia by the Century Co., New York, to $375 for *Virginia, Marylandia et Carolina in America Septentrionali . . .* by Joh. Bapt. Homan, circa 1714. Prints range in price from $10 to $75. We should point out that the sample list we saw was for Delaware, Maryland and Virginia, and our price scale is based solely on that. The Lanes do not have a general catalogue but will send specialized lists on request.

L-4

HANNIBAL LEE COLLAGES, Dept. CC
    P. O. Box 1092
    Easton, MD 21601

Brochure, free, 4 pages, black and white.

Artist Hannibal Lee has no catalogue but will send on request colored slides or photos of collages available at the time of enquiry and the small black-and-white brochure that shows his style. The brochure describes how he creates his collages of fabric, often combined with grasses, bark and stones, from his original drawings. A major collage can contain up to 1,600 pieces of fabric. Mr. Lee's subject matter embraces endangered animals, waterfowl, sea shells, mythology, people living and dead, houses and buildings of historic interest. He accepts commissions and will create personalized collages for clients on any subject in sizes from table-top art to wall-size murals. He has signed, numbered low-edition prints available, including the charming *Orpheus and the Animals,* edition of 150, in a hand-burled walnut frame. An unusual, personal art form well worth collecting.

L-5
THE LEFT HAND, INC., Dept. CC
140 West 22nd Street
New York, NY 10011

The Left Hand Catalog, $1, refundable with purchase, published annually, 30 pages, illustrated, black and white.

A catalogue designed especially for southpaws, full of all kinds of useful and amusing gadgets and objects—sports equipment, housewares, books on left-handed knitting, crochet and needlepoint, wallets, left-handed moustache cups, mugs and pitchers. Poster collectors will find black-and-white photographic posters, 2½' x 3½', of "legendary lefties" such as Chaplin, Garbo, Babe Ruth, Paul McCartney, Marilyn Monroe and Mark Spitz, $2.50 each or $3 in full color. There are also bumper stickers, T-shirts and sweatshirts, buttons and patches, left-handed playing cards and greeting cards (they open from the left, like the catalogue), watches, clocks and cameras, even guitars (full-size, $45). A find for "sinister" people and their friends.

L-6
LEMAN PUBLICATIONS, INC., Dept. CC
Box 394
Wheat Ridge, CO 80033

Quilts and Other Comforts, 50¢, published annually, 32 pages, illustrated, black and white.

This little catalogue offers the greatest selection of quilt patterns available anywhere and all the necessary accessories for making them—metal templates and packs (metal with window), template sets (some of posterboard), patterns and kits. Among them are two authentic Hawaiian quilt designs (an exclusive), the State Flowers quilt pattern, Pennsylvania Dutch and Early American patterns and a delightful embroidered snowflake pattern. A kit for an American Glory appliqué quilt, inspired by

one in the Philadelphia Museum, is around $25 (this includes the cotton percale quilt top and calico appliqués), and star quilt kits are $16.95. Also available are kits for patchwork pillows and quilts, and supplies such as quilting frames, hoops, threads, needles, batting, markers and graph paper, quilting designs and stencils, and quilting and needlework books.

L-7
LENOX CHINA, Dept. CC
Prince & Meade Streets
Trenton, NJ 08605

Free brochures of limited edition plates. Lenox China/Crystal Pattern Book, free, published annually, 36 pages, illustrated, color.

For plate collectors, two small brochures describe the limited edition of the Lenox Boehm plates in the Wildlife (the Beavers) and Bird (the Robins) series, issued only during 1977. Plates are not sold directly by Lenox but may be ordered or obtained from china dealers and stores carrying these plates. Presumably, the 1978 plate brochures will be current now. *The China/Crystal Pattern Book,* also available free from Lenox, shows current patterns and gives suggested retail prices for place settings and stemware.

L-8
THE LION MARK, Dept. CC
721 Elm Street, P. O. Box 276
Winnetka, IL 60093

The Lion Mark. English Sterling Silver, free, revised spring and fall, 128 pages, illustrated, black and white.

An extremely handsome and beautifully produced large catalogue, for which there is no charge at the time of writing, although this policy may change. The Lion Mark specializes in British sterling silver pieces of the highest quality, antique, semi-antique (late Victorian, Edwardian or later, but mostly fine reproductions of traditional eighteenth- and nineteenth-century designs, the finish softened and enriched by time and use) and modern reproductions. Each piece or set of pieces is meticulously described and clearly illustrated with large black and white photographs so you can really see the detailing. All antique pieces are authentic, properly hallmarked and in excellent condition. There is a wide range of antique sterling—coffee sets and pots, trays, tea caddies, sugar baskets and cream jugs, sauce boats, platters, serving dishes, salts, butter shells, mustard pots, salvers, candlesticks, bowls, cake baskets, mugs, snuff boxes, goblets, wine coasters and lots of exquisite wine labels. In flatware you'll find services; sets of forks; dessert spoons and forks; teaspoons; skewers; marrow scoops; tea caddy

Above, ship surgeon's brass candleholder from Mystic Seaport Museum Store, M-34. Below left, candleholder in the form of a monk, reproduced from fifteenth-century French silver original; Boston Museum of Fine Arts, B-18. Below right, "Tree of Life" wooden candelabrum from Finland; Stockmann, S-38.

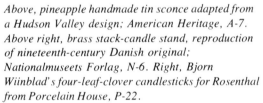

Above, pineapple handmade tin sconce adapted from a Hudson Valley design; American Heritage, A-7. Above right, brass stack-candle stand, reproduction of nineteenth-century Danish original; Nationalmuseets Forlag, N-6. Right, Bjorn Wiinblad's four-leaf-clover candlesticks for Rosenthal from Porcelain House, P-22.

spoons; serving, dressing and other special spoons; sugar nips; soup, gravy and sauce ladles; fish slices; butter knives; asparagus tongs; grape shears; sugar tongs; a splendid large Georgian toasting fork; cheese scoops; knife rests; mustard or egg spoons—just about everything for the table that could be made in silver. Prices range from $22 for a mustard or egg spoon to $11,000 for a magnificent and rare set of four candlesticks made in London in 1771 by Ebenezer Coker. Antique silver comprises almost 100 pages of the catalogue.

L-9
LIROS GALLERY INC., Dept. CC
628 North Washington Street
Alexandria, VA 22314

Brochure, free, illustrated, black and white.

This gallery specializes in eighteenth- and nineteenth-century prints and paintings, maps, and Russian icons. They list hand-colored lithographs by Currier & Ives; icons, including brass traveling icons ($40 to $2,000); engravings from the Civil War and post-Civil War years from *Harper's Weekly* including works by Winslow Homer and Thomas Nast ($5 to $50), Audubon prints, English hunting prints, and music manuscripts. Prices range from $5 to $4,800.

L-10
LIST COMMUNICATIONS, Dept. CC
P. O. Box 916
New York, NY 10023

Collectors Series, free, updated periodically, 10 pages.

List Communications specializes in "hard-to-find" domestic LPs. However, a closer look at the offerings shows them to be an outlet for re-issues from Columbia Records archive material, a good deal of which may be available in your local record shops. There are many Broadway shows, soundtracks, complete plays, a good selection of jazz, folk and classical, but no opera. There is also a selection of budget records. Prices are list with a 5 percent discount on sales over $10, 10 percent on orders over $26 and 15 percent over $60. Shipping is a flat $1 per total order.

L-11
LITTLE NEMO COMIC ART SHOP, Dept. CC
108-30 Ascan Avenue
Forest Hills, NY 11375

Cartoonists and Illustrators Portfolio, $4 (refundable with purchase), published 4 to 6 times a year, 82 pages, illustrated, black and white.

A terrific source for lovers of comic strips and illustra-

tions. The shop has newspaper pages, originals, book covers, comic book excerpts, movie posters, etc. A Sunday page of *Blondie,* October 9, 1932, is $450; a Sunday page of *Little Nemo,* May 27, 1906, is $4,000. Al Held illustrations dated 1931 sell for $1,000; a powerful drawing of Conan the Barbarian by Barry Smith is $2,050. An acrylic painting for a poster advertising *Diamonds Are Forever* (not used for the Bond film) is listed at $750. Among the hundreds of other offerings are George Herriman's Krazy Kat, Al Capp's Fearless Fosdick, Milton Caniff's Terry and the Pirates, Mandrake and Spiderman, Captain America, and Batman and Robin. Pencil drawings by Dean Cornwell, studies for later painted illustrations, are $350.

L-12
**LOS ANGELES COUNTY MUSEUM—
MUSEUM SHOP,** Dept. CC
5905 Wilshire Blvd.
Los Angeles, CA 90036

Gift Selections From the Los Angeles County Museum of Art, $1, 23 pages, illustrated, color.

The Los Angeles County Museum offers such things as greeting cards, wrapping paper, note cards, books, scarves, needlepoint kits and jewelry related to the museum's collections. A handsome tote bag decorated with an ancient Peruvian design costs $20. You can buy an original page from a nineteenth-century Koran—an example of the great calligraphic tradition of Islam—for $30 (limited supply). Also available: a limited number of authentic ancient Egyptian amulets and scarabs set in traditional or contemporary 14k. gold mountings, no two alike, listed at $350 to $950. A signed, limited edition silk scarf designed by the contemporary artist Billy Al Bengston is priced at $27.50. Some items require a small additional mailing charge.

L-13
JEAN-PAUL LOUP, Dept. CC
400 Lathrop Avenue
River Forest, IL 60305

Art Limited Editions, free, published seasonally, 38 pages, illustrated, color.

Jean-Paul Loup specializes in original, hand signed and numbered prints by many of the big names of modern art along with prints by a number of lesser-known artists. In the current catalogue, there is a study of lovers by Chagall in an edition of only 50 prints (plus 5 artist's proofs); a gay *Candy Canes* by Calder (150 plus 15 artist's proofs); a handsome Miró that incorporates his name in the design (150 plus 15 artist's proofs); a vivid Vasarely abstraction, a serigraph limited to 250; and a Henry Moore study of reclining figures, in a total edition of 70. Other artists whose works are available include Peter Orlando, Ernest Trova, Salvador Dali, Arbit Blatas, Margoni, Uriburu and Oliveira. Prices range from $30 to $5,500.

L-14
LOVELIA ENTERPRISES, INC., Dept. CC
P. O. Box 1845
Grand Central Station
New York, NY 10017

Tapestry Catalogue, $1, published annually, 16 pages, illustrated, color.

Lovelia produces limited-edition tapestries of Dutch interiors, harvests, hunts, scenes from Italy, Spain, France and Belgium, all machine-woven on old looms in cotton or wool, some copies of museum masterpieces. Sizes vary from 20" x 20" to 39" x 118" and prices from around $8.50 to $425.

L-15
LYNCHBURG HARDWARE & GENERAL STORE,
Dept. CC
P. O. Box 322
Lynchburg, TN 37352

Lynchburg Hardware & General Store Catalog, $1, published annually, 32 pages, illustrated, color.

Americana Tennessee-style, heavy on the barrels, bottles and insignia of Jack Daniel, of sour-mash whiskey fame. The founder of the store, Lem Motlow, was a nephew of Jack Daniel and worked with his uncle at the distillery until Prohibition turned him storekeeper. Among the items in this amusing collection are a small match-box sleeve for kitchen matches ($3.50 delivered, with matches); old-fashioned wooden kitchen tools, including an ice pick in a wooden sheath; rustic weather vanes ($18.50 delivered); a little gadget called a Tennessee match striker; a Jack Daniel's barrel-bung paperweight ($1.25 delivered); a solid oak whiskey barrel planter; stoneware jugs like those Mr. Daniel's whiskey used to come in, from quart to two-gallon sizes; old-time riverboat playing cards in a tin card case; poker cards and a gentleman's poker kit; a "volunteer chest" designed to sling against a pack saddle and double as a camp stool (or hold six straw-packed bottles of you-know-what); and old posters and handbills for saloons, a mule auction, and Mr. Daniel's Silver Cornet Band. There's also the *Silver Cornet Band Album,* a reconstruction of the musical favorites and playing of the original band formed in 1890, in up-to-the-minute stereo ($5).

Top, Lapp dolls from Stockmann, S-38. Center, folk art handcrafts; Heather Hill Crafts, H-14. Bottom, Ecuadorian straw angels; Gifts from the Andes, G-10.

Above, Sacred Butterfly china, adapted from the Chinese Export porcelain; Historic Charleston Reproductions, H-22. Below left, chain-link clear glass bowl, pitcher and decanter copied from originals in Old Sturbridge Village collection from American Heritage, A-7. Below right, antique Georgian silver from Denise Poole, P-21.

M-1
HUGH MACPHERSON (SCOTLAND) LTD.,
Dept. CC
17 West Maitland Street
Edinburgh, EH12 5EA
Scotland

Price list.

This distinguished Scots firm specializes in making bag-pipes, kilts, tartan hose and scarves. They also offer tartan travel rugs, ties, sashes, Highland dancers' outfits, pipe-band uniforms and various accessories. Kilts for both day and evening are made to measure of 100 percent wool. Prices range from around $5 to $200 and are given in pounds sterling, subject to current exchange rates. Post-age, packing and insurance are extra.

M-2
MAGNOLIA HALL, Dept. CC
726 Andover
Atlanta, GA 30327

Yester-Year Furniture, $1, refundable with pur-chase, published three times a year, 80 pages, illustrated, black and white.

Reproductions of Victorian furniture and accessories such as mirrors and lamps. There's the usual complement of chairs and tables, beds and chests, sofas and stools, in-cluding the always popular gout stool (about $80), and for the china and glass collector, a big assortment of curio cabinets. An elaborately scrolled and mirror-backed corner wall cabinet is around $50; a lighted curio console cabinet with curved glass doors and front, 42'' wide and 30'' high, about $200; an old-fashioned curved glass china cabinet, 80'' tall and 47'' wide, around $530. Also, there are various kinds of clocks: a station-master's clock with calendar, a saw clock that runs on gravity and never needs winding and a couple of elegant museum clock reproductions—one a Louis XV pendulette clock, 11½'' high, about $40; the other a copy of the Frederic Japy clock of 1740 on display in the Museum of Decorative Arts, Paris, about $60. The price of the catalogue includes twenty-four fabric samples, and you receive a $2 cer-tificate with the first order.

M-3
MALICK'S FOSSILS, INC., Dept. CC
5514 Plymouth Road
Baltimore, MD 21214

Malick's Fossils, Inc., $3, 106 pages, published annually, illustrated, black and white.

A catalogue for knowledgeable collectors, researchers and teachers that includes a geological time scale, table of contents, teaching aids and detailed lists providing name, period, formation, locale. The catalogue covers animals, plants, minerals, artifacts of early man, literature on fos-sils and artifacts, and a few decorative accessories such as paperweights. Prices are given in most cases and are available on request in others.

M-4
MANHATTAN DOLL HOSPITAL, Dept. CC
176 Ninth Avenue
New York, NY 10011

*Doll Houses, 4 pages, color. **Houseworks Ltd.,** 24 pages, sepia-tone. **The X-Acto House of Minia-tures Collectors Series. Tidewater Collection of Accessories. Tidewater Collection of Miniature Furniture.** Folders, illustrated in color and duotones. **Brick and Stone,** catalogue sheet, illus-trated. **The Concord Collection,** 28 pages, illus-trated, color. **E-Z-Lectric,** folder, illustrated. **Chrysnbon Miniatures,** illustrated fact sheet. **Miniature Vinyl Floors and Walls,** illustrated fact sheet. **Realife Miniatures,** 4-page catalogue sheet, illustrated, color. **Lundby of Sweden,** 16 pages, color. $1.50 for any or all catalogues, refundable with purchase. Published annually.*

Want to build a better doll house? Doll up the one you have? All you need is right here in this treasury of catalogues. Doll houses by Walmer or Halls are priced from $45.99 to $229.99. Williamsburg doll house kits start at $109 with a choice of finely detailed window, door, staircase and dormer window components, shingles and brass hardware. The *X-Acto* catalogues offer rug kits, fireplaces, wallpaper and furniture kits in 1'' to 1' scale.

Mini-stone, mortar, pebbles, vinyl tiles for floors and walls are found in the *Brick and Stone* sheet. From *Concord* comes a vast selection of scaled furniture, accessories and dolls for the serious collector of miniatures as well as the doll-house enthusiast. *E-Z-Lectric* offers a 12-volt lighting system for miniature rooms. *Chrysnbon* has period miniature furniture kits, while *Realife* offers complete room kits at $11.95 that can be adapted to your own doll house. *Lundby's* line of furniture and accessories is designed specifically for their own houses, which start at $32.99, but with some imagination, you can use them in your own settings as well.

M-5
THE MAP STUDIO AT WHITLOCK FARM,
Dept. CC
20 Sperry Road
Bethany, CT 06525

No catalogue, information on request.

Owners Cliff Sahlin and Tony Williams don't find it feasible to print a catalogue, as their field and township maps from the 1860s, '70s and '80s are all originals (they took over and are reviving a business founded in 1899).

Instead, they will research requests for maps of individual towns, counties and states in their files and provide maps with good color and scads of local detail of interest to collectors and students of local history.

M-6
EPHRAIM MARSH COMPANY, Dept. CC
P. O. Box 266
Concord, NC 28025

Ephraim Marsh Distinctive Furniture, *$1, updated semiannually, 144 pages, illustrated, black and white.*

Ephraim Marsh is a mail-order business selling reproduction period furniture directly to the consumer. Among the many pieces of interest to collectors in this catalogue are curio cabinets in Queen Anne and American Colonial styles, a Queen Anne lowboy with curio-cabinet top, a Queen Anne-style cocktail table with glass top and velvet lining for safe display of precious objects ($219), a Chippendale-style wall shelf and a curio console ($330). There are some reproduction clocks such as shelf clocks and the good old regulator wall clock ($209).

"Moonstar," an unusual modern transistor clock. Despard Designs, D-9.

Far left, Aaron Willard mantel clock reproduced by Colonial of Zeeland, and left, Lancaster County tall-case clock, in the style of John Bachman, both from Edison Institute, E-4.

M-7
MASON & SULLIVAN CO., Dept. CC
39 Blossom Avenue
Osterville, MA 02655

The Mason & Sullivan Collection of Clocks, *50¢, published twice a year, 36 pages, illustrated, black and white.*

Mason & Sullivan supplies all the components for you to make clocks yourself—materials, blueprint, movements and dials, and assembled cases, either finished or unfinished. There are grandmother and grandfather clocks, the Willard banjo clock, shelf clocks in kits, an English carriage clock, octagonal wall clock and school clock, steeple clock, regulator clock, mantel clock and Eli Terry pillar-and-scroll clock. Choice of woods is mahogany, cherry or walnut for most of the clocks. Also available are tools and finishing accessories, dials and brass numerals (including moving moon dials) and lyre pendulums. Prices are reasonable—depending on the wood selected, the Willard Grandmother case clock set is $137 to $190, which does not include dial and movements; the blueprint is $1.50. A lovely contemporary glass clock, 65″ high, 16½″ wide and 9⅜″ deep, designed by Milton Gunerman, in cherry that can be finished in natural stain or glossy enamel, is $63.75 for the do-it-yourself set, plus movement. In addition to clocks, Mason & Sullivan has a miniature piano, 8¾″ long, 5½″ wide and 3½″ high that comes in a kit with cherry parts preshaped and ready to join (keyboard and pedals are completely assembled), some good-looking barometers in kit form, Swiss music box movements and brass parts for clock cases.

M-8
MATURANGO MUSEUM OF INDIAN WELLS VALLEY, Dept. CC
P. O. Box 1776
Ridgecrest, CA 93555

Publications list, free.

Publications available from the Museum, priced from $1 to $5.95, cover such subjects as the flora and fauna of the desert, fossil mammals and rock paintings, sand paintings and Indian uses of wild plants.

M-9
MAXWELL MUSEUM GIFT SHOP, Dept. CC
University of New Mexico
Albuquerque, NM 87131

No catalogue, but you can write to the manager of the museum gift shop for information about the high-quality, one-of-a-kind Southwestern arts and crafts for sale, such as pottery, old and new rugs and jewelry. A number of the items are unique to the area. Slides of items will be sent to serious buyers.

M-10
PAUL McAFEE & FRIENDS, LTD., Dept. CC
841 West Genesee Street
Skaneateles, NY 13152

Vanishing Arts, *brochure, free, published annually, illustrated, black and white.*

The brochure features the work of four craftsmen, William Burke, Sid Bell, Allan Sustare and Gail Wiltshire. Burke works in crystal. His 8″ long *Frolicking Dolphin* is $98; a limited-edition eagle, 5¾″ high with a 12″ wing span, costs $770 in clear crystal, $1,400 in translucent satin crystal. Sid Bell makes small pins and pendants. A trout is $15, an Indian-head-and-bearskin pendant, $65. Sustare and Wiltshire collaborate on scrimshaw etchings set in sterling. An eagle pendant, limited to fifty examples, is around $213; a 1½″-high unicorn head, $74.80. (Please note that scrimshaw may no longer be shipped to states prohibiting its import.) There is a small shipping charge.

M-11
McDONALD'S COLLECTABLES, Dept. CC
1229 17th Street
Manhattan Beach, CA 90266

Catalogue, free, 16 pages, published seasonally, illustrated, black and white.

Joyce McDonald's catalogue covers a wide range of old and current limited-edition plates, mugs, bells, thimbles, figurines and Christmas decorations by all the famous companies from Arabia to Wedgwood. The price range is wide, but as prices change with each list, we will not quote those in the current catalogue. Discounts are offered on many items. Frames for plates and books for collectors are included in the catalogue. We also received with McDonald's catalogue a color catalogue put out by the National Association of Limited Edition Dealers, with photographs of a selection of current limited editions, frames and books.

M-12
ROD McLELLAN CO., Dept. CC
1450 El Camino Real
South San Francisco, CA 94080

Acres of Orchids, *free, published in spring and late summer, 8 pages, illustrated, color.*

Compared to other orchid catalogues, this one is fairly small. Prices range from $7 to $40 for the most expensive, Mericlone BLC Greenwich 'Cover Girl,' a very fine green Cattleya.

M-13
MERCER MUSEUM SHOP, Dept. CC
Bucks County Historical Society
Pine and Ashland Streets
Doylestown, PA 18901

Catalogue, 50¢, 16 pages, illustrated, black and white.

A charming little catalogue of sketched objects from the Mercer Museum Shop, many made by local craftsmen using the old Pennsylvania Dutch techniques. Authentic reproductions from the kitchen and dairy collection include a round ladle, butter paddle, black iron sausage hook that would be great for hanging up pans in a country kitchen ($45) and a copper saucepan with rattail handle ($16.50). Maplewood candlesticks, some with brass tops and bottoms, converted from bobbins used in old textile mills for twisting and spinning, cost from $2.50 to $3.25. Among other collector's items are glassware in the styles of Revolutionary America, all free blown and no two pieces exactly identical; slip and sgraffito plates; a crimped-edge pie plate and candleholder in red ware made from clay dug from an Eastern Pennsylvania hillside, hand-shaped on a potter's wheel, signed and dated; miniatures of country furniture in the Museum; reproductions of Bucks County prints and *fraktur*, old butter-mold prints ($6.50); tinware lamps, lanterns, primitive six-arm Moravian chandelier (electrified, $125), boxes and scoops; hand-wrought iron; pewter spoons, buttons and porringers made from old molds. Lots more items such as cookie cutters, corn-husk dolls, lead soldiers, decoys and patchwork pillows are crammed into this compact catalogue, a small treasure trove. Included with the catalogue is the Historical Society's publications list of books on local crafts, tools, architecture and place names.

M-14
MERRY GARDENS, Dept. CC
P. O. Box 595
Camden, ME 04843

The Merry Gardens Pictorial Handbook of Rare Indoor Plants, *$2, 36 pages with availability list, illustrated, black and white. List alone, 50¢.*

Unfortunately, we cannot describe the handbook offerings as all we received was the cover and one inside spread. However, a card about the Merry Gardens literature describes the availability list as including over 300 indoor foliage, flowering and vines, 200 begonias, 80 fuchsias, 80 hedera, 200 cacti and succulents, 40 ferns and mosses, and 75 gesneriads, and the pictorial handbook as having 300 black-and-white photos of indoor plants with their botanical and common names and a key to culture.

M-15
THE MERRY MUSIC BOX, Dept. CC
20 McKown Street
Boothbay Harbor, ME 04538

Musical Wonder House Recordings, *free brochure, also catalogue, 75¢, 24 pages, published annually, illustrated.* **Collector's Series Catalogue of Musical Gifts,** *$1, published annually, illustrated, color.*

The Merry Music Box is a store that proclaims it has "America's largest selection of imported musical boxes." They also sell by mail imported and custom-built Swiss musical boxes and stereo albums and stereo cassette tapes of music played on antique musical boxes and Edison cylinder records. The brochure we received (we were not sent either catalogue) lists the stereo albums, which cover religious music; Christmas, concert and opera favorites; waltzes and polkas; classical music; ragtime and cakewalks and old songs and ballads. Records are priced at $7.45 each, which includes postage but not insurance. The illustrated catalogue of recordings and the Collector's Series catalogue can be ordered from a form in the brochure, or they will be sent free on request with a mail order of the stereo recordings listed in the brochure.

M-16
THE METROPOLITAN MUSEUM OF ART,
Dept. CC
Box 255, Gracie Station
New York, NY 10028

American Decorative Arts, *$1 for four catalogues a year (or 25¢ a catalogue), 48 pages, illustrated, black and white.* **Spring,** *$1 for four catalogues a year (or 25¢ a catalogue), 48 pages, illustrated, black and white and color.* **The Treasures of Tutankhamun,** *free on request, 48 pages, illustrated, color.*

The regular sales catalogues of this internationally renowned museum are, as you would expect, filled with beautiful objects of the highest quality reproduced or adapted from the Museum's collections. There are prints after great paintings, facsimile sculptures, china, silver, glass, tiles, pewter, jewelry, needlepoint and embroidery designs. The current Decorative Arts catalogue has a glorious Sandwich glass flower pot and stand (from the only known example, pre-1830); crystal ship's tumblers, dated around 1845; a crystal champagne glass, jar and salt and pepper shakers all with a superb Victorian design of

Antique crystal paperweight from L. H. Selman, S-11.

Art glass paperweights by Steven V. Correia, Boston Museum of Fine Arts, B-18.

"Spirit of '76" and "Bicentennial" glass paperweights from Holly City Bottle, H-23.

Wooden paperweight from Hagley Museum Store, H-1.

Whimsical and personal memorabilia are clustered in a shadow box made from an old Victorian picture frame by James Lee. Photographer: Otto Maya.

three faces of the same woman; a handsome silver beaker reproduction of a New England 1695 original; a group of silver miniatures; a marvelous brass candlestick, and an interesting piece of Americana—a cast-iron effigy of an Indian, believed to have been a "treaty token," to be placed on the houses of those protected by Penn's treaty with the Indians.

The *Spring* catalogue contains, among many other items, a 37¼" x 30" unframed print of Van Gogh's great painting of irises; note cards of full-color gravure of works in the collections; plaques of an owl and the profile of an Egyptian king; a splendid Egyptian cat cast in bronze, complete with detachable earrings; an eighteenth-century octagonal Meissen cup and saucer in the kakiemon style; lovely American glass pitchers; sterling silver bowls, cups, spoons, etc.; stained-glass roundels; an Etruscan acrobat, 4⅜" long, in bronze or silver, taken from the handle of a box; a limited-edition (1,000) leaded crystal paperweight decorated with a winged bull, and a silk-screened wool challis shawl from the design of a nineteenth-century Chinese export trade platter. Prices in these catalogues range from $1.25 to $495, with a small charge for shipping and handling.

The Treasures of Tutankhamun catalogue presents the finest and largest collection ever achieved of jewelry and other objects-in-replica from ancient Egypt. It includes a number of objects in the exhibition that opened at the Metropolitan in December 1978 and a few from other treasure rooms of the Egyptian Museum in Cairo. For the first time ever, craftsmen were permitted to make molds directly from the fragile, priceless originals of these fabulous works of art. In other cases, an ancient motif has been adapted for a modern use or a model created from photographs and drawings. The jewelry is especially striking and beautiful—amulets, in 18k. gold or 24k. gold electroplate, of Anubis, Ptah, Hathor and Uraeus; a gold half-shell pendant, the original of which was worn by Queen Mereret of the Twelfth Dynasty ($16.50 for the pendant in 24k. gold electroplate and $16.50 for the torque to wear it on); rings; buckles; bracelets, necklaces and earrings; pins and fascinating hieroglyph charms. Other superb replicas are a lotus goblet, sterling silver with 24k. gold electroplate, 4" high ($115); a fascinating silver pomegranate vase; a lotus cachepot of alabaster glass; limited edition (2,500) plate by Haviland-Parlon of Limoges depicting the sun god in the form of a falcon, turquoise, lapis lazuli, carnelian and 24k. gold on cobalt blue background ($150); and an exquisite gilded statue (38" high including base) of the goddess Selket, for which production will be limited to about 100 copies over the next two years ($1,500). You can also order books on the tomb and its treasures, a 176-page catalogue of this unique exhibition and needlework adaptations of motifs from the treasures. The catalogue may be obtained for no charge, if specifically requested.

M-17
KONRAD MEUSCHEL, Dept. CC
Kaiserplatz 5
Bonn 1, West Germany D-5300

Einblattdrucke und Flugblätter, *free, 80 pages plus inside back cover;* ***Wertvolle und Seltene Bücher/Graphiken alter Meister,*** *free, 76 pages;* ***Autographen,*** *free, 40 pages. All published yearly or as acquisitions require.*

Konrad Meuschel is one of West Germany's leading antiquarian book and autograph dealers and has exhibited at the thirteenth annual Bookfair in New York in 1977. The three catalogues, in German, are well-produced. Prices are in Deutschmarks and some seem quite high. Collectibles in *Einblattdrucke* date from 1513 to 1848; *Wertvolle* offers a worldwide assemblage of books and prints, and the 238 entries in the *Autographen* catalogue include a manuscript signed by Charles Darwin at 6,000 marks and a handwritten extract from Heinrich Heine at 7,000.

M-18
MICHELE GIFTS, Dept. CC
56 Meadowbrook Avenue
Greensburg, PA 15601

Brochure, free, published annually, 4 pages, illustrated, black and white.

Pewter sculptures by Swiss artist Walter Judith, some free-standing, others mounted on plaques or framed as wall decorations or pendants. The sculptures are mostly of animals, birds and sportsmen and are rather simplistic, one of the more attractive being a sculptured pewter swan on a wood base, 6" high, $60. There are also some pleasant flower-shaped candleholders in pewter ranging in price from $18 to $30. Many of the items in the brochure are also available in sterling silver or gold, prices on request.

M-19
MILL POND PRESS, INC., Dept. CC
204 South Nassau Street
Venice, FL 33595

Art for Collectors, *$1, published 2 to 4 times a year, 48 pages, illustrated, black and white and color.*

Mill Pond Press publishes signed, numbered prints by contemporary artists in limited editions as well as unlimited "decorator prints." They specialize in studies of wildlife, flowers and western scenes. A haunting study by Robert Bateman of a young barn swallow perched in an open window, 20½" x 27½" in an edition of 950, is $75. A number of handsome paintings of birds by Roger Tory

Peterson, in an edition of 950, are priced from $125 to $225. An atmospheric scene of a ranch hand and horses by Melvin C. Warren, 23'' x 31'', in an edition of 750, is $150. "Decorator prints," 14'' x 11'', sell for $15. Major credit cards accepted.

M-20
MINIATURE SILVER, Dept. CC
317 South Prospect Avenue
Park Ridge, IL 60068

Miniature Reproductions of Antique Silver, $1, published periodically, 25 pages, illustrated, sepia.

Sterling-silver replicas of famous pieces of museum silver, done to a scale of 1'' to 1', include a sauce boat by Joseph Richardson, circa 1711–1784, in the Metropolitan Museum, $13, and Martha Washington's tea board, engraved with the Washington crest, from the same museum collection, $24. Also available are such things as tea pots, stirrup cups, candlesticks, baskets, etc. All pieces are signed by the artist. A simulated wood curio cabinet in which to display your miniatures, copied from an eighteenth-century silver shop, with a concealed light inside, is 17'' x 11'' x 6'' or 9'' ($110 or $115, depending on size). Add $1 per piece for handling and insurance.

M-21
THE MINNEAPOLIS INSTITUTE OF ARTS,
Dept. CC
2400 Third Avenue South
Minneapolis, MN 55404

Arts, free, published annually, 4 pages, illustrated, black and white.

The Minneapolis Institute sells reproductions, calendars, postcards, books, playing cards, a tote bag, a "Friends" cookbook and posters. Among the offerings are an Art Deco poster in browns, greens, orange, blue and white, earrings cast from an eighth-century Tang Dynasty pair, a portfolio of six Ukiyo-e paintings from the floating world and a poster of Picasso's *Harlequin*. Books include a work on *Fakes & Forgeries, Imperial Robes & Textiles of the Chinese Court* and *Prints 1400–1800*. Prices range from 15¢ to $50.

M-22
MIXED-MEDIA, LTD., Dept. CC
P. O. Box 11190
Chicago, IL 60657

Catalogue of Fine Art Posters, $5 (refundable with purchase), 64 pages, illustrated, black and white.

Mixed-Media is a wonderful source for posters of art

exhibitions, musical events and the 1972 Olympics. Twenty-eight Olympic posters by such artists as Hockney, Vasarely, Wesselman and Hundertwasser are available in a hand-signed edition of 200 (prices on request) and an edition of 4,000 signed in the stone (most at $50). A number of Dali posters designed for the Teatro Museo Figueras are listed at $20, a Norman Rockwell of a runaway boy and policeman at $20, Andy Warhol's *Flowers* at $25 and Georgia O'Keeffe's stunning posters for the Santa Fe Chamber Music Festivals at $20. There are also brilliant works by Klimt, Matisse, Braque, Miró, Picasso, Chagall, Shahn and many others, over 700 in all, and posters by earlier artists like Lautrec, Delacroix and Homer. Minimum shipping fee, $5 per order.

M-23
ROBERT MORLEY & CO., LTD., Dept. CC
4 Belmont Hill
London SE13, England

Connoisseurs Collectors Section at Morley Galleries; Early Keyboard Instruments; Harps; Pianos. $6 (refundable with purchase), published seasonally, illustrated.

The $6 fee for the four illustrated brochures is meant to discourage all but the serious collector of period antique and reproduction musical instruments. The lists are concise and choice. The *Connoisseurs* folder (6 pages) features eighteenth- and nineteenth-century keyboard instruments, including a "Baker Harris Londini Fecit 1775" spinet, a 1770 Longman and Broderip harpsichord and a square piano by William Southwell, circa 1800. The *Early Keyboard* collection (4 pages) shows fine reproductions of spinets, virginals, clavichords and harpsichords. Both modern and antique harps are available from the *Harp* catalogue. Included are Gothic, double-action, 45–46-string harps, circa 1850; 43-string Grecian pedal harps; single-action "ramshead"; late-eighteenth-century, plus reproduction Irish harps. The piano catalogue boasts some fine early Bechsteins. All prices are quoted in pounds sterling.

M-24
MORTON'S OF NEW ORLEANS, Dept. CC
133 West Franklin Street
Chapel Hill, NC 27514

Morton's of New Orleans, free, 14 pages, illustrated, black and white.

This gallery is a subsidiary of Morton's Auction Exchange, Inc., of New Orleans, and the present catalogue is devoted to paintings such as *A Shoeshine Boy's Best Friend* by John George Brown (1831–1913), a study of a boy in vest and high-button shoes watching his dog stand on its hind legs; *Cabin Scene,* a study of black rural life by William Aiken Walker (1838–1921); and still-life studies of fruit, tobacco, a pipe and mug by Thomas H. Hope. Subjects are mainly portraits, landscapes, genre and sporting scenes, and prices range from around $600 to $6,500.

M-25
THOMAS MOSER, Dept. CC
30 Cobb's Bridge Road
New Gloucester, ME 04260

Thomas Moser, Cabinet Maker, $2, published annually, 38 pages, illustrated, black and white.

Although the superb hand-crafted pieces made by Thomas Moser are squarely rooted in Shaker and other traditional American forms, there has been a subtle movement toward the contemporary that is clearly apparent in this latest catalogue. The collection is now made in naturally-aged oiled cherry, a wood Mr. Moser regards as the finest medium because of its color and clarity of grain. Each piece of furniture is built entirely by one man, using methods of joinery that have been practiced since ancient times, and signed and dated by him. Pieces include the traditional harvest table, chair table, trestle table, ladder-back chairs, pencil post and trundle beds. The prices range from $80 to over $1,000, with crating charge extra. Moser will also do custom work to your specifications from a photograph or measured drawing.

M-26
MOUNT VERNON LADIES' ASSOCIATION,
Dept. CC
Mount Vernon, VA 22121

List of publications, free, 3 pages.

The Association offers a series of books and booklets, a few hardcover but mostly paperback, about Mount Vernon and George Washington, and some prints suitable for framing, such as color reproductions of the Stuart portraits of George and Martha Washington, 11″ x 14″ (75¢), a full-size facsimile of Washington's 1793 map of his Mount Vernon Farms, 16″ x 23″ ($1), and the kitchen garden plan. Also available are postcards, color photos and 35mm slides, a three-minute 8mm movie and a twenty-eight minute 16mm sound movie of Mount Vernon.

M-27
MUNICIPAL MUSEUM OF BALTIMORE, INC.
(The Peale Museum), Dept. CC
225 Holliday Street
Baltimore, MD 21202

Price list, free, 2 pages, black and white.

The Peale Museum, as the Municipal Museum is more generally known, offers publications, books, prints and maps relating to Baltimore, the Peale family and the Museum, and a drink and hors d'oeuvre cookbook compiled by the Women's Committee of the Museum ($1.75). A set of reproductions of three early maps of Baltimore is $7.50; a sterling silver commemorative medal honoring the 150th anniversary of the two great monuments that earned Baltimore the name, ''The Monumental City,'' costs $15.

M-28
MUSEUM COLLECTIONS, Dept. CC
140 Greenwich Avenue
Greenwich, CT 06830

Museum Collections, $1, published annually, 36 pages, illustrated, color.

The current edition of this handsome catalogue has nearly 400 examples of sculpture and jewelry reproduced from works in major museums and private collections in the U.S. and abroad, ranging from Ancient Egypt to contemporary. The company which produces the pieces, Alva Museum Replicas, Inc., is the only authorized U.S. producer of reproductions from the Louvre. Casts are made directly from impressions of the originals and each is accompanied by a certificate of authenticity. Rodin's *The Kiss,* 12½″ high, is $50. Gaston Lachaise's *Acrobat,* 17½″ high, from the Indianapolis Museum of Art, is $60. An Ashanti fertility doll from Africa, 14″ high, costs $37.50; a bowl in the form of a jaguar, cast in weatherstone so it can be used outdoors or indoors, the original of which came from Panama, is $30. A pre-Columbian stylized eagle from Costa Rica, gold or silver electroplated on pewter, can be bought either as a pin ($8.50) or a dog collar ($10). Postage and handling charges are given after the price of each object and for orders of $50 or more there are bonus gifts.

M-29
MUSEUM OF AFRO-AMERICAN HISTORY,
Dept. CC
Dudley Station, Box 5
Roxbury, MA 02119

Brochure, $1, refundable with purchase, published seasonally, 4 pages, illustrated, black and white.

The Museum in the African Meeting House, a historical part of Black culture in Boston (it dates back to 1806), offers a number of unusual posters and publications dealing with the history of American Blacks, with special emphasis on Massachusetts and Boston. You'll find a black-and-white glossy poster of the Meeting House, 12″

PURCHASING PRINTS

Signed, limited-edition prints are, generally speaking, the most valuable. However, there are exceptions and variations, such as Old Master prints (Dürer and Mantegna, for example); artist's proofs, which precede the numbering process and are therefore earlier (the printing surface wears down as the number of impressions increases) and prints pulled by the artist rather than by the printer (the word refers literally to the pulling away of the paper from the lithographic plate or stone, wood block, etching plate, etc.).

While some original prints are not signed (this was often true at the end of the last century), usually they are signed on the margin, most often along with the date, the title, the number of the print and the total edition. A good many prints are signed in the stone (lithographs) or signed in the plate (etchings), which means that the artist signed his work within the printed image and the signature is a printed, not a unique, handwritten one.

If you are a beginning print collector and want to know where to start, consult your local museum about the best places to purchase prints. Many firms in the mail-order business have long been noted for the quality of the works they sell, but, again, if you are in doubt, consult a museum or a reputable gallery.

"Le Repos," original lithograph by Jean-Pierre Cassigneul. Original Print Collectors Group, O-9.

x 17'' ($1); a calendar in color citing important dates in Afro-American history ($3.50); T-shirts with the African Meeting House/Museum logo silkscreened on cotton knit in white, red, blue, green and gold; a history of Afro-America in newspaper format, *Black Chronicle,* created by educators and historians, 14 packaged issues for $4.75; and *City Games,* a coloring game and guidebook to introduce children to Boston's neighborhoods ($1.50). For stamp collectors, there is a collection of nine U.S. postage stamps commemorating such Black Americans as Booker T. Washington, Salem Poor and George Washington Carver, plus descriptive booklet, for $2, and a first day commemorative stamp card honoring Salem Poor, who fought at the battle of Bunker Hill, 6'' x 8'' ($1.50).

M-30
THE MUSEUM OF MODERN ART, Dept. CC
11 West 53rd Street
New York, NY 10019

Gifts, $1, 20 pages, published annually, illustrated, color.

Each year the Museum of Modern Art (MOMA) brings out a unique line of Christmas cards, note paper and calendars that have taken the fancy of many collectors. In this beautifully produced catalogue you will find limited-edition signed and framed lithographs by Chagall, Matisse and Cocteau priced from $125 to $300. There are also a dozen of the Museum's own fine art books and a group of art-related books for children. Game collectors will find some unusual games and puzzles priced from $6.95 to $50 for a Bauhaus chess set designed by Josef Hartwig, a handsome handmade reproduction of a set designed fifty years ago at the Bauhaus woodwork shop that is in the Museum's Design Collection. Members receive generous discounts, and membership forms are included with the catalogue.

M-31
MUSEUM OF THE AMERICAN INDIAN, MUSEUM SHOP, Dept. CC
Heye Foundation
Broadway at 155th Street
New York, NY 10032

Books about Indians, descriptive price list, $1, 60 pages. Color Slides, $1, 42 pages.

Although the American Indian crafts at the Museum Shop are not sold by mail because of the limited quantity, the Shop will supply a complete listing of books about Indians, comprising over 2,000 titles, and a complete listing of over 3,000 35mm color slides that may be ordered. Slides are 75¢ each or $8 a dozen and cover some Indian paintings and a wide range of arts and crafts from pre-

Columbian cultures in the U.S., Canada, Mexico, the West Indies, Central and South America, and Indians of prehistoric times. Also available by mail are greeting cards with eighteen reproductions of American Indian paintings, $3.50 a dozen ppd. An excellent source for anyone interested in the history and culture of the Indians of the Americas.

M-32
MUSEUM OF THE CITY OF NEW YORK, Dept. CC
Fifth Avenue at 103rd Street
New York, NY 10028

Museum Shop Catalogue, free, published annually, 16 pages, illustrated, black and white.

The items in this catalogue—prints, reproductions, old-fashioned toys, dollhouse miniatures, note cards, books, Delftware, jewelry—reflect the Museum's collections. There's a cyclorama of New Amsterdam on canvas for needlepointing, 17″ x 23″, available with or without yarn and needle; Delft pillboxes and cow cream pitcher; a cast-iron toy fire pumper from the original nineteenth-century mold; enchanting reproductions of nineteenth-century rag toys such as a tabby cat or pug dog, hand-screened in color on cotton muslin, flat for framing or stuffed; and Currier & Ives prints reproduced from the Museum's collection of originals—the largest in the world. Other offerings include a set of eight song-sheet covers from the originals, a poster of Broadway, and Pollack's toy theaters to cut out and assemble. For doll collectors there are doll families, a Jenny Lind doll made of cloth and dressed in calico, a hand-painted wooden ''penny'' doll, and all sorts of dollhouse furniture. The books listed deal with every aspect of New York City, past and present, neighborhoods and people, from the riverfront to the theater. Prices range from $1 to $60, with a small charge for postage and handling.

M-33
MY GRANDFATHER'S SHOP, LTD., Dept. CC
2415 Ennalls Avenue
Wheaton, MD 20902

Best Selections from your Limited Edition Dealer, free, published seasonally, 30 pages, illustrated, color.

My Grandfather's Shop sends out the standard small catalogue issued by the National Association of Limited Edition Dealers, Inc., whose members are retail and wholesale merchants in the specialized field of exchanging and selling limited-edition plates, bells, figurines and other collectibles. Shown in color, with size, issue price (subject to change without notice), the number made in the edition and an asterisk for first editions, are plates,

Ars Libri, A-21, offers unusual photographs from their collection, from 1839 to the present.

PRECAUTIONS FOR PRINT COLLECTORS

When framing original prints, it is of primary importance not to cut, or allow the framer to cut, the paper surrounding the printed image, as to do so reduces the value of the print. If the margins differ in width or are otherwise irregular, mat the work in such a way as to correct this. Be sure to use only 100 percent pure rag paper when you mat a print. Other papers may ''burn'' through and cause discoloration of the margins.

You should also be careful, when mounting a print, never to use glue, Scotch tape or masking tape, or rubber cement. The best adhesive is standard library paste, or your own paste mixture of flour and water.

Never hang prints, drawings or watercolors where they will be constantly exposed to strong natural or artificial light, which can cause disastrous fading. Preferably, keep the works in portfolios with glassine paper between them and view them by turning the pages, the way you'd leaf through a magazine. If you insist on hanging prints, circulate and replace them every few weeks.

119

Pewter amulet, shaped and decorated like a Persian cartouche. Jewish Museum, J-4.

"Sky Above Sinai" and *"Jerusalem,"* lithographs by Israeli artist Michail Grobman. Spertus Museum of Judaica Store, S-29.

"Haggadah for Passover," hand-signed lithographs by Ben Shahn. Kennedy Galleries, K-5.

bells, Christmas ornaments and steins by the well-known companies, such as Wedgwood, Rosenthal and Bing & Grondahl.

M-34
MYSTIC SEAPORT MUSEUM STORE, Dept. CC
Mystic, CT 06355

Gift Catalogue, 50¢ for a 2-year subscription, 32 pages, published annually, illustrated, black and white and color. **Book Catalogue,** *50¢ for a 2-year subscription, 22 pages, published annually.*

This museum store has some very high-quality offerings for collectors of maritime art and things relating to the sea. The current edition has a limited number of superb captain's spirit chests of mahogany and brass, velvet-lined, signed, dated and numbered, and containing six hand-blown lead crystal decanters and two pairs of crystal tumblers and stemmed glasses. A special edition for 1978 features limited-edition prints in full color of the Tall Ships paintings by Charles Lungren ($60 each, unframed; $145 matted and framed), nineteenth-century sailing charts struck from the original copper plates, and hand-colored reproductions of an Antoine Roux watercolor in an edition of 300 ($45 for the print, $157 matted and framed). (Roux was acclaimed as the finest painter of ships in the early 1800s.) There's some beautiful scrimshaw, particularly one of the ship *Volusia* of Salem in a squall, executed by artist Scott Krieger on an old whale's tooth, about 5″ tall with stand, $400. Mystic Seaport is endeavoring to find an ivory substitute for whale's teeth. The U.S. government, however, allows the sale of scrimshaw made from stocks of whales' teeth certified to have been in existence before the whale was declared an endangered species, and a copy of the exemption accompanies each of the Krieger whale teeth, among the few still available.

The book catalogue lists every conceivable subject relating to the sea, from whalers to fisheries to shipbuilding to maritime histories and period architecture. Prices for items in the catalogue range from a few dollars up to the hundreds. A small shipping charge is added.

M-35
MY UNCLE, Dept. CC
133 Main Street
Fryeburg, ME 04037

Doll Houses of My Uncle, 25¢, 8 pages, illustrated, black and white.

Delightful doll houses, scaled 1″ to 1′, in a variety of authentic architectural styles—New England saltbox, Victorian mansion, Beacon Hill townhouse and Nantucket Cape. Two are sold as kits, one as a kit or completely finished, and the Victorian mansion with two floors and attic, bays and dormers, a porch with hand-turned columns, is assembled and painted, ready to furnish, for $495 plus shipping charges collect. Kits range in price from $45 for the Cape to $195 for the saltbox. For the saltbox and Victorian mansion you can also get, for a small charge, glossy photos and floor plans drawn to scale. The finished houses may be decorated to taste with your own miniature furniture, wallpaper, curtains, fixtures and decorative hardware.

Tea towels in linen with designs from tavern signs in Colonial Williamsburg, C-28.

121

N-1

GEORGE NADER ART GALLERY, Dept. CC
92, Rue du Magasin de l'Etat
P. O. Box 962
Port-au-Prince
Haiti

Contemporary Haitian Art, $4, 106 pages, illustrated, black and white. Look Haiti, $1, 32 pages, illustrated, color. The Primitivisme Haitien, $10, 96 pages, illustrated, sepia and color.

Three from among a number of publications offered by a gallery that specializes in the brillant and imaginative works of Haitian artists. Scenes of village and country life, portraits, studies of fruit and flowers, voodoo rites, religious subjects, are among the paintings illustrated. Many of the famous names are included such as Hector Hyppolite, Philomé Obin and Wilson Bigaud, and there are a number of younger painters doing vivid, delightful work. Original Haitian paintings are not subject to duty in the U.S. or Canada. Prices on request.

N-2

**NATIONAL ARCHIVES AND RECORDS
SERVICE,** Dept. CC
Washington, DC 20408

Documents From America's Past: Reproductions from the National Archives, free, published periodically, 38 pages, illustrated, black and white.

A fascinating source of Americana. Among the many items offered in facsimile are doodles and documents by John F. Kennedy, including a handwritten draft of his inaugural speech and remarks scheduled to be made in Austin, Texas, on November 22, 1963; Franklin D. Roosevelt's correspondence with Einstein on atomic energy and his "Day of Infamy" speech; the 19th Amendment, 1920; the Emancipation Proclamation, 1863; the Monroe Doctrine, 1823; the Declaration of Independence; Washington's official map of Yorktown, 1781. You can also send for color reproductions of old Navy prints and watercolors from Roosevelt's extensive collection at Hyde Park; war posters; a Mathew Brady portfolio of eminent Americans; prints of sail and steamboats; and cassettes of the voices of Lindbergh, Churchill, Hitler and several Presidents. Prices range from $1 to $6 (for cuff links of the first Great Seal of the United States).

N-3

NATIONAL AUDUBON SOCIETY, Dept. CC
Service Dept., 950 Third Avenue
New York, NY 10022

Audubon Christmas Catalogue, free, published annually, 24 pages, illustrated, color, also separate flyers for books, magazines, bird feeders.

The Society mails out an interesting little catalogue of which the theme, naturally, is nature. There are clothes, jewelry, tote bags, a backpack with the Audubon emblem, note cards, memo pads, calendars, bookmarks and all kinds of small gift items. Collectors of playing cards would be interested in a deck with illustrations of egret and Louisiana heron exclusively printed for the Society from paintings by Robert Gillmor ($5 a set), naturalists in the LP record albums in the *Sounds of Nature* series, the *Field Guide of Eastern and Western Bird Songs* on cassettes, the series of field guides and the many books. Among other items in the catalogue are glass Christmas tree balls illustrated with pairs of birds by wildlife artist Charles Ripper (set of three, $8.95); amusing crystal salt and pepper shakers with pewter screw-on tops of frog, pig, elephant or hippopotamus heads; an animal orchestra of tiny figures, 1½" high, each playing a different instrument; sand-cast solid brass paperweights in the shape of a shark or whale; the Bronze Menagerie, miniature animals, 2½" high, sculpted in cold-cast bronze by Norman and Herman Deaton, cottontail rabbits, skunks, prairie dogs, beaver, red foxes or chipmunk, gift-boxed, $20 each; and wood carvings from the Lawtons of a penguin, lemming, puffin, polar bear with cub, dolphin and baby, hawksbill sea turtle and humpback whale, $9 to $45. (Numerous other carvings are available from the

"Phoenixes," a needlepoint kit adapted from a Ming dynasty silk tapestry. Freer Gallery of Art, F-14.

From an oval Imari platter, a needlepoint kit for an oval footstool. Creative Needle, C-38.

Needlepoint pillow kits, designs adapted from historical textiles, Jane Whitmire, W-12.

Left, brass and glass display cases handmade in Mexico. Right, display stands for minerals and fossils. All from Dover Scientific, D-14.

Right, collector's table in mahogany lined with velvet, Classic Crafts, C-21. Below, folding mahogany stand and tray to display needlework. Sudberry House, S-42.

Lawtons; write directly to Lawtons, P. O. Box 21, Essex, CT 06426 for catalogue.) You can also become a member of the Society. The annual membership fee—$15 (individual), $18 (family) or $8.50 (student)—also brings you a year's six issues of the Society's nature magazine, *Audubon*.

N-4

NATIONAL GALLERY OF ART, Dept. CC
6th and Constitution, N.W.
Washington, DC 20565

Catalogue of Reproductions and Publications, *free, 64 pages, illustrated, black and white.*

This great museum publishes a number of catalogues and publications relating to its collections, exhibitions and lectures. Books by such eminent writers as Kenneth Clark, Mario Praz, Sigfried Giedion and John Pope-Hennessy are listed along with booklets covering the major schools of painting in the gallery collections and catalogues devoted to both the permanent collections and temporary exhibitions such as *English Drawings and Water Colors from the Collection of Mr. and Mrs. Paul Mellon* and *African Art in Motion*. The range of color reproductions and postcards is vast and represents artists of every school and period, from Botticelli and Bellini to Degas and Cézanne to Morris Louis and Jackson Pollock. Prices vary from 10¢ for a postcard to $50 for Anthony Blunt's book on Poussin. There is a charge of $1 for postage and handling.

N-5

NATIONAL HANDCRAFT INSTITUTE, INC.
Dept. CC
1425 Grand Avenue
Des Moines, IA 50337

Woodcraft Collection, *50¢, refundable with purchase, published seasonally, 24 pages, illustrated, color.*

National Handcraft Institute specializes in kits that include miniature antique furniture (a Chippendale chest-on-chest 4¼" high by 2¾" wide is around $8), a Lifetime thirty-one-note music box with a starter set of discs for five traditional melodies (from around $90 to $100, depending on whether the wood is pine, cherry or walnut) and a schoolhouse clock, as well as more prosaic things like planters and butcher-block pieces. They also have kits for decoy ducks (a canvasback and a wood duck), three-quarters life size, complete with paints and painting guides.

N-6

NATIONALMUSSEETS FORLAG, Dept. CC
Radvad, DK-2800 Lyngby
Denmark

Museum Copies from the National Museum of Denmark, *free, published periodically, 22 pages, illustrated, black and white.* *Broadsides from the National Museum of Denmark,* *free, published periodically, 20 pages, illustrated, black and white.*

Handsome copies of Bronze Age artifacts from the museum collection include a miniature sword from around 1000–800 B.C., which was placed in a grave as real swords were too precious; a variety of knives and swords; ornaments depicting Thor's Hammer, dating from the tenth century A.D.; intricate keys; a very modern looking necklace, circa 1000 B.C., deposited as a sacrifice in Jebjerg bog; and figurines of bulls and lions. Other offerings are a silver gilt copy of a Late Roman ring, silver clasps, cufflinks or earclips, wooden candlesticks copied from nineteenth-century folk art and a fascinating nineteenth-century "stack-candle stand" with a length of candle coiled upward around a rod and held by a kind of pincer. The broadsides are reprints of popular sheets of cut-out dolls, soldiers, Christmas tree decorations, historical events, ships, jumping jacks, games and cut-out farms. Prices are published separately and vary according to exchange rate changes.

N-7

NATIONAL TRUST FOR HISTORIC PRESERVATION, Dept. CC
740 Jackson Place, N.W.
Washington, DC 20006

The National Trust for Historic Preservation Gift Collection, *free, published annually, 22 pages, illustrated, color.*

Among the many beautiful and useful objects offered by the National Trust for Historic Preservation are pewter blazer buttons patterned after a set created to commemorate George Washington's inauguration in 1789 (set of seven, three 1" in diameter, four ¾" in diameter —$13.50); needlepoint kits including one taken from Frank Lloyd Wright's design for an art glass window in his Oak Park, Illinois, studio; a Dong Kingman lithograph celebrating the 1976 Operation Sail in an edition of 500, numbered and signed; a reproduction of Washington's "camp cup" in sterling ($105) or pewter ($15, or $14.50 each for set of twelve); drinking cup designed by Jefferson in 1810 in several sizes from a 2-oz. miniature to 10 oz. Also listed are a wide selection of publications on such subjects as *Victorian Cut & Use Stencils, Wooden Ship-*

125

building & Small Craft Preservation, America's Forgotten Architecture and *American Advertising Posters of the 19th Century.* All proceeds from sales go to further the preservation goals of the National Trust.

N-8
THE NATURE COMPANY, Dept. CC
1999 El Dorado Avenue
Berkeley, CA 94707

Nature Company Catalog, *free, published semiannually, 32 pages, illustrated, two-color.*

Primarily a catalogue for naturalists. There are some unusual items here that would interest collectors, such as sand-cast bronze wind bells from the deserts of the American Southwest, designed by world-famous architect Paolo Soleri. Each bell bears the Soleri workshop stamp of his Cosanti Studio and differs very slightly in surface design. Weathering in the desert air gives a rough earth-tone finish. The bells can also be used indoors as mobiles. Prices run $14 for a small bell, $32 for medium and $42 for large. There is also a Soleri bell sculpture incorporating the largest of the bells with linkages and sculpture for $250. The Copenhagen Sundial, which would make a stunning piece of garden sculpture, is a beautiful dial cast in solid bronze, adjustable to tell solar time anywhere in the Northern Hemisphere, 14½" diameter, 20" high, $165. Three prints of watercolors by R.W. Tyler, *Wildflowers of the California Mother Lode, Wildflowers of Alaska* and *Wild Berries of Alaska,* in full color on a white background, 18" x 30", are each $8. For owl collectors, a wonderful abstract lead crystal owl from Norway, 2" high, costs $17.50. There are also some fascinating nature recordings of the sounds of a tropical rain forest, the language and music of wolves, songs of the humpback whale, sounds of the sea and a frog pond, ranging in price from around $5 to $7. A most intriguing and well presented catalogue, with some great gift ideas.

N-9
NATURE HOUSE, INC., Dept. CC
Griggsville, IL 62340

Pocket Portfolio, *$2 (refundable with purchase), published annually, over 50 loose pages, illustrated, color.*

Color prints of birds, animals and flowers by three artists are the specialty of Nature House. The prints are 22" x 28" and published in editions of 5,000, signed and numbered. Richard Sloan does paintings of North American birds. An attractive study of male and female bluebirds by their nest is $400; a pair of cardinals in a snowy evergreen, $150. Richard Timm paints North American mammals. His *Gray Fox,* puzzling over a monarch butterfly, is $50;

Eastern Cottontail, searching for grasses in a light snow, $75. Maryrose Wampler does flowers in their natural settings of fields and woods. Nature House also offers a series of dog prints by E. H. Hart, edition of 2,500, $60 per print. Flower prints by Andrey Avinoff are limited to 1,250 and range from $12.50 to $30. Prices on all prints vary with availability.

N-10
NEEDLEWORKS NEEDLEPOINT, Dept. CC
P. O. Box 12427
Atlanta, GA 30355

Needleworks Needlepoint, *$3, refundable with purchase, 20 loose-leaf pages in cover, with order forms, illustrated, color.*

Elegant, imaginative, beautiful designs for rugs, bell pulls, pillows, chair seats, purses, even a lamp base (which can also be painted with a design to match your wallpaper) are the specialty of Needleworks Needlepoint. There are Chinese designs, such as an oriental scroll rug, 38¼" x 54" ($400) or Ming medallion pillow, some fascinating shaped shell pillows, approximately 15" across ($40), shaped baskets of eggs, flowers, vegetables and fruit, delicate pastel floral squares with cane border, a paisley patchwork rug and needlepoint Christmas stockings and shaped Christmas ornaments that would make family gifts to treasure (stockings are $45 and $50, ornaments $7.50). The price of the kit includes the design hand painted in oils on finest quality cotton canvas, yarn, needle and stitch instructions when necessary. Mounting is not included, but the company will be happy to give quotes.

N-11
NEPAL CRAFTS EMPORIUM, Dept. CC
G. P. O. Box 1443
Kathmandu, Nepal

Handmade Artistic Products of Nepal, *$5, refundable with purchase, 28 pages, illustrated, black and white.*

Works in brass and copper; gilded images of Buddha and other gods; studded filigree boxes; masks; necklaces; temple dogs, elephants, birds, owls and other animals; carved-wood mythological figures; pots; lamps; windows; screens; doorways; paintings on cotton, silk and paper; and wool rugs are among the many items offered by the Emporium. Elaborately carved window frames and shutters are available in many designs and sizes. There are enchanting little sculptures of rabbits, mice and peacocks. Carpets, known as Tibetan rugs, generally measure 3' x 6' but can be woven to order. Prices on request.

N-12
THE NEWARK MUSEUM, Dept. CC
49 Washington Street
Newark, NJ 07101

Publications of the Newark Museum, *free, published annually, 8 pages, black and white.*

The Newark Museum publishes various catalogues of its shows, many pertaining to New Jersey, and the *Newark Museum Quarterly* which costs $7 a year. The publications list also gives available back issues of the *Quarterly* from 1949. Four interesting books which may be ordered through the museum are: *New Jersey's Money* by George W. Wait, 434 pages, 460 illustrations, $17.50; *The Movies Begin: Making Movies in New Jersey 1887–1920* by Paul Spehr, 172 pages, 211 black-and-white and 3 color illustrations, $13.95; *Ancient Glass at the Newark Museum* by Susan H. Auth, 238 pages, 10 color plates, $15.95 hardcover, $9.95 softcover; *Survival: Life and Art of the Alaskan Eskimo* by Barbara Lipton, 96 pages, 44 black-and-white and 14 color illustrations, $7.95. Museum members receive a 20 percent discount.

N-13
THE NEWBURYPORT GUILD, Dept. CC
96 High Street
Newburyport, MA 01950

The Newburyport Guild, *50¢, published annually, black-and-white illustrated price lists.*

The Newburyport Guild is a promotional mail-order business that offers the work of a group of independent merchants, manufacturers and individual crafts people in the Newburyport area. Their selection, chosen to reflect the spirit of the area, is vast and interesting. A sampling of the collectibles includes reproductions of New England and Shaker furniture, including sleigh seats, campaign chests, trays; reproductions of copper lanterns, jailer's keys, nautical bells, tavern signs, solid brass striding-man doorstops; genuine wheelhouse deck-grating tables, hand-carved nautical figures, hardwood children's toys, foot-racers made from antique hardwood shoe lasts, doll houses, including one based on the Betsy Ross house, completely assembled ship models, New England prints, paintings and custom handcrafted "Quarterboard" signs. Prices are very reasonable.

N-14
NEW CHINA ARTS CORPORATION, Dept. CC
225 Park Avenue South, Suite 816
New York, NY 10003

Brochures, *free, illustrated, color.*

Bold, brightly colored woodblock prints by peasant painters of Huhsien County, the People's Republic of China, depicting scenes from their daily lives. Editions of one hundred examples, authenticated by the seal of the individual artist, are $175. One-of-a-kind watercolors on silk copied from Chinese paintings of the past range from $40 to $300.

N-15
NEW YORK BOTANICAL GARDEN, Dept. CC
Bronx, NY 10458

The New York Botanical Garden Fall-Winter Gift Catalogue, *free, published seasonally, 16 pages, illustrated, color.*

A small, delicious and unusual catalogue with all kinds of Christmas gift ideas that are a bit out of the ordinary —potted bulbs, sprouting seeds from the English seedsmen Thompson & Morgan, a calendar, stationery, aprons, place mats and chopping board with horticultural motifs, sunflower-design tote, apron, luncheon set, pillbox and poster, and flowery sachets and soaps. Collectors will appreciate the Poster Print Series of full-color lithograph posters of plants and herbs from fifteenth-, sixteenth- and seventeenth-century woodcuts and engravings ($6 each) and the plant ecology wall charts from the Natural History section of the British Museum ($5 each or 3 for $13.50), the Warhol silk screen flower prints ($20) and utterly enchanting naive posters of cats—in a bed of iris or in the tropics—at $22.50. There's also a handy "No-Frame" poster hanger of two slip-on strips of plastic, 30" long, to cut to any desired size, $5 for two sets.

N-16
NOR'EAST MINIATURE ROSES, INC., Dept. CC
58 Hammond Street
Rowley, MA 01969

Nor'East Miniature Roses, *free, published spring and fall, 16 pages, illustrated, color.*

For the horticultural hobbyist, miniature roses are a natural. These dwarf roses grow only 12" to 15" tall at most, sometimes only 5" to 8", and reflect, in miniature, the classic hybrid teas. They are cared for like any other roses but have the added advantage of being growable both indoors and out—miniatures in the garden can be potted in fall and brought inside. Prices for these exquisite, colorful little miniatures are very reasonable, from around $2.50 to $3.50 each. You can order a basic indoor miniature rose kit (four plants, four pots, three quarts of potting mix and instructions) for $12.95 ($13.25 west of the Mississippi) and various collections selected by Nor'East Roses. A collection of twelve of the highest rated miniature roses is around $27. Some of the roses make splendid plants for hanging baskets. Nor'East also sells their own special potting mix and *The Complete Book of Miniature Roses* by Charles Marden Fitch ($12.95), which tells you all you need to know. We can see that this would be a fascinating and rewarding hobby.

N-17
NORTHEAST BEAD TRADING COMPANY,
Dept. CC
12 Depot Street
Kennebunk, ME 04043

Northeast Bead Trading Company Catalogue, free, published annually in fall with spring supplement, 24 pages, illustrated, black and white.

This company's catalogue lists a wonderfully wide range of beads. There are beads of carved camel bone and sandalwood with extra large holes, sterling silver beads, brass beads, gold-filled beads, handmade Venetian glass beads, flower beads from Japan, agates from India, Mexican onyx, semiprecious gem beads such as turquoise and jade, clay beads, porcelain beads, stoneware and shell beads, pasta beads and nut bread beads, beads of buffalo and cow horn. There are also natural, undyed feathers and a number of cords, chains, pins, clasps and wires, even jeweler's tools for sale. Prices are listed in three categories —retail (singly or by the dozen), 25 percent discount on larger quantities, 50 percent discount on large quantities for resale. Prices vary from around 13¢ each to $48 per thousand. There is a minimum order of $10 and a small charge for postage and handling.

N-18
NORTHEASTERN NEVADA MUSEUM, Dept. CC
P. O. Box 503
Elko, NV 89801

Northeastern Nevada Historical Society Quarterly, $1.50 (free to members), published quarterly, 59 pages, illustrated.

The Northeastern Nevada Museum offers a selection of books relating to northeastern Nevada and the west in general. There are the usual cookbooks and field guides,

books on local Indian tribes, the Basques (who came to Nevada as sheepherders), Nevada ghost towns, railroads of Nevada and much more. Members receive a 10 percent discount on purchases. The *Quarterly* makes interesting reading.

N-19
M. NOWOTNY & CO., Dept. CC
8823 Callaghan Road
San Antonio, TX 78230

Catalogue, $1, published annually, 22 pages with separate price list, black and white, no illustrations.

It is a pity there are no illustrations in this catalogue, for the subject matter is wide-ranging and intriguing. Among the groups of items are all kinds of stones, polished, cabochons and faceted, polished agate and bloodstone eggs from India, snuff bottles in glass, ivory and jade, marbles, minerals and fossils and Indian artifacts such as arrowheads, mostly flint, but also jasper, chalcedony and obsidian. There are onyx carvings by Mexican Indians, Mexican pottery and carved stone fetishes, and, listed under antiques, oddities and novelties, offbeat things like old iron keys, branding irons, nails, spurs, railroad spikes, ox yokes, horseshoes, mounted and polished longhorn steer horns and Western-style brass badges. Prices, quoted by the single unit, dozen or hundred, according to the item, are reasonable. There's a fascinating list of trade beads, such as 100- to 300-year-old Venetian millefiori, traded in Africa for ivory, gold and slaves, and also to the American Indians between the 1600s and 1800s (an average strand of thirty-five to seventy beads, 24″ long, is $10), Dutch and Hudson's Bay trade beads and old silver-bead necklaces from Ethiopia. Nowotny also sells display stands and frames of different kinds, specimen boxes, display lights, adhesives and clear sprays, books related to their merchandise, and even barbed wire in bundles of ten assorted varieties—which someone must collect as there's also a "Barbed Wire Bible" that lists over 500 varieties with patent dates.

Amusing poster from Cauldron Promotions, C-9.

Above, contemporary Finnish ceramics based on old rustic designs by Pohjanpiika; Stockmann, S-38. Below left, puzzle jug made at Greenfield Village; Edison Institute, E-4. Below right, Pennsylvania Dutch sgraffito plate reproduced from the collection of the Philadelphia Museum of Art, P-11.

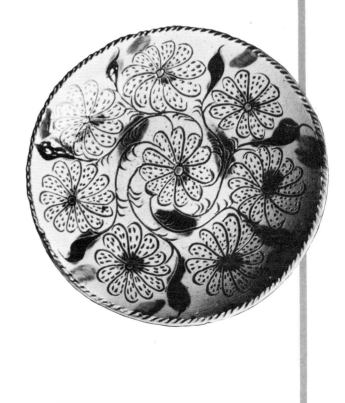

O-1

THE OHIO RIVER MUSEUM, Dept. CC
c/o Campus Martius Museum
Marietta, OH 45750

Price list, free.

Part of the Ohio Historical Society, the River Museum lists publications, color reproductions, recordings, post-cards, notepaper, sterling silver charms and boat-model blueprints. A charm of a steamboat with a paddle wheel that turns is $6; the blueprint of a ⅛″ scale model packet excursion sternwheeler named *Belle of Louisville* by Alan Bates is $5.25; a paperback album of *Americana River Boats,* after sixteen paintings by William Reed, complete with histories is $20; a showboat poster, 46″ x 24″ is $5. Stereo recordings of steamboat whistles, calliope tunes and riverboat sounds average $6 each. The normal charge for postage and handling is $1.

O-2

OKLAHOMA INDIAN ARTS & CRAFTS CO-OPERATIVE, Dept. CC
P. O. Box 966
Anadarko, OK 73005

Set of brochures, published annually, 4 pages, il-lustrated, black and white.

The co-operative produces beaded handbags, bracelets and buckles, and partially and fully beaded men's and women's horsehide moccasins, all the work of individual craftspeople. Homer Lumpmouth fashions jewelry of en-graved German silver. Donna Tsatoke creates dolls rep-resenting various tribes. James Querdibitty makes feath-erwork war bonnets, bustles and war dance costumes. One of his bustles, 30″ in diameter with felt draggers 41″ long, is made of eagle feathers, dyed plumes and yarn. Prices on request.

O-3

OLD HALL GALLERY LTD., Dept. CC
Crown Lodge, Crown Road
Morden, Surrey SM4 5BY
England

Old Hall Gallery Ltd., $10 (for four issues), pub-lished annually, 16 pages, illustrated, black and white.

Among paintings currently offered by this English firm are a splendid *British Men-of-War & a Steam Yacht near Naples Harbour* signed Tomasso de Simone and dated 1865; a portrait by Sir Peter Lely (1617–1680) of a lady in an oyster satin dress; Sir John Everett Millais' canvas of a woman in a white dress with a large bowl of roses, and an eighteenth-century study by George James of two young sisters on a terrace with their King Charles spaniel. For color transparencies, send a $1 bill for two (returnable). Prices on request.

O-4

THE OLD PRINT GALLERY, INC., Dept. CC
1212 31st Street, N.W.
Washington, DC 20007

Showcase, $2, published bimonthly, 96 pages, il-lustrated, black and white.

This is an excellent catalogue of original antique Ameri-can prints and maps published between 1600 and 1890, almost all one-of-a-kind and many backed with rice paper to flatten and strengthen the folds. The cover of a current issue shows an amusing patriotic lithograph, *The True American Sailor,* published by N. Currier ($165). There are Currier & Ives lithographs of American scenes rang-ing in price from $125 to $200; a composite lithograph showing the exterior, office, composition and press rooms of Clark & Brady's Brookville *Democrat,* from an 1878

"*Maiko,*" *a serigraph by Japanese artist
Junichiro Sekino. The Yoseido Gallery, Y-2.*

Chinese painting on silk. CRDO Handicrafts, C-37.

Man on turtle replica netsuke. Peabody Museum, P-7.

Centennial Quilt in patchwork and appliqué, by G. Knappenberger, 1876.
Hirschl & Adler Galleries, H-18.

Handmade tufted tapestry. Gentry-Lucas, G-8.

Mola tapestry from San Blas Islands. Pan-Am
Exhibits, P-3.

atlas of Jefferson County, Pa. ($100); an original broadside advertising the exhibit of the *Great American Mastodon* ($250), and a delightful theatrical print of Mme. Rentz's Minstrels in *H.M.S. Pinafore. Telegraph Chart, America-Europe* is a wonderfully complex lithograph celebrating completion of the first oceanic telegraph, published in 1858 by Charles Magnus, N.Y.; and *L'Amerique,* a black-and-white aquatint engraved by C. Roemild and published circa 1825 shows Europeanized Incas worshiping the sun amid lush American foliage and strangely drawn llamas ($125).

O-5
THE OLD SHELL GAME, INC., Dept. CC
P. O. Box 252
Milton, MA 02186

The Old Shell Game Catalogue, 25¢, published annually, illustrated color folder with supplemental catalogue sheets added monthly.

A company that gives you the names and addresses of its competitors and suggests you shop them first for quality and price must be pretty sure that collectors will come back to them. Their listings are straightforward, their guarantee of A-1 condition or money back in ten days is firm, and their prices seem reasonable. Advanced collectors with special needs receive special attention.

O-6
OLDSTONE ENTERPRISES, Dept. CC
77 Summer Street
Boston, MA 02110

Oldstone Enterprises, free, brochure, published annually, 4 pages, illustrated, black and white.

Oldstone offers rubbing materials for headstones, historical markers, coins, and other relief designs. The rubbing kit contains paper, wax, tape, a brush for clearing surfaces, and a booklet guide to creative rubbing. You can also order wax (in eight colors including silver and gold) and paper separately. A children's rubbing kit and *The Last Word,* a study of early New England graveyards complete with fold-out map showing locations of hundreds of graveyards, are also available. Prices range from $1.25 to $7.50. There is a small shipping charge.

O-7
THE OPERA BOX, Dept. CC
Box 48
Homecrest Station
Brooklyn, NY 11229

The Opera Box, free, 28 pages, published twice yearly, black and white.

This extensive list of books not only includes a very complete selection of volumes on opera, but also covers a wide range of musical subjects including biography, history and musical training. Prices range from $1 to $55.

O-8
ORIENTAL INSTITUTE, UNIVERSITY OF CHICAGO, Dept. CC
1155 East 58th Street
Chicago, IL 60637

The Suq, The Oriental Institute, University of Chicago, 35¢, 16 pages, illustrated, black and white.

The catalogue we received, the first to be published by the Oriental Institute, on the occasion of its tenth anniversary, has reproductions from the collection of the Institute, old and new, and from other collections. The opening picture, on the cover, shows three Egyptian cats of Bastet (goddess of love and joy) from different periods and dynasties, and the inside pages have mummy bead necklaces; canopic jars in white Alvastone, 13″ high ($40 each); jewelry; a sphinx; royal figures; the Horus Falcon Oracle; a terra-cotta Dead Sea Scroll jar containing one complete scroll (reduced scale), 5½″ high, 14-page pamphlet with history included ($6.50); a goat with bell, 3½″ × 2½″, original of bronze from Luristan, 1400–700 B.C.; seals; tablets, amulets; a Sumerian libation cup; rider on a horse from the Achaemenid period, 6¼″ high ($18), and ageless brass camel bells with glass evil-eye beads, imported from Turkey ($7.50). If you send with your order a separate check for $15 membership fee payable to the Oriental Institute, you are entitled to the members' 10 percent discount.

O-9
ORIGINAL PRINT COLLECTORS GROUP, LTD., Dept. CC
120 East 56th Street
New York, NY 10022

Catalogues and newsletters, free to members, published bimonthly, 16 pages, illustrated, color.

An excellent source for original graphics by contemporary artists (and, from time to time, fine old master prints as they become available) and well worth the annual membership fee of $25. Actually, if you are a serious buyer, membership costs you nothing, as the fee is applied to your first order within one year of joining. You also get a $25 credit for each initial purchase of prints that can be applied to subsequent orders within one year of joining. If you are interested in receiving literature describing the membership plan, an application form, sample catalogues and newsletter, just write to the Original Prints Collectors Group, or OPCG for short. Who are the OPCG? According to their direct-mail letter, they are "a relatively small group of art lovers who have banded together to take advantage of our collective buying power so that, with professional expert advice, we can acquire the finest modern graphics by both known and yet-to-be-recognized artists at the most advantageous prices... because of our contacts in the art world, and because we purchase graphics directly from the source, we can offer our members truly great works of art before the general public even knows of their existence."

Certainly, judging by the two catalogues we received, numbers 3 and 4 in volume VI, we think their expertise provides a valuable service for those not *au courant* with the art market, and the selections are reasonably priced, especially when you consider that all prints are sold framed and the price includes framing and insured delivery to any address in the continental United States. Some of the prints cost less than $100, others less than $200. An original lithograph by the lyrical French artist André Brasilier, *Pays de Neige,* signed edition of 125, framed size 28½'' x 35½'', is $275. Prices, naturally, vary according to the artist and the size of the edition. An original 1971 Joan Miró lithograph, *Le Lezard aux Plumes d'Or,* signed edition of 50, was $1,695; a Calder lithograph, signed edition of 99, $950; an Anuszkiewicz serigraph, signed edition of 100, $485; and a Dali etching, *Invention of the Lightbulb,* signed edition of 450, $600. Orders, which may be charged to major credit cards, are filled in sequence, beginning with the lowest serial number of each print, until the edition has been exhausted. The OPCG newsletter quotes annual rates of appreciation for the work of various artists. Prints by Calder, LeRoy Neiman and Gatja Rothe they sold a few years ago have since doubled, tripled or quadrupled in price. An extra service of benefit to members is a listing in the newsletter of prints sold out in previous offerings that members wish to buy. The original price of the print is given along with the bid, which can be anything up to $500 over the price initially paid.

O-10
ORNAMENTAL BOXES, Dept. CC
11789 West Pico Boulevard
Los Angeles, CA 90064

Ornamental Boxes, 50¢, refundable with purchase, 24 pages, published annually, illustrated, black and white.

These ornamental boxes and figurines collected from around the world are mostly crafted in the homes or shops of artisans. Many are painstaking reproductions, finely detailed and aged for an antique look, and some can be made into music boxes, with a choice of tunes. There are hundreds of boxes to choose from, plus carved wood animal figurines and some Korean brass figures. The designs cover many periods and, judging by the clear photographs, these are good, reasonably priced buys. A fourteenth-century bullhide map case, 6'' x 10'' x 5'', costs $17.50. A solid brass cricket box is $10, and stamped metal 'English tins' can be had for as little as $2. The most expensive box, a brass-bound and inlaid dispatch case, 8'' x 12'' x 4'', goes for $50.

O-11
OSIRUS, Dept. CC
Box 308
Santa Ynez, CA 93460

Osirus, $1, refundable with purchase, published annually, 80 pages, illustrated, black and white.

The organization known as The Order of Osirus was established in 1572 in Newbury, England, and spread over the years to the United States and many other parts of the world. There are now hundreds of covens of these "white witches," who use their powers, spells and potions only for good and useful purposes. The catalogue is crammed with elixirs, ritual candles, herbs, oils, incense, amulets and talismans, ouanga bags (part of voodoo practice), powders, stones, books, tarot cards, records of psychic music and many other things relating to the occult. Prices are low, the most expensive item being a "God of the Witches" statue, 18'' high, around $70.

O-12
OVAL STUDIO, Dept. CC
1018 Beacon Street
Brookline, MA 02146

Peiter Smart's Portfolio of Wildlife Etchings, free, 8 pages, illustrated, black and white.

The detail and accuracy of English artist Peiter Smart's wildlife portraits, etched on black scraperboard, has attracted the interest of museums of science and natural history, naturalists and conservationists. The catalogue shows his portraits of a fox, mouse, owl, cat, panda, and squirrel with mouse. Although both originals and lithographs, with some of the first-edition prints signed, are mentioned, prices given are only for the prints. These cost 75¢ each and may be ordered in a portfolio of the six, with postage of $1.50 extra.

O-13
OZARK MOUNTAIN COLLECTION, Dept. CC

7 Downing Street
Hollister, MO 65672

Ozark Mountain Collection, $2, refundable with purchase, published annually, 14 pages, illustrated, color.

A great variety of things is produced by this group of some fifty artists and craftspeople. A flintlock gun of curly maple, handmade by Danny Caywood, is decorated with silver wire and engraved brass. Rhonda Ravenscroft-Dixon creates windows of colored glass into which she incorporates antique bottles or jars so that a plant or flowers can be arranged in them. Other items include sculpture-like, free-form wooden boxes by Bob Bolles; authentic patchwork quilts from craftspeople in the hills of Arkansas and southwest Missouri; original sculptures; jewelry; ceramics; handmade furniture and tools; a witty chess set, the players mountain people, the pawns hound dogs. Objects are one-of-a-kind or in limited and unlimited editions and prices range from $10 to $1,000. Shipping charges are given after the price.

Above, zoomorphic painted vessel, reproduced from the Casa Grande region original. Artiques, A-23.

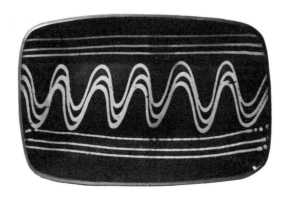

Top left, ceramic fruit bowl from nineteenth-century original, and left, pottery platter from original circa 1700, in Collections of Greenfield Village and the Henry Ford Museum. Edison Institute, E-4.

A study of nature in art and reality combines botanical prints with a collection of house plants. Windows with opaque backing and grow lights frame the greenery like large-scale living paintings.

Japanese camellia in stained glass. Philadelphia Museum of Art, P-11.

Cattleya orchid available, in bud, by mail. Rod McLellan, M-12.

P-1
PALEONTOLOGICAL RESEARCH INSTITUTION, Dept. CC
1259 Trumansburg Road
Ithaca, NY 14850

Bulletins of American Paleontology, $40, two volumes a year, illustrated. Paleontographica Americana, average price $35, published periodically, illustrated.

Over 200 bulletins numbering 72 volumes have been issued by the Institution since 1895. Elaborately illustrated, they deal with Cenozoic and Mezozoic fauna of the southern and eastern United States, Cuba, Colombia, Costa Rica, Ecuador, Jamaica, Panama, Peru, Trinidad and Venezuela; also the Paleozoic fauna and flora of North America, South America and Australia. Published studies deal with the various phases of taxonomy, microorganisms, paleobiology, paleoecology and plants. A series of large, illustrated quarto monographs covers such things as trace fossils, bivalves, corals, sponges and fish. Other books on related subjects are also listed. Bulletins are available individually or by volume, and prices vary. Price lists are available for all publications. The Institution also offers some cast trilobite jewelry reproduced in silver for $3.50 for a small charm to $10 for a set of cuff links, plus postage.

P-2
PALMETTO COLLECTIBLES WAREHOUSE, Dept. CC
Highway 301
Ulmer, SC 29849

Nostalgia Unlimited, $1.50 (refundable with purchase), 60 pages, published seasonally, illustrated, black and white.

Collectors of advertising gimmicks, war memorabilia, political campaign buttons and general "junque" will have a field day browsing these collectibles. Palmetto seems to have a line on all of the old Coca-Cola advertising promotions: golf tees at 39¢ each (a dozen at 29¢ each), serving trays, knives, clippers, bottles, bottle openers, mirrors. There is a "Wallace in 1972" belt buckle for $8.50; old heavy metal "reward" signs from Texas, $4.75; American bygones like the red turpentine earthenware urns and pots from the 1850s in two styles, $18.50 for one of each. The catalogue also has military relics from World War II: helmets ($24.95), belt buckles, medals and insignia, most of them from Nazi Germany, but a couple from Italy and Russia.

P-3
PAN-AM EXHIBITS, Dept. CC
3743 Highcliff
San Antonio, TX 78218

Pictorial Review, free, published annually, 8 pages, illustrated, black and white.

Pan-Am offers handmade Mola tapestries by the Cuna Indians of the San Blas Islands, Panama. Motifs range from gods, animals and birds to flowers and geometrics, all brilliantly colored. There are also hand-woven tapestries by the Salasaca Indians of Ecuador featuring stylized figures from Inca and pre-Inca designs. Both types of tapestries are suitable for wall hangings, clothing or pillows. Prices run from $2.95 to $24.95.

P-4
F. PANCER, Dept. CC
6514 W. Cermak Road
Berwyn, IL 60402

Brochure, free, published annually, illustrated, black and white.

A unique brochure devoted exclusively to things Czechoslovakian. Egg collectors will delight in the variety of hand-painted egg shells, each one different in design, boxed five or six and priced at $6.05 (5) and $7.20 (6). There are also hand-painted white or black goose egg shells, individual chicken egg shells painted by a Czech artist with peasant figures and attached to a decorative ribbon, 2 eggs for $6.55. Two packs of playing cards, Tarock with roman numerals and Mariasky, $3.45 and $1.95 respectively, will interest card collectors. For the doll collector, delightful girl-dolls dressed in native

Czech costumes come in sizes from 7'' to 12'', $7.20 to $11.45. There is also a small but nice selection of hand-cut crystal—a 14''-diameter crystal plate signed by the artist is $213.50, toothpick holders at $6.90 and a Labut swan for $22. All prices include postage. The brochure is in Czechoslovakian and English.

P-5
PAPILLON, Dept. CC
56 East Andrews Drive N.W.
Atlanta, GA 30305

Papillon Needlepoint, *$3, refundable with purchase, published annually, 30 pages, illustrated, color.*

Some of the most delightful needlepoint designs we have ever seen are in the Papillon catalogue, a marvelous source for the unusual and stylish. There's a beautiful Della Robbia wreath, an adaptation of the Florentine original, with holly leaves and glazed fruits, 14'' circle, approximately $70; a marvelous 48'' octagonal rug with shell silhouettes, $375; and classic designs taken from a China Trade plate, Peking tapestry, Nanking vase, scalloped Imari plate. Among our favorites are the needlepoint Oriental backgammon board with fire-breathing dragons and lacquer-red spires ($195); the French Provincial bellpull, taken from a hand-carved panel in a French chateau, 6'' x 60'' ($132); the amusing Zodiac signs, 14'' circles (each $53), and the exquisite Japanese Noh bird, Edo fish and nui haku bird pillow patterns. Each kit contains the painted canvas, stainless-steel needles, printed instructions showing both the continental and basketweave stitches, a Papillon tote bag for your handwork and Paternayan Persian needlepoint yarn.

P-6
THE PARKER GALLERY, Dept. CC
2 Albemarle Street
Piccadilly
London W1X 3HF
England

A General Catalogue of Recently Acquired Prints, Paintings, Relics and Models, *free, 112 pages, illustrated, black and white.*

Studies of battles and military garb, views of towns and houses, portraits of people and animals, paintings of sailing and steam ships, models of ships are among the hundreds of items carried by the Parker Gallery. Does a watercolor of Corfu tempt you? Or an oil of a dashing 17th Lancer on horseback? Or a Brazilian steamer on the Amazon? There are also prints and paintings of sporting events, hunting expeditions and railways. Prices range from about $50 to $8,000.

P-7
PEABODY MUSEUM OF SALEM, Dept. CC
East India Square
Salem, MA 01970

The Peabody Museum of Salem, *sales catalogue, 50¢, published annually, 24 pages, illustrated, black and white.*

This New England museum, founded in 1799 by the ambitious Salem sea captains to house the collections of ''natural and artificial curiosities'' they gathered from the four corners of the earth, has a sales shop that offers, at the museum and by mail, a wide selection of reproductions, prints, books and unusual gifts with a marine motif. Their ship reprints and marine reproductions, offered in limited editions, are especially interesting. A reproduction from an original watercolor by Antoine Roux, 1808, of the brig *Topaz,* built at Newburyport in 1807, 21¾'' x 14¾'', in a limited edition of 300, is $30. A chart of the harbors of Salem, Marblehead, Beverly and Manchester, from an 1804–1806 survey by Nathaniel Bowditch, reproduced from the original copperplate engraving, is just $7. *Canton Factories,* a lithograph taken from an amusing reverse painting on glass by an unknown Chinese artist of the factories where Europeans traded, with Chinese junks in the foreground and foreign flags flying, limited edition of 1,000, is $25. Marine books from the Museum's collection include *A History of American Marine Painting* by John Wilmerding, 279 pages, 186 illustrations, 18 color plates, $25, and *Scientific Instruments* by H. Wynter and A. Turner, an invaluable volume for the collector of instruments used in navigation, astronomy, surveying, 239 pages, 238 photographs, color and black and white, $27.50. There are polymer reproductions with ivory finish of Japanese netsuke ($20 and $15), polymer reproductions of a shaman charm from the Haida Indians of the Northwest coast (the original was carved from sperm-whale tooth) and scrimshaw teeth. Plate collectors will appreciate the handsome set of six ship plates of famous American sailing vessels made by Vista Alegre of Portugal, reproduced from colored engravings in the National Maritime Museum, Greenwich, England ($120 the set of six). There are also some beautiful reproductions of early Canton ware by Vista Alegre: plates, teapot, cup and saucer, creamer, sugar, master salt, leaf tray and tile, ranging in price from $10 for the tile to $60 for the teapot. The quality of gifts in this catalogue is exceptional.

P-8
PEKING GALLERY, Dept. CC
    5022 Hidden Branches Drive
    Dunwoody, GA 30338

Loose sheets, free, 4 pages, illustrated, black and white.

Reproductions of works by Chinese artists—studies of crabs and crustaceans by Che Pai-sheh, a galloping horse by Hsu Pei-hung, a series of playful pandas. Sizes range from 8½" x 11" to 15" x 23". Prices vary according to size and number of prints per set. A set of two horses (11" x 14") costs $4; a set of six pandas (11" x 14"), $9.

P-9
PEMBERTON & OAKES, LTD., Dept. CC
    150 Barton Avenue
    Evanston, IL 60202

Special mailings on limited editions, free.

While Pemberton & Oakes has no catalogue, the company sends out regular mailings to customers recommending limited-edition works of art, most often collector's plates, when, as they say, "an especially attractive opportunity presents itself." For instance, a 1978 mailing we received concerned a first plate by children's artist Donald Zolan, *Erik and the Dandelion,* which was to be made during a twenty-two-day firing schedule, the shortest ever announced for a plate. With such a limited edition, the plate would undoubtedly sell out fast and increase dramatically in value from its original price of $19 within a few years. (One example cited by Pemberton & Oakes, the 1971 Goebel Hummel Annual, with an issue price of $25, was worth $900 in 1978.) By sending in a firm reservation order and check or money order, a collector can be assured of obtaining the plates recommended by Pemberton & Oakes, and there's a one-year warranty during which you can return the purchased piece.

P-10
PENSACOLA HISTORICAL SOCIETY, INC.,
    Dept. CC
    405 South Adams Street
    Pensacola, FL 32501

Pensacola Historical Society Newsletter, *free, published annually (November), 6 pages.*

Publications, maps and cookbooks pertaining to Pensacola, its history and society. A limited supply of Christmas cards by local artists is also available.

COMMEMORATIVE PLATES: *Top, Boy Scout plate by Norman Rockwell from Hickory House, H-17. Center, D'Arceau-Limoges 1978 Girl of the Seasons, "Summer Girl," from The Bradford Exchange, B-20. Bottom, Gorham's "The Battle of Rhode Island, The Black Regiment, 1778," from Joy's Limited Editions, J-6.*

Mongolian silver snuff bottles inlaid with coral and turquoise.
A. Goto, G-17.

"Red and White Poppies," a color reproduction of the Japanese painting
in the style of Nonomura. Freer Gallery of Art, F-14.

P-11

**PHILADELPHIA MUSEUM OF ART, MUSEUM
SHOP,** Dept. CC
P. O. Box 7858
Philadelphia, PA 19101

The Museum Shop, *25¢, published annually, 40
pages, illustrated, color.*

Among the offerings of the Museum Shop is a five-piece
dinner service adapted from an eighteenth-century Imari
plate, with dinner, dessert and bread-and-butter plates,
tea cup and saucer, $40 a place setting or from $6.50 to
$12 for individual pieces. There's also a coupe soup at
$10. A handmade wooden giraffe, 15″ high, a reproduc-
tion of a nineteenth-century toy in the museum's collection of Pennsylvania Dutch art, limited quantity, no two
alike, is $56. Among the other items sold by the shop are
needlepoint and embroidery kits, pottery, glassware,
stained glass panels, jewelry, greeting cards, appointment
and wall calendars and four delightful jigsaw puzzles, one
taken from a patchwork quilt, another from a painting by
Henry Rousseau ($6.50 each). There is a small handling
and shipping charge.

P-12

**THE PHILLIPS COLLECTION, PUBLICATIONS
DEPARTMENT,** Dept. CC
1600–1612 21st Street, N.W.
Washington, DC 20009

The Phillips Collection, *25¢, published annually,
illustrated, black and white.*

The Phillips Collection, which opened in Washington in
1921, was the first major museum of modern art in the
United States. The more than 2,000 works of art cover a
wide range of artists, from Impressionists to contemporary American painters like Georgia O'Keeffe, Frank
Stella and Robert Motherwell. All the big names are
here—Cézanne, Renoir, Van Gogh, Monet, Picasso,
Matisse, Roualt, Braque, Klee, Kandinsky, to name a
few. The Publications Department sells reproductions of
the art in the form of prints, large and bookplate size,
postcards, note cards and slides, and has various publications relating to the Collection. Renoir's *Luncheon of the
Boating Party,* for instance, is available as a slide ($1),
postcard (15¢), note card (50¢), bookplate-size print
($1.25) and large print ($10).

P-13
PHOENIX ART MUSEUM, Dept. CC
1625 North Central Avenue
Phoenix, AZ 85004

The Museum Shop—Phoenix Art Museum, *50¢, published annually, illustrated, black and white.*

This museum shop offers two bells designed by the architect Paolo Soleri, $10 and $50 respectively, with a biography of the designer. A cylindrical cherry-bark box lined and sealed with tin is $15, Japanese rice paper wallets depicting various Japanese scenes, $2.50. Trays, greeting cards, needlepoint boxes and frames, jigsaw puzzles and wrapping papers are also part of the shop's stock-in-trade. There is a small postage and handling charge.

P-14
PIONEER MUSEUM, Dept. CC
P. O. Box 613
Ashland, KS 67831

No literature, write for information.

The Pioneer Museum has two books for sale. One is *Notes on Early Clark County, Kansas,* compiled by the Clark County Historical Society, six volumes of stories of the early settlers, from 1874 ($4 each). The other, compiled by Florence E. Hurd, Curator of the Museum, is *Kings and Queens of the Range,* a pictorial record with reprints of pictures taken between 1894 and 1904 of cattle ranches, early trail drives and similar subjects ($7 in soft cover, $10 in hard cover). Postage is not included.

P-15
PIPESTONE INDIAN SHRINE ASSOCIATION,
Dept. CC
P. O. Box 727
Pipestone, MN 56164

Brochure, free, published every two years, 10 pages, illustrated, black and white.

The Association is at the Pipestone National Monument, which occupies the site of the famed pipestone quarries of Minnesota. Indians traveled as much as 1,000 miles by foot or horse to get the sacred red stone to make the pipes they used on many ceremonial occasions. The brochure shows nineteen pipes of different styles and shapes (not all ceremonial) such as plains pipes, the most common style, elbow pipes (a personal or pleasure pipe), elaborately carved buffalo and claw pipes, hatchet pipes, stone reproductions of the metal pipes traded to the Indians in the late 1700s by the British and French, disk pipes, and micmac pipes. Prices range from $8 to $32. There are also various

items in catlinite, effigies of bears and bison, turtles and owls, a tomahawk paperweight, arrowheads of various sizes and war clubs.

P-16
DONALD T. PITCHER, Dept. CC
P. O. Box 64
North Haven, CT 06473

Massachusetts—Old Maps and Prints, *free, 12 pages, black and white.* **Early Prints—(Local Scenes),** *free, 10 pages, black and white.* **Early Maps—1800's,** *free, 10 pages, black and white.*

Donald Pitcher specializes in early Americana dealing specifically, though not entirely, with the New England and mid-Atlantic states. He publishes approximately a dozen different catalogues a year on various regions and specific titled subjects such as original woodcuts by Winslow Homer, Thomas Nast, etc. *Massachusetts* is a collection of woodcuts, maps, prints and books covering virtually all areas of the Commonwealth dating from the early 1800s. *Early Prints (Local Scenes)* lists 123 woodcuts and prints from the 1800s of the New England States, New York and New Jersey. *Early Maps—1800's,* with more than 120 listings, includes regional maps of North America and a fine group of world maps. Prices listed in all three catalogues are modest, from $2.75 for a 1937 guide to Salem, Massachusetts, to $50 for an 1839 *Historical Collections of Massachusetts* by J. W. Barber. Collectors with specific interests in the New England and mid-Atlantic states may write to Mr. Pitcher for his special listings.

P-17
PITT PETRI, INC., Dept. CC
378 Delaware Avenue
Buffalo, NY 14202

Newsletters on collectors' items, free.

Pitt Petri publishes and mails regular newsletters on Boehm, Cybis porcelains, collectors' plates and fine paperweights by Baccarat, Perthshire, St. Louis, Ysart and other companies, each accompanied by order form and reply envelope. They also have books of interest to collectors. The writing of the newsletters is detailed and informative, the illustrations are clear and the quality of the offerings high. Some current newsletters showed the delightful series of "portraits in porcelain" of famous women from the Cybis Studio, works from the Boehm Tutankhamun Collection and seven special Baccarat paperweights in limited editions of 300.

P-18
PIZAZZ LTD., Dept. CC
1510 West 15th Street
Amarillo, TX 79102

Pizazz Ltd., $3, 33 loose-leaf pages in folder with index and price list, published annually with additional pages mailed when ready, illustrated, black and white.

Surprisingly enough, this miniature shop is in the heart of the Texas Panhandle, and the owners issue a friendly invitation to stop by for coffee, if you happen to be in that part of the world, and see some of their unlisted miniatures—antique salesman's samples, cabinetmaker's samples, children's chairs, guns and many other items. Judging by the catalogue, they have a wide-ranging selection of furnishings with an unusual five-panel hand-painted screen and hand-painted wall murals by Richard Reynolds. There are four murals; two Chinoiserie, one a view of Boston Harbor in the 1800s, the fourth a hunt scene, each 50'' long, to be installed in a three-walled miniature room, or you can custom order them to any size. Modern furniture crops up among the antique—a Barcelona chair ($130) and chrome cube table ($16) in a room with a zebra rug and jungle mural and a bar, complete with miniature liquor bottles. Miniature Staffordshire figures, tiny china and porcelain reproduction Fitzhugh and Imari plates, various accessories, complete kitchens and bathrooms, minuscule cakes and candy boxes, handmade rugs and petit point rug kits are all part of this staggering collection. There are also one-of-a-kind sterling silver boxes, some topped with semi-precious stones ($20 to $40), portraits on ivory with oval silver frames that could double as lockets and lots more fun things. Miniaturists will agree this is a source with plenty of pizazz!

P-19
PLAYER PIANO CO., INC., Dept. CC
704 East Douglas
Wichita, KS 67202

Player Piano Co., Inc., $2.50, published every two years, 120 pages, illustrated, black and white.

A marvelous catalogue for mechanical-instrument collectors and hobbyists from a company that offers the largest selection of player piano parts and accessories in the world. The list of contents starts with tubing and hose and ends with an invaluable section on identifying features in determining types of player actions, a special package deal of a beginner's outfit for $62 and a lengthy and comprehensive index of every item in the catalogue. Each listing is well and informatively written, and the item numbered and priced. The company offers a large selection of player piano rolls, including Ampico and Duo-Art reissues of popular tunes, some classical music and selections from musicals like *No, No Nanette* and *Pal Joey,* ranging in price from $1.76 to $2.96.

P-20
PONY EXPRESS SYSTEM, Dept. CC
2986 Navajo Street
Yorktown, NY 10598

Pony Express Clock News, $1, refundable with purchase, 8 pages, published annually, illustrated.

According to owners Sy and Shirley Wittner, this is the first and only catalogue of genuine antique clocks published in America. Shown in the catalogue are authentic reconditioned and fully guaranteed schoolhouse, parlor, railroad station, barbers', bankers', post office, Ionic and miniature clocks circa 1900. Most have regulator pendulums and many are available with a thirty-one-day calendar face at a slightly higher price. An old schoolhouse clock, 22'' long, 13'' wide, 4½'' deep costs $98. A railroad station gallery clock, 14'' in diameter and 4½'' deep, is $95. A 20'' long, 9½'' wide, 4'' deep parlor clock is only $75. All clocks are fully guaranteed and come with a certificate of age and ownership. One especially amusing barbershop clock has a face on which time runs backward—it was intended to be hung on a wall opposite a mirror and was used in turn-of-the-century bars and barbershops throughout America. The mirror image, of course, reflected the correct time. Approximately 22'' long, 13'' wide and 4½'' deep, this clock sells for $135. Packing and shipping are extra. Major credit cards are accepted and telephone orders welcomed. If you happen to be in the vicinity of Yorktown, the Pony Express showroom has over 300 of these clocks on display (many of which are not available by mail) and also a full line of Victorian and turn-of-the-century furniture and accessories collected by the owners, who have for years run an antique auction business.

P-21
DENISE POOLE, Dept. CC
Timberland House
Horncastle Road
Woodhall Spa
Lincs. LN10 6UZ
England

Old English Silver, Old Sheffield Plate, free, revised several times a year, 16 pages, illustrated, black and white.

The catalogue and price list of old silver and Sheffield plate consists, naturally, of one-of-a-kind items, but it is constantly revised, and if the item you order is sold, your money will be returned or a similar piece may be chosen.

*Louisburg Eagle, hand-carved
by Willard Shepard.
Shep's Ship Shop, S-17.*

Scrimshaw eagle by Allan Sustare. Paul McAfee & Friends, M-10.

*Hand-sculptured copper and brass eagle with bronze accents. Addison
Greene, A-1.*

An arrangement of eighteenth-century English and Chinese enamel boxes on a low cocktail table allows the delicate details and sentimental mottos to be viewed and enjoyed from above. Photographer: Guerrero.

It is advisable to give a second and third choice. The selection of eighteenth-, nineteenth- and twentieth-century pieces shown in the current catalogue covers just about every type of tableware, from tea pots and coffee sets to pitchers, toast racks and napkin rings. It includes a set of five Georgian silver dessert spoons by Hester Bateman, a George III meat skewer, a Victorian sauce ladle, an unusual Victorian mug with slightly concave sides embossed with bright ovoids on a matt ground with a beaded base and molded rim. An excellent source for the collector. Prices, quoted in sterling, range from one pound to over 300 pounds and shipments are made by air, fully insured. Any item may be returned within seven days for a cash refund. Bear in mind that while antiques (anything 100 years or more old) are not subject to duty, more recent pieces are. Check current rate with your local customs office.

P-22
THE PORCELAIN HOUSE, LTD., Dept. CC
41 Madison Avenue
New York, NY 10016

Rosenthal Studio-linie: Joy to the World, free, published annually, 32 pages, illustrated, color.

Elegant, fanciful and unusual, the objects in this Rosenthal collection, by such famous designers as Bjorn Wiinblad, Tapio Wirkkala and Natale Sapone, are true works of art. Works by Wiinblad include his stunning new series of collector plates, *Oriental Night Music,* illustrating musical motifs from the Arabian Nights ($55 for a 6″ plate, gift-boxed); his imaginative stone-glaze ceramic candleholder, *The Juggler;* his elongated lady-with-flowers vase, her empty head the receptacle; and his beautiful embossed *Fantasy* bowl ($125). Circo II, a swirl of crystal that can be either free-form sculpture or an ashtray ($25), was designed by Italian artist-sculptor Natale Sapone. *Inca,* by Tapio Wirkkala, a group of interlocking crystal candleholders like stylized ice temples and Wolf Bauer's vibrant vase *The American Beauty Rose* are other gems of contemporary design worth collecting. Presumably, the objects shown in this beautifully assembled and well-written catalogue change each year, but it's certainly one to look out for.

P-23
PORTLAND ART MUSEUM SHOP, Dept. CC
1219 S.W. Park
Portland, OR 97205

Price list, free, published annually, 8 pages, illustrated, black and white.

The Museum Shop offers books, catalogues and pamphlets —a number published by the museum —together with postcards, posters and pendant Coptic crosses from originals circa 1800. The books include *Art in the Life of the Northwest Indians,* illustrated in black and white and color, and a *Cookbook of the Portland Art Museum 1974,* one hundred recipes, loose leaf pages suitable for framing with an easel, slip and clear plastic sheet for display of recipes. Among the posters are Indian masks and blankets, Japanese prints, a Baskin sculpture, and a nautilus shell advertising the museum. Prices vary from 10¢ to $21.50.

P-24
POSTER ORIGINALS, LIMITED, Dept. CC
924 Madison Avenue
New York, NY 10021

Poster Originals, Limited, $3.50, 92 pages, published seasonally, illustrated, black and white and color.

A handsomely produced catalogue of poster art featuring American art posters, 1972 Olympic posters, Polish circus and zoo posters, a special collection published in France called New Images, Pop Art, Super Environmental Graphics and special posters by Milton Glaser and Seymour Chwast. There is also a wide selection of European art posters, shown in black and white. The book also features a helpful glossary and detailed instructions on framing and preserving prints. Prices are generally in the $15 to $40 range, with a few exceptions. Framing kits are also available.

P-25
THE PRADO (MUSEO DEL PRADO), Dept. CC
Madrid
Spain

Catalogue of Slides, Catalogue of Postcards and Catalogue of Artoleos (reproductions on canvas), free brochures.

Spain's magnificent museum of art offers lists of slides, postcards and reproductions, mostly of works in its collection. There are numerous titles by painters of the Spanish school such as El Greco, Goya, Murillo, Velasquez, Zurbarán and Ribera along with those by artists of other countries—Fra Angelico, Mantegna, Botticelli, Raphael, Titian, Veronese, Tintoretto, Van Eyck, Van der Weyden, Brueghel, Rubens, Poussin and Bosch. Many slides are of details of the paintings. The brochures are in Spanish and prices, where given, are in pesetas, subject to current rates of exchange. Slides, etc., are sent "on request, cash on delivery, postage to be paid by the client."

P-26
PRESTON'S, Dept. CC
Main Street Wharf
Greenport, L.I., NY 11944

Of Ships and Sea, 25¢, 130 pages, published biannually, illustrated, color and black and white.

Preston's *Of Ships and Sea* is a real treasure gallery for the marine collector. There are over thirty pages of ship models in kit and completed form with prices starting at $8.95 for a scale model of a Hobie Cat, 14″ long by 22″ high, that really sails, to $84.95 for a kit of the whaling ship *Charles W. Morgan,* 26″ long by 20″ high. Completed models, some one-of-a-kind, signed and available with brass name plates for presentation purposes range from $150 for a schooner-rigged pilot boat to $395 for a 39″ model of *The Great Republic.* Ships in bottles, books on the sea, reproductions and original prints and pictures of the sea, handsome scale-model reproductions of Civil War guns, naval cannon, whaling harpoons and replicas of ship's figureheads ($29.95 to $165) are also available. There are brass clocks and barometers, replica electrified brass ship's lamps, scrimshaw, weather vanes, nautical weather instruments, ship's wheels, plus decorative wall figures.

P-27
THE PRINT MINT, Dept. CC
1147 Greenleaf Avenue
Wilmette, IL 60091
and
Route 4
Bridgewater, VT 05034

Print Mint, brochure, free, published annually, 16 pages, illustrated, black and white.

Print Mint lists a number of delightful items of interest to the collector. There are limited-edition candlesticks made of spool bobbins from a nineteenth-century mill in Vermont; spoon sculptures in silver plate of animals, birds and insects; hand-printed silk-screen and lithograph reproductions of work by American Indian artists of the Southwest; reproductions of prints by Canadian Eskimos; stone rubbings; prints of Chicago and San Francisco scenes; a series of prints depicting ski slopes all over the U.S.

Print Mint Jr. offers graphics for children along with American Indian coloring books, train art, mobiles, handmade bubble gum machines and kites from China. Prices on request.

P-28
PRINT WORLD, Dept. CC
P. O. Box 6601
Philadelphia, PA 19149

19th Century Engraved Prints, $1 (refundable with purchase), 12 pages.

The catalogue lists steel engravings, wood engravings, photogravures and typogravures based on paintings. Historical scenes, scenes from Shakespeare, portraits of Presidents of the United States, illustrations for famous literary works, great paintings are included among the various prints. A portrait of Queen Victoria after Winterhalter, 7″ x 10¼″, is $21; George Washington after Stuart, 15½″ x 19¾″, is $25; and a Madonna by Raphael, 8½″ x 12″, is $13.50. Civil War scenes and portraits, 7¾″ x 10¾″, include some made after ambrotypes done expressly for the engravings by Mathew Brady. There is a 10 percent discount on orders over $100.

P-29
PUCKIHUDDLE PRODUCTS, LTD., Dept. CC
Oliverea, NY 12462

Craftskills from the Catskills, 50¢, published annually, 20 pages, illustrated, black and white and color.

A charming portfolio of handcrafted decorative and practical items with some things of special interest to collectors. The Log Cabin quilt, 96″ x 96″, in warm earth tones, made by hand with Dacron interlining, $300, is handsome enough to hang on a wall. There's a smaller version, a patchwork blanket of the same design, 31″ x 47″, for $35. Handmade, amusing stuffed animals include a 22″-tall Mother Goose of washable canvas decked out in calico apron and sun bonnet, $17.50. Rugs, handloomed by the Amish, washable, colorfast, in three color combinations, 28″ x 54″, are $19.50 each. Hand-blown glass bells, 3″ long, $2.25 each, might add sparkle to a Christmas tree collection.

Nineteenth-century scrimshaw-style knife box. John F. Rinaldi, R-14.

R-1

**RADIO YESTERYEAR, THE RADIOLA
COMPANY,** Dept. CC
Box C
Sandy Hook, CT 06482

*Brochure, free, published periodically, illustrated,
black and white.*

An orgy of nostalgia for vintage radio show enthusiasts
from the Thirties, Forties and Fifties. Tune in The Amos
'n Andy Show; Jack Benny vs. Fred Allen; George Burns
and Gracie Allen; The Immortal Sherlock Holmes by the
Mercury Theater on the Air, starring Orson Welles (September 1938); The Shadow; The Whistler; Judy Garland
on Radio; and CBS Lux Radio Theatre versions of movies
like The Thin Man and To Have and Have Not. Remember the Andrews Sisters, Baby Snooks, Fibber
McGee and Molly? They're all here on records, each with
an hour of programming that can be played on mono or
stereo. No prices are given in the brochure, so request the
price list. Updates and supplements are sent to the mailing
list four to six times a year.

R-2

**RAGGEDY ANN ANTIQUE DOLL & TOY
MUSEUM,** Dept. CC
171 Main Street
Flemington, NJ 08822

Brochure on museum, free.

This is primarily a museum of antique dolls of bisque,
wax, wood, china and other materials and of antique toys.
There are no mail-order sales, but certain collector dolls
and toys are sold in the museum toy shop. There is a doll
repair hospital, and the museum will buy old dolls in any
condition.

R-3

F. RANDOLPH ASSOCIATES, INC., Dept. CC
1231 Race Street
Philadelphia, PA 19107

Footnotes: A Newsletter of the Performing Arts,
free, 48 pages, published quarterly, illustrated,
some color.

Whatever your interest in the performing arts, you'll find
it well represented in this jam-packed catalogue. Books
on dance, theater, music and art administration, instruction, history, comment, biography, scripts, libretti, etc.
There is a vast collection of dance records listed by ballet
title, choreographer, company and year of production. In
the other record listings are original-cast albums (including some hard-to-finds), opera, original sound tracks,
plays, Shakespearean comedies on cassettes and a sound
effects library. In a section on Eastern Theater, the company offers video tapes for sale or rent. The catalogue also
lists motion-picture souvenir programs, dance and theater
posters (some priced slightly lower than at their original
source), miniature theaters, postcards, stationery and
T-shirts. *Footnotes* offers a rebate plan on purchases over
$30. This is one of the most complete catalogues of its
kind we have seen.

R-4

RASHID SALES COMPANY, Dept. CC
191 Atlantic Avenue
Brooklyn, NY 11201

Arabic Music, $1 (refundable with purchase), pub-
lished annually, 84 pages, illustrated, color.

Established in 1934, Rashid Sales Company is the largest
source of original Arabic records and tapes in America.
Their catalogue, nicely produced in English and Arabic
by EMI Greece SA, lists hundreds of albums and tapes
including pop, filmtracks, original cast recordings, some
religious and one classical disc: *Peter and the Wolf* in
Arabic. Labels represented are *Voix de l'Orient, Soutel-
phan, Voice of Lebanon, Cairophon, Voix de l'Islam,
Baidaphon, Sout El Hob* and, naturally, *EMI*. Costs in
1978 were $5.98 per disc, cassette or eight-track tape.

R-5

J. F. RAY'S FOSSILS, Dept. CC
P. O. Box 1364
Ocala, FL 32670

Ray's Fossils, price list, free with stamped, self-
addressed envelope, 2 pages.

Fossils such as shark teeth, dinosaur bone fragments,

bones of various other mammals, gastropods, cephalopods, petrified wood, beetle cocoons, sold singly or in lots up to one hundred, at prices ranging from 75¢ to $37.50 for a giant 4'' to 5'' shark tooth from South Carolina. Ray's has hundreds of fossils not listed, so if you have a particular need, they will be happy to hear from you. Minimum order $5 ppd.

R-6
THE RED LANTERN SHOP, Dept. CC
236 Shimmonzen Street, Higashiyama-ku
Kyoto, Japan 605

Contemporary Japanese Prints, free, published twice a year, 20 pages, illustrated, black and white and color.

Subjects and styles ranging from landscapes, animals and figures to abstractions and surreal fantasies, done in delicate to bold techniques, are fully illustrated. There are woodblocks, etchings, stencil and embossed prints in limited and unlimited editions. A series of snow scenes by Koichi Sakamoto, etchings measuring from 2¾'' x 5'' to 7'' x 9½'', sell from around $15 to around $76. A *Ballerina—U* lithograph and silkscreen print in an edition of eighty by Kosuke Kimura, 15½'' x 21½'', costs around $133. Prices range from $7.60 to $304.18 and are "subject to the exchange rate on the business transaction without notice." The prints, which are not dutiable, are shipped by air or sea, as requested.

R-7
REFLECTION MARKETING, Dept. CC
3767 Oakdale Avenue
Pasadena, CA 91107

Pub Mirrors!, $1, revised as new styles are added, 6 pages, illustrated, color.

These are updatings of the classic British pub mirrors designed to advertise different brands of spirits and beer. Some have American versions, such as Michelob, Colt 45, Jack Daniel's whiskey and Coca-Cola, others have automobile insignia, zodiac signs, pictures of Chaplin and Monroe (Marilyn), saloon signs, all permanently silk-screened on the back of the glass before the silvering is applied—not painted on the surface or glued on as decals. Reflection Marketing emphasizes that there are considerable savings in ordering directly from them rather than buying the mirrors in retail stores, as through mail order they have eliminated the markups and passed on the savings to the customer. No mirrors sell for over $35 (for the 18'' x 24'' size) and the small, 6'' x 8'' and 6'' x 9'' sizes are only $7. Sizes are glass size only; the mirrors are a few inches larger framed.

R-8
REMINGTON ART MUSEUM, Dept. CC
303 Washington Street
Ogdensburg, NY 13669

Frederic Remington Museum, brochure, free, 4 pages, illustrated, black and white, sepia and color.

This museum specializes in art prints, postcards, books, tiles, wall plaques, plates, etchings and slides depicting the work of the famed artist of the Old West. One item of particular interest, in an authorized edition of 15,000, is a bronze plate sculpted by Roger Brown interpreting Remington's *The Bronco Buster,* cast in Italy by the same foundry that cast the original three-dimensional work. Prices vary from 15¢ to $55, and there is a small charge for postage and handling.

R-9
THE RENAISSANCE GILDE, Dept. CC
Box 5
Cambridge, WI 53523

The Renaissance Gilde, free, 8 pages, published periodically, illustrated, black and white.

The art of the lute-maker is lovingly practiced by Marilyn and William Daum at The Renaissance Gilde. Their elegant newssheet *cum* newsletter shows a montage of photos of their craftsmanship, and a lengthy article by Mr. Daum describes their methods, philosophy, apprentice programs and price structure which starts at $375 for apprentice-made lutes, and at $600 for a Daum-made six-course lute. Prices rise to $3,000 for a thirteen- and fourteen-course baroque lute, and custom work can go even higher.

R-10
REPLICAS OF ANTIQUITY, INC., Dept. CC
760 Summer Street
Stamford, CT 06901

King Tutankhamun by Replicas of Antiquity, free, catalogues published annually with supplements, 12 pages, illustrated, color.

This particular catalogue is stunningly illustrated in full color with photographs of the Tutankhamun mask miniature reproduction in 18k. vermeil (gold on sterling silver) with hand glazed enamel or in solid gold, the former in an edition of 7,500, the latter in an edition of 2,500; a scarab bracelet, also in vermeil or gold; 11'' high statuettes of the

The simplest construction of shelves on brackets is all that is needed for a unique and fascinating collection of authentic pre-Columbian pottery in a room designed by Bernard Gelbort. Photographer: Max Eckert.

"Domino Players" by Horace Pippin, reproduced as a postcard or a large poster from The Phillips Collection, P-12.

Oil portrait of John Gardner, late 1750s, by John Singleton Copley. Hirschl & Adler Galleries, H-18.

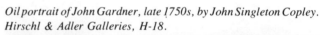

king riding a leopard or as a harpooner, available in bronze in an edition of 1,000, in silver in an edition of 600, and in solid gold in an edition of 150 (all bases are pewter); a solid 14k. gold ring depicting the falcon-headed god Ra-Harakhty; and a blue and gold vulture-goddess necklace with a cabochon sapphire set as the eye (in vermeil or gold). Prices range from $175 to $2,600. The firm also welcomes commissioned replicas "to create your own preferred treasures."

R-11
WALTER REUBEN INC., Dept. CC
410 American Bank Tower
Austin, TX 78701

Rare Maps, $5, published twice yearly, 88 pages, illustrated, black and white.

A fascinating catalogue of around 550 old and rare maps from all over the world, ranging in price from $15 to $1,250, with many between $100 and $200. In a current catalogue, a crisp, hemispheric map of the northernmost regions of the world, showing the routes of early explorers in some detail (Herman Moll, ca. 1720, London) is $100. The first map of the West Indies to appear in any atlas (from the *Theatrum of Abraham Ortelius,* Antwerp, 1519–1595, full original color, with two maps of Mexico and the West Indies on one 14″ x 19½″ sheet) costs $350. A very good source for map collectors. Walter Reuben, who is listed under Antiquarian Booksellers, also puts out a catalogue called *Rare Americana,* priced at $5.

R-12
RIJKSMUSEUM, Dept. CC
Department of Reproductions
Hobbesmastraat 21
Amsterdam,
The Netherlands

Catalogue of reproductions, slides, and books, free, 12 pages.

A compact brochure listing color and black-and-white postcards of Dutch paintings, frescos, Asiatic art, drawings, etchings and engravings, sculpture; Christmas cards; reproductions of paintings on paper, canvas and cardboard; posters; books and exhibition catalogues from this famous museum's collection. If you are not familiar with the collection, there's a complete illustrated catalogue with over 5,000 black-and-white reproductions of all the paintings for 195 guilders. All prices are quoted in Dutch currency, and profits go entirely to the acquisition fund of the Rijksmuseum.

R-13
RILEY COUNTY HISTORICAL MUSEUM,
Dept. CC
2309 Claflin Road
Manhattan, KS 66502

List of publications, free, 2 pages.

The books sold by the Riley County Historical Museum sales shop, many by local authors, present a wide range of Riley County and Kansas history. Also available are prints of pen-and-ink drawings of the churches of Manhattan and vicinity, and various scenes in Manhattan and Riley County, a china collector's plate of Riley County scenes, and a pewter collector's plate of Riley County ($17.76).

R-14
JOHN F. RINALDI, Dept. CC
Box 765
Dock Square
Kennebunkport, ME 04046

Nautical Antiques & Related Items, $2, published spring and late fall, 26 pages, illustrated, black and white.

All manner of top-quality nautical antiques, such as quadrants, sextants, telescopes, compasses, ship's clocks, scrimshaw, carvings, whaling newspapers, figureheads, ship models, sail-making equipment, lanterns, lap desks and marine paintings, plus collectors' reference books on scientific instruments, marine chronometers, English barometers and marine antiques. Each item is completely and clearly described, sometimes with a brief rundown on its history. Prices range from around $6.50 for a whaling newspaper of 1898 or 1900 to around $2,500 for a classic ship's figurehead of a woman, circa 1830, or a sailor's quality bone ship sailing model from the early 1900s. Most prices run in the hundreds. Rinaldi will also buy nautical antiques, from a single piece to an entire collection.

R-15
ROBERTS INDIAN CRAFTS AND SUPPLIES,
Dept. CC
P. O. Box 98
Anadarko, OK 73005

Price list, 15¢ in stamps, published seasonally.

This supplier offers many kinds of beads in a wide range of colors along with shells, feathers, bells, shawl fringe, buckskin thongs, horsehair, real hair bone pipes, needles, thread, etc. You can choose from Indian seed beads, cut beads from Czechoslovakia, rainbow beads, Crow necklace beads, tubular or tile beads, imitation bone tube beads and several others. Prices range from 3¢ to $2.75. There is a small charge for insurance and postage. You can write for information about items not listed on the price sheet.

R-16
ROCKY MOUNTAIN LODESTONE, INC.,
Dept. CC
P. O. Box 1375
Englewood, CO 80150

Rocky Mountain Lodestone, $1, refundable with purchase, published seasonally, 18 pages, illustrated, color.

An interesting catalogue with a Western bent, specializing in handcrafts and limited-edition sculptures and art glass. Among the Lodestone exclusives in the current catalogue are George Northrup's wildlife bronze of two Wyoming red ducks on a log, signed and numbered in an edition of twenty ($400); a stained-glass prairie rose cut from German antique crackle and seedy-clear hand-blown glass in a hand-turned 2'' mahogany frame with copper chain, signed and numbered by the artist, Jacqueline Lloyd Wright ($240); some enchanting bronzes of animals by Carla Boyle; a reproduction of a Mason decoy duck, carved and hand finished in ponderosa pine by Thomas Taber; art deco glass vase, decanter and oil lamp by Hot Glass; and a stunning 16'' square mirrored etching in Art Nouveau style by Mucha, bordered with antique stained glass and banded with brass-clad lead ($175). Lodestone also has unusual wildlife belts and buckles, clothing, amusing wooden toys and beautiful sculptural jewelry in 14k. gold and precious stones.

R-17
RICHARD ROESSLEN, Dept. CC
Taunusstrasse 47
6000 Frankfurt/Main
West Germany

German Collector Items, $2 (refundable with purchase), published seasonally, 4 illustrated color leaflets, 9 illustrated black and white leaflets.

The Roesslen leaflets feature German steins and tankards, collectors' plates, Hummel dolls, figurines and candles and Dresden porcelain figures, with descriptions in English and prices in U.S. currency. There are some very attractive Merian City steins ($12.90 with pewter lid, $6.40 without lid) of such cities as Heidelberg, Vienna and Innsbruck, some in dark brown or light green, others in full color; dolls in German, Bavarian and Black Forest costumes; Berlin Design plates, bells, steins and unusual lead crystal goblets with medallions of Old Masters of music (Beethoven, Mozart, Wagner, Bach, Schubert, Liszt) in a limited edition of 3,000, each goblet numbered

and with certificate; and the Wildlife Collection of bird figures, ranging in price from $9.40 to around $42. There is a minimum order of $50, which includes packing, but not shipping. Delivery takes about a month, you pay on receipt and duty on the items runs around 4 percent.

R-18
ROMBINS' NEST FARM, Dept. CC
117 W. Main Street
Fairfield, PA 17320

Catalogue, 25¢, published annually, 40 pages, illustrated, black and white.

A gift catalogue with many items that would be of interest to collectors. In addition to the usual Hummel dolls, plates, figurines and Christmas-tree balls, you'll find a locally handcrafted limited-edition Pennsylvania Dutch Christmas Plate, hand-carved German figurines, a porcelain cardinal bell from Germany and an unusual ruby-fired crystal hummingbird bell from Corning, New York (6¼'' high, $9.95). Delightful life-size majolica cats from Portugal are $11.95 and $21.95. Under the heading of nostalgia are replicas (made in a local foundry) of old cast-iron wheel toys such as a coal wagon, tractor, fire engine, train set and country doctor, ranging in price from $6.95 to $32.95, and the hand-painted cast-iron banks that are now so hard to find. Among the replica banks, we especially liked the covered bridge and two mechanical banks—a Victorian boy on a trapeze and an organ bank complete with dancing children and monkey (around $36). There is a most amusing lithographed tin bank of a thieving crow who pops out and takes a coin in his beak ($6.50). This jam-packed catalogue also has all kinds of dolls—a Victorian wooden jointed doll, Pennsylvania Dutch costume dolls, bisque baby doll replicas of the old Byelo dolls, Polish folk-art dolls, antique china doll kits, an unusual, witch-faced apple-head doll kit, and dollhouse furniture, some in kit form.

R-19
RONIN GALLERY, Dept. CC
605 Madison Avenue
New York, NY 10022

Two pamphlets, The 32 Aspects and Social Customs of Women, and Landscapes of Kiyochika, each $1, illustrated, black and white and color. Also 2 major catalogues, Images of the Floating World, $5, 38 pages, illustrated, color and black and white; Autumn of Ukiyo-e, $6, 40 pages, illustrated, black and white and color.

The serious collector can select from a large group of superb Japanese woodblock prints dating from the seven-

Top and bottom row, miniature metal soldier kits from The Soldier Shop, S-26.

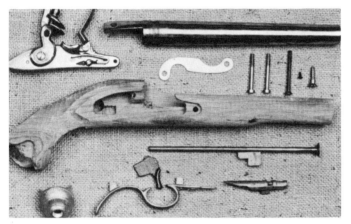

Brass mounted reproduction kit of American Revolutionary War flintlock pistol. Replica Models, CJM Arms, C-20.

At the right, a replica of a nineteenth-century powder can from the Hagley Museum, H-1.

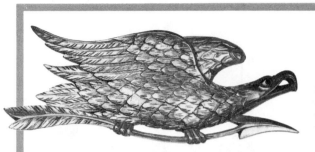

Kittery eagle, hand-carved pine, from Shep's Ship Shop, S-17.

Below, painted-tin note holder, an exact reproduction of the one in Washington Irving's "Sunnyside" kitchen. American Heritage, A-7.

"Spirit of '76" Bicentennial bottle by Wheaton for Holly City Bottle, H-23.

teenth century to the present day. Every subject of Japanese printmaking is covered, from geishas in the Meiji period to scenes by moonlight or in snow to modern studies of women and boats at anchor. All prints are originals and by many of the great names—Utamaro, Hokusai, Hiroshige, etc. One of Yoshotoshi Taiso's *32 Aspects,* a woman overwhelmed by whirls of smoke (1801–1803), costs $625. Prints average from 6" x 12" to 18"x 13", and most are signed and dated.

R-20
ROSE ROCK COMPANY OF OKLAHOMA, INC.,
Dept. CC
Box 6496
3016 N. Eastern Avenue
Moore, OK 73160

Beautiful Rose Rocks of Oklahoma, *folder, 50¢, published seasonally, illustrated, black and white.*

The reddish-brown "rose rocks" of Oklahoma, so called because of their likeness to a rose in bloom, are petal-like clusters of sandy barite crystals known to geologists as sand-barite rosettes. Well-formed specimens, which are usually from ½" to 4" in diameter (although the largest known is 17" across and weighs 125 pounds), are much prized by collectors. The rosettes occur mostly in the Garber Sandstone, deposited during the Permian period about 250 million years ago, and are most abundant along the north–south outcrop of the Garber in central Oklahoma. The percentage of good-quality roses, single or in cluster form, is very small, and once the deposits are exhausted there will be no more, so for a modest price you can have something unique. Single and double roses are 75¢ for small, $1 for medium, $1.25 for large, unmounted clusters from $10 to $100, and clusters mounted on walnut, maple or polished rock base, $20 to $125.

R-21
ROSES COLLECTORS RECORDS, Dept. CC
300 Chelsea Road
Louisville, KY 40207

General Collectors Catalogue, *free, published annually, 24 pages plus supplements, tabloid newspaper format, some illustrations.*

Paul Willenbrink began this family owned and operated business in 1964. The objective of the company is to help people find the records that are not readily available in their local record shops, locate albums that are factory discontinued and research rare old-time records for those willing to wait. There are over 5,000 titles listed in the catalogue, but, as Mr. Willenbrink points out in a letter to us, "the hard-core collector would not be interested in us." Mr. Willenbrink sums up his catalogue as follows:

"We appeal to 98 percent of folks who cannot find what they want in their local record store; particularly two types of records, (a) low-price budget albums the major labels do not promote, (b) nostalgia; hard to find, out of the ordinary country/western such as Carter Family originals, old-time Rodgers, Vernon Dalhart, Sons of the Pioneers, Spade Cooley, etc., the Big Band albums from the 30s and 40s, old-time radio programs. The regular record business is about 85 percent rock and roll and the other 15 percent jazz and pop, and naturally, they promote what the kids buy. In our kind of business it's different." Prices range from $3.98 on up. There is a large selection of classic comedy material, top pop artists, but no hard rock or classical.

R-22
ROYAL ONTARIO MUSEUM, BOOK AND GIFT SHOPS, Dept. CC
100 Queens Park
Toronto, Ontario M5S 2C6
Canada

Gift Guide, *free, 6-page pamphlet, illustrated, black and white.*

The museum offers such things as Tibetan bracelets, Indonesian sarongs, African ivory, Peruvian pottery, Eskimo carvings, dolls, clay birds from England, an Art Nouveau paperweight from New Brunswick, a porcupine quill box from the Ojibway, gold-plated or sterling silver jewelry reproduced from work excavated in the People's Republic of China, and a number of scale models of dinosaurs. You can also order prints after four watercolors by Lady Elizabeth Gwillim (ca. 1800), Christmas cards after watercolors by an anonymous artist, postcards and books. Prices run from 75¢ to $450 with a small charge for postage and handling.

R-23
JOSEPH RUBINFINE, Dept. CC
RFD #1
Pleasantville, NJ 08232

Autographs, *$1, 36 pages, published twice a year, illustrated, black and white.*

Mr. Rubinfine offers a collection of letters and autographs from Abigail Adams to Orville Wright in a handsomely produced catalogue with excellent illustrations and fascinating descriptions. Included in the current catalogue are an 8-page letter from Susan B. Anthony on women's rights ($850), a letter from Jack London describing California as "God's country" ($475), and a collection of thirty-three presidential autographs from Washington to Eisenhower for $3,750. Naturally, all items are subject to prior sale. There is also a want-list service.

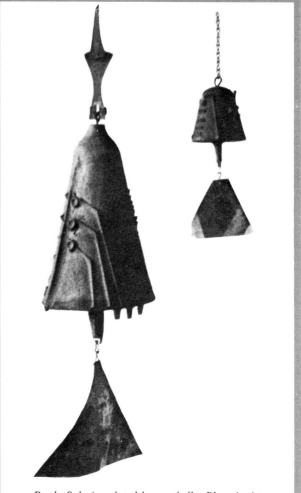

Paolo Soleri sculpted bronze bells. Phoenix Art Museum Shop, P-13.

Handsome decoys, finished or in kit form, from Bay Country Woodcrafts, B-8.

155

S

THE ST. LOUIS ART MUSEUM SHOP, Dept. CC
Forest Park
St. Louis, MO 63110

Mailer and price list, free.

The Museum Shop offers a number of publications such as *Tsutsumu: The Japanese Package* ($5); *The Artist in the Kitchen,* a cookbook with 400 recipes ($8.95); and *Handbook of the Collections* ($12), plus postcards and reproductions of works in the museum's collection. Prices range from 20¢ for cards to $1.75 to $15 for reproductions, with a small charge for postage and handling.

S-2
SALLIE'S SPECIALTIES, Dept. CC
Box 7732
Atlanta, GA 30357

Collectible Playing Cards from Around the World, *50¢, published annually, printed in sepia, illustrated.*

A fascinating collection of playing cards from around the world, many of them reprints of historical decks. Each deck is represented by an actual-size illustration and description. Prices range from $1.50 to $12. In addition, Sallie's Specialties offers 'backs only' in several sets and one-of-a-kind backs that may be ordered from a special list. The company also has two collectible card club plans that offer a new deck of playing cards each month.

S-3
SAN DIEGO MUSEUM OF MAN, Dept. CC
1350 El Prado
Balboa Park
San Diego, CA 92101

List of publications, free.

The publications are paper-bound San Diego Museum papers on such subjects as Peruvian embroidery, Chumash fishing equipment, Diegueno coiled baskets, Yuman pottery making, raine technology along the southern California coast and peyote paraphernalia. Prices, which are subject to change without notice, range from $1.50 to $4.

S-4
JACQUES C. SCHIFF, JR., INC., Dept. CC
195 Main Street
Ridgefield Park, NJ 07660

Especially for Specialists, *catalogues of public stamp auctions, $6 a year, published 8 to 10 times a year.*

The auction catalogues presumably show and describe the stamps offered for auction, for which bids can be made by mail or phone, but all we received were covers.

S-5
SCHMID BROTHERS, INC., Dept. CC
55 Pacella Park Drive
Randolph, MA 02368

Limited Editions, *free folder, published annually, illustrated, color.*

A folder of commemorative collectibles of the year, many of them in limited editions. There is a wide variety of Christmas ornaments, candles, music boxes, bells, plates by Sister Berta Hummel and Juan Ferrandiz Castill and the Anri woodcarvings of Italy. The collection also offers limited editions of sculptured figures by Ferrandiz and Anri; Berlin Design porcelain blue-and-white plates, steins and mugs; and Bavarian beer steins. Prices are very reasonable.

S-6
FRANK S. SCHWARZ, Dept. CC
1806 Chestnut Street
Philadelphia, PA 19103

Philadelphia Collection, *and* **19th Century American Paintings,** *$2 each, published semiannually, around 32 pages, illustrated, black and white and color.*

Schwarz specializes in fine paintings, furniture and silver. The painting catalogue includes *Greek Head* by Elihu Vedder, oil on panel, 12½'' x 9½'', signed and dated 1871, price on request, and *Impressionist Landscape, 1888,* by William Wendt, $750. Among other painters listed are John Joseph Enneking, George Cochrin Lambdin, Thomas Doughty, Herman Herzog and Charles Par-

To accentuate the iridescence of Roman glass, designer Bernard Gelbort fitted an architectural niche with clear acrylic shelves lit from each side. Photographer: Max Eckert.

Left, Currier & Ives jumbo playing cards. Museum of the City of New York, M-32.

Below, wooden games and puzzles. Berea College Student Craft Industries, B-11.

Porcelain ''Egyptian'' dominoes with incised hieroglyphics. Brooklyn Museum Gallery Shop, B-28.

tridge Adams. Prices range from $550 to $2,500. The *Collection* catalogue includes paintings, silver and furniture. Works by Rembrandt Peale, Ernest W. Longfellow (the son of the poet, Henry Wadsworth Longfellow), James Peale and Maxfield Parrish are among the paintings illustrated. Among the other pictured items are a mahogany tall clock by George Crow, Jr. (1720–1802), Alaskan ivories, a pair of New Orleans silver pitchers, and a punch bowl and ladle incorporating Hawaiian 1883 silver dollars made in the late nineteenth century by George C. Shreve of San Francisco. Prices on request.

S-7
F. A. O. SCHWARZ/FRANZ CARL WEBER INTERNATIONAL, Dept. CC
745 Fifth Avenue
New York, NY 10022

Holiday Gift Selections, free, published annually, 60 pages, illustrated, color.

The next best thing to visiting the main store of F. A. O. Schwarz is browsing through their annual holiday catalogue. This is one of the largest and finest collections of toys and hobbies in America. Among the collectibles are nine pages of dolls, doll houses and furnishings from all over the world. The famous, exclusive, 1″ to 1′ scale Schwarz Colonial doll house is $995 furnished, or $750 unfurnished. The fabulous Steiff line of animals is here as are toy soldiers and imported and unusual chess sets. There are motorized miniature cars and boats, a heat- and weather-resistant over-scaled train with steam locomotive ($249.95), period functional model trains from $40, tracks and accessories, corn-husk sculpture figures from $4.95, nesting dolls, plus more mundane toys of our time.

S-8
SCIENTIFIC MODELS, INC., Dept. CC
340 Snyder Avenue
Berkeley Heights, NJ 07922

Model Kits and Miniature Furniture Kits, 25¢, published annually, 8 pages and 4 pages, illustrated, color.

The model kits are for ships and planes. Clipper ships, galleons, schooners, are among the ship models. There's Columbus' flagship, the *Santa Maria;* the *Robert E. Lee* Mississippi steamboat; in the collector's series of wood ship models, the *Cutty Sark,* H.M.S. *Bounty* and U.S.S. *Constitution* (Old Ironsides); among the historic ship models, the *Golden Hind* of Sir Francis Drake, the clipper ship *Sea Witch* and the whaler *Charles W. Morgan.* The airplane kits are of three kinds: the carved body series, made of balsa; the built-up series with pre-formed metal parts; and rubber-powered EZ-Bilt models that fly 500 to

1,000 feet. *Miniature Furniture* consists of various doll house furniture kits, either whole rooms of furniture—such as a country kitchen, old fashioned bathroom with wood-encased fittings, traditional living room and dining room—or the single-piece series of furniture.

S-9
THE SCULPTURE STUDIO, INC., Dept. CC
441 Lafayette Street
New York, NY 10003

William Bowie, The Sculpture Studio, Inc., 50¢, 6 pages, illustrated, color.

William Bowie specializes in metal wall sculptures, such as a decorative *Starburst* in six sizes and a two-tier or three-tier version. In most cases the sculptures are gold-leafed steel with silver-leaf accents and brazed bronze joints. There are stylized studies of birds, flowers, trees and sailboats as well as abstractions. Prices range from $60 to $1,200. Different sizes and finishes can be made to order. Shipments are made collect unless otherwise prearranged, with 4 percent crating charge. On-approval orders are accepted if crating and shipping are paid both ways.

S-10
SELECT BOOKS, Dept. CC
5969 Wilbur Avenue
Tarzana, CA 91356

Publications, free brochure, published periodically, 2 pages.

Paper editions only of craft- and hobby-related books, among them Betty Jacobs' *Growing Herbs and Plants for Dyeing,* which includes information on harvesting and dyeing along with sources of hard-to-find seeds; *Your Hand Weaving* by Elsie Davenport, especially good for beginners who want to use a four-harness loom; and the comprehensive *Your Handspinning* by Elsie Davenport on all aspects of working with a spinning wheel. Prices are $2 to $5, and there is a small charge for postage and handling.

S-11
L. H. SELMAN LTD., Dept. CC
761 Chestnut Street
Santa Cruz, CA 95060

Price Guide and Catalogue of Collector's Paperweights, $3, published annually, 50 pages, illustrated, color.

A stunningly beautiful catalogue of choice antique and contemporary glass paperweights, all shown in color, identified, described and priced. The design, illustration and writing of the catalogue is to be highly commended for style and clarity. For the beginner, the first pages have useful, factual information and advice about collector's paperweights (their background, investment value, where to buy them, how to know if they are genuine) and there's a basic library of books and periodicals and a glossary of terms. The antique paperweights shown were made during the classical period of the 1840s by Baccarat, Clichy and St. Louis, with a few American examples, such as a New England fruit weight on white latticino ground with quatrefoil faceting ($350). Prices range from around $100 for a Baccarat rock weight to $2,600 for a rare mushroom double overlay by Clichy. All are exquisite works of art. In contemporary paperweights, Selman has those of Perthshire, a small Scottish craft concern, priced from $20 to $350, Baccarat (including some sulphide cameo weights), St. Louis, D'Albret sulphide paperweights, the beautiful flower weights of Paul Stankard and Francis Dyer Whittemore, Jr., the Art Nouveau designs of Lundberg Studios in California and the French-style paperweights of Ray and Bob Banford. There are also some paperweight-related objects such as iridescent glass vases from Lundberg Studios and an antique Whitefriars wineglass and inkwell with millefiori motifs. Accessories for collectors include Lucite display stands ($2.50 each), a self-lighted magnifier and a cataloguing kit. Paperweights listed are offered subject to prior sale. Selman will look for a specific type of weight for you, do insurance appraisals and cataloguing, and purchase fine paperweights.

S-12
THE SEWING CORNER, INC., Dept. CC
1313 South Killian Drive
Lake Park, FL 33403

The Sewing Corner, *25¢, published 2 to 3 times a year, 48 pages, illustrated, color.*

If you expect The Sewing Corner to have supplies for seamstresses, you're wrong. The catalogue is devoted almost entirely to a vast collection of collectors' thimbles and spoons, with display cabinets and vitrines for collections. The range of thimbles is staggering. There's a King Tut treasure thimble, a 14k. gold mask on a sterling silver thimble, limited edition of 5,000 ($59); a Royal Silver Jubilee thimble with profile portraits of the Queen and Prince Philip, limited, numbered edition of 250 ($85); Hummel thimbles; Coalport thimbles; jade, soapstone, gemstone and pottery thimbles; French sterling silver thimbles with designs from the fables of La Fontaine; a fluted lead crystal thimble; a ceramic English-cottage thimble; Limoges thimbles; a hand-turned lapachus wood thimble; Bilston and Battersea enamel thimbles, and many, many more, a truly fascinating array. The Sewing

Corner also has books on thimbles and a scrapbook with printed record sheet and pricing portfolio for your collection. In the spoon selections are replicas of century-old apostle spoons; a Welsh love spoon; Czechoslovakian silverplated spoons with cloisonné reproductions of paintings by Old Masters in the bowl (set of six, $37.50); a Stieff reproduction of the 1675 Copeland spoon, the oldest piece of pewter made in America ($11.95 for original 7¾'' size); Oneida presentation spoons for anniversaries and birthdays; a flower-of-the-month set of twelve spoons ($75, or $6.95 each); spoons for each state in the Union; Bicentennial spoons and a silverplated spoon from Holland with a scrimshaw insert ($13.95). With the order form there's an application for membership in the Collector Circle, an international club of thimble collectors, which brings you the *Collector Circle Gazette* four times a year and a Collector Circle thimble. In case you want to use, rather than just look at, your silver or gold thimbles, there's a thimble size comparison chart for thimbles made in the U.S., Germany, England and France.

S-13
SHAFFER'S TROPICAL GARDENS, INC.,
Dept. CC
1220 41st Avenue
Capitola, CA 95010

Lists of plants, free, published annually.

Shaffer's specializes in orchids, and for their fortieth year in business they issued an attractive color catalogue, which they told us would not be repeated. What you will receive is their annual listing of plants—the parents of the various crosses, the first-bloom seedlings with crosses listed below and Cymbidiums. They also have books on orchid culture.

S-14
THE SHAKER MUSEUM, Dept. CC
The Shaker Museum Foundation, Inc.
Shaker Museum Road
Old Chatham, NY 12136

Booklist, broadsides list, notepaper designs, free.

The booklist covers a varied range of topics on Shaker life and includes two titles published by the Foundation. Subjects include architecture, furniture, iron and tinware, spinning wheels, music, garden seeds, herbs, baskets and a how-to book on Shaker furniture. Pamphlets and booklets are also offered. Prices are reasonable. The broadsides range in size from 5'' x 9'' for "Thoughts on Living in a Shaker House," 10¢ plus 50¢ postage, to a 29½'' x 23''Shaker Bicentennial Poster for $1.50, 75¢ postage. The notepaper designs are charming, intricate and yet

Unicorn wire sculpture. Barr Art Studio, B-4.

Tiger collage by Hannibal Lee, L-4.

Lion print, Fogelsong Studios, F-9.

Top, sterling silver thimbles, and etched crystal thimbles, all from The Sewing Corner, S-12.

Apostle spoons, authentic replicas in antique silver plate. The Sewing Corner, S-12.

Antique sterling silver wine labels. The Lion Mark, L-8.

162

simple. They sell for $2 a box, 50¢ postage. However, the blue-and-black flyer does not indicate how many are in a box or if the designs are in color.

S-15
SHAKER WORKSHOPS, INC., Dept. CC
P. O. Box 1028
Concord, MA 01742

Shaker Furniture, 50¢, published periodically, 16 pages, illustrated, black and white.

The Shaker Workshops make authentic reproductions of the finest Shaker pieces in museums and private collections, most of which are sold in kit form. There is a precedent for this—it was the way the Shakers themselves used to ship their furniture from village to village. The kits contain everything needed to assemble and finish pieces—glue, hardware, sandpaper, stains, tapes for chair seats—and step-by-step instructions. Prices are very reasonable, from around $15 for a small stool to around $340 for an 8-foot trestle table, plus shipping and handling costs. Two pieces in the catalogue, a kitchen desk cupboard and a tall clock, are sold assembled and finished, not in kits. The cupboard is around $800, the clock around $700.

S-16
SHELBURNE MUSEUM, Dept. CC
Shelburne, VT 05482

List of publications, free.

The publications mostly relate to the collections at the Shelburne Museum, such as hat boxes and bandboxes, pieced work and appliqué quilts, decoys, tools, horse-drawn vehicles, paintings and drawings. Also available are a pictorial history of the Museum, 128 pages, 32 color and over 325 black-and-white illustrations ($5), catalogues of exhibitions, article reprints and color postcards of the Museum.

S-17
SHEP'S SHIP SHOP, Dept. CC
Jordan Cove
Waterford, CT 06385

Shep's Ship Shop, free, 1 page, illustrated, black and white.

Shep is Willard Shepherd, master woodworker, who carves such pieces of old-time Americana as figureheads, name boards, eagles, all in pine and brass, or gold-leafed (only gold leaf, he warns, is weatherproof). He will also execute carved designs to order. Prices range from about $21 for a brass-leafed sperm whale, 8'' long, to $1,380

for a gold-leafed Chesapeake eagle with 6-foot wing span. Among our favorites are the Saucy Sally rudderhead and the horn-blowing Goody Two Shoes (28'' long, $63).

S-18
SHIP 'N OUT, INC., Dept. CC
Harmony Road
Pawling, NY 12564

Ship 'N Out, free, published annually, 8 pages, illustrated, color.

A treasure-trove of objects reproduced from nautical originals—ships' wheels of old teak or solid acacia with solid brass hubs, ships' lanterns, portholes, brass candlesticks and bells. More land-based offerings include brass hatracks, a bentwood clothes stand, solid brass door knockers and bar foot rail, and baggage racks, including one after the New South Wales Railroad and Ferry original. Prices on request.

S-19
SHOPPING INTERNATIONAL, Dept. CC
Norwich, VT 05055

Shopping International, 25¢, published seasonally (spring and fall), 48 pages, illustrated, color.

Handcrafts, gifts, clothes and jewelry from all over the world fill the pages of this handsome catalogue. There are delightful handcarved colored gourds and ceramics from Cuzco, an Ecuadorian *Cruz de Vida* handwoven wall hanging, 16'' x 43'', $36, a Mexican abalone jewel box and a charming carved ayacahuite-wood pueblo from Tepotzlan, Chinese woven bamboo baskets and Taiwan cinnabar lacquerware, a brass-accented pewter duck box from Hong Kong, 5'' long, $21, and, from Greece, a graceful prancing elefsis horse crafted in brass, $24.50. A special artists' collection includes a Lippizaner horse, crafted by Franco Dragoni, in alabaster (large size, 12¾'' high, $132; small, 8'' high, $62), an owl etched on solid lead crystal from Sweden, and an amusing toucan basket from China in lacquered bamboo and wood, $125.

S-20
JOHN SINCLAIR LTD., Dept. CC
266 Glossop Road
Sheffield S10 2HS
England

Leaflets, free.

Mr. Sinclair specializes in annual decorative and commemorative plates, mugs and bells by such companies as Wedgwood, Spode, Coalport, Royal Copenhagen, Bing & Grondahl. Shown in the leaflets we received are the first four plates in Wedgwood's Castles & Country Houses

Paper model of the Hohenzollern Palace. John Hathaway, H-11.

Chinese animal ornaments, reproduced from the originals. Freer Gallery of Art, F-14.

series ($22 ppd.) in a limited edition of 5,000, the Wedgwood Charles Dickens Characters plate in Queen's Ware ($15.50), a Coalport first edition Father's Day mug ($17) and a special item, the elegant Wedgwood Cutlers vase in three-color jasper (pale blue, portland blue and white), in a limited edition of 200 priced at $350.

S-21
SLEEPY HOLLOW RESTORATIONS, INC.,
Dept. CC
150 White Plains Road
Tarrytown, NY 10591

Books from Sleepy Hollow Restorations, *free, published twice a year, 16 pages.*

Sleepy Hollow Restorations, Inc. is a non-profit institution which owns and maintains Sunnyside, Washington Irving's home in Tarrytown; Philipsburg Manor, Upper Mills, in North Tarrytown; and Van Cortlandt Manor in Croton-on-Hudson, New York. The titles in this catalogue include a facsimile of the 1875 first edition of Washington Irving's *Old Christmas,* $10; three volumes of *The Van Cortlandt Family Papers,* $12 for Vol. I and $19 each for Vols. II and III. There are commentaries, books on the specific homes, general accounts of life in the Hudson Valley, facsimile documents, maps and twelve full-color prints of the most famous characters and scenes from Washington Irving's *Rip Van Winkle* and *The Legend of Sleepy Hollow* by nineteenth-century artist Felix O. C. Darley, 10⅝" x 8⅜", $4.50.

S-22
G. SMITH & SONS, Dept. CC
74 Charing Cross Road
London WC2H 0BG
England

The Snuff Center, *free, folder with price lists.*

This century-old firm offers thirty-seven snuffboxes and snuff-takers' accessories, forty-eight kinds of snuff and twenty-four tobaccos. A Cornish pewter snuffbox with embossed hunting scene on the lid costs around $35, a rosewood box with plain lid is $10, while a sterling silver snuff spoon is $5. A set of copper etchings of five snuff-taking ladies reproduced from a print in the Smith collection is around $11. Prices are given in pounds sterling; postage and insurance are extra. In case you want to know how to take snuff, there's an amusing reprint in the folder on *How to Partake of a Pinch of Snuff* credited to A. Steinmetz, Tobacco, London, 1857. Just the list, names and descriptions of the various snuffs make fascinating reading.

S-23
JOHNSON SMITH CO., Dept. CC
35075 Automation Drive
Mt. Clemens, MI 48043

Catalogue of Surprises, Novelties, Funmakers,
25¢, published 3 times a year, 80 pages, illus-
trated, black and white and color.

Among the novelties of special interest to collectors are all
kinds of belt buckles, from trucker and motorcycle buckles to military and coin buckles (average price, $2.95),
and cloth patches (79¢ each or five for $3.49). Replica
model roadster and tractor, steam-driven, are $84.95 and
$59.95 respectively. Various other model vehicles, some
radio controlled, range from $2.19 to $59.95. Shipping
and handling charges depend on amount of purchase.

S-24
THE SMITHSONIAN INSTITUTION, Dept. CC
P. O. Box 1641
Washington, DC 20013

The Smithsonian Associates' Catalogue, *free,*
published twice a year, 32 pages, illustrated, color.

A jewel of a catalogue, beautifully produced, with a
stunning selection of things that could conceivably cover
everyone on your gift list, collectors and non-collectors.
For the collector, there are sculptures, glass, silver and
pewter reproductions from the Smithsonian Collection, a
limited edition millefiori paperweight ($175) and some
delightful boxes in different materials and shapes—one is
a butterfly in many-hued woven straw from the People's
Republic of China ($25). In addition you'll find every-
thing from the customary Christmas and note cards,
calendar and engagement book to the totally unexpected.
A vibrant red and green enamel bowl ($35), modern
jewelry and a 36"-square silk scarf in the same red and
green (or black and white) were designed by artist Richard
Anuszkiewicz. Tree trimmers will discover a crocheted
snowflake ($5), silver bell and herald angel and an irides-
cent glass butterfly ($45), and for those who also serve in
the kitchen, there are cookie cutters, ceramic cookie
stamps or wooden springerle molds, with recipes. Among
the gifts a child would love are puzzles, a doll house kit
and doll house furniture, and soft-sculpture toy kits you
sew yourself—the dinosaur family is an enchantment.
There are also needlepoint kits, desk accessories, books,
jazz records from the Smithsonian's American Music
series, a man-sized umbrella with the Smithsonian logo,
the Hirschhorn tote bag with great names of modern art
printed on heavy canvas ($15) and a couple of exquisite
necklaces, one of Chinese cloisonné beads, the other
blue-and-white porcelain Peking beads ($65). A lasting

A 1920s Royal Dux lamp, Hollywood style, and a
1930 Donald Deskey lamp in polished nickel
chromium, both from 21st Century Antiques, T-14.

gift would be a Smithsonian membership, which for a mere $12 a year brings the monthly *Smithsonian* magazine and other benefits. Members get a discount on gifts ordered; postage is extra.

S-25
JANE SNEAD SAMPLERS, Dept. CC
Box 4909
Philadelphia, PA 19144

Jane Snead Samplers, 25¢, published annually. 48 pages, illustrated, black and white.

"Keepsake needlework" is the way Jane Snead describes her delightful, old-fashioned sampler kits, many with Pennsylvania Dutch motifs and mottos. A quaint family-tree sampler with spaces for twelve names, 17″ x 22″ finished size ($8); a wedding sampler; a map sampler depicting symbols of American history such as a covered wagon, steamboat, locomotive and Indian in war bonnet, finished size 16″x 20″ ($6.50) and antique automobile samplers are among the many shown in the catalogue. An eight-page center section shows a selection of decorative needlepoint kits of flowers, birds, animals, outdoor scenes, all reasonably priced from $2.50 up. This company will also custom make any size frame up to 17″ x 22″ in a choice of finishes.

S-26
THE SOLDIER SHOP, INC., Dept. CC
1013 Madison Avenue
New York, NY 10021

The Soldier Shop Catalog, $3, published annually, 162 pages, illustrated, black and white.

In the past fifteen years The Soldier Shop catalogue has grown from its original sixteen-page brochure to this handsomely produced, enormous compendium of militaria. The company offers original helmets going back to 1812, stirrups of the Mexican War and general period militaria, many of them one-of-a-kind. There are medals, belts and buttons, both original and replicas; hand-molded plates, mugs and porringers; decorative figures and hangings; paperweight reproductions of eighteenth-century militaria and much more. Thousands of books on every phase of the military form a large part of this catalogue, along with records of military music from around the world. There's a fine selection of military uniform prints by A. Rigodaud, official artist for the French Army, at $2.95 each; hand-colored military plates by Eugène Lelipevre at $3.95 each, plus other handsome prints of period military uniforms from around the world. The hobbyist and collector of figures and figurines will find ninety-eight pages devoted to toy soldiers and modeling kits including Imrie/Risley miniatures. Prices go as high as $2,000.

S-27
SOTHEBY PARKE BERNET, INC., Dept. CC
980 Madison Avenue
New York, NY 10021

Auction catalogues, illustrated, black and white and color, by subscription. Information on request.

This world-famous auction house sells over 50,000 different objects over the course of a single season (September through June), and the list of categories covers everything from wine to houses. More than a hundred catalogues are published each year and can be subscribed to either by category (i.e., "all prints and photographs," $50 per year) or in their entirety for $450 a year, including post-sale price results.

S-28
SOUTH STREET SEAPORT MUSEUM, Dept. CC
16 Fulton Street
New York, NY 10038

List of museum publications, free.

The publications of this waterfront museum all relate, naturally, to the sea and to the historic South Street area of New York. Most are paperback; three are hardcover. Some of the books listed are *Counting House Days in South Street,* by Ellen F. Rosebrock, about the historic buildings of South Street in the nineteenth century ($2.50); *South Street around 1900,* a pictorial history photographed by Thomas W. Kennedy ($1.50); *The Wavertree, an Ocean Wanderer,* an account of the voyage of the *Wavertree* around the Horn in 1907–08, from a narrative of Captain George Spiers (hardcover, $4.50), and the *South Street Seaport Museum Cookbook,* recipes from the volunteers and staff of the Museum ($1.50). There's a postage and handling fee for each book, and shipments are insured.

S-29
SPERTUS MUSEUM OF JUDAICA, MUSEUM STORE, Dept. CC
618 S. Michigan Avenue
Chicago, IL 60605

No catalogue as most of the pieces in the museum shop's extensive collection of paintings, graphics and fine silver by Israeli artists are one of a kind, imported from Israel. There's also a small selection of Judaic and Israeli antiques. Write for information about specific items you might be interested in. Among the Israeli artists whose works have been shown and sold at the Museum are Michail Burdzelan and Michail Grobman, both immigrants from the USSR.

Above, custard glass hand-painted and signed by the artist. Fenton Art Glass Company, F-3. Right, Art Nouveau reproductions in silver, copper and hand-blown glass from Collectors' Guild, C-26.

Coca-Cola memorabilia mirror from Reflection Marketing, R-7.

S-30
STACK'S, Dept. CC
123 West 57th Street
New York, NY 10019

Rare Coins, public auction sale catalogues and price lists, illustrated, black and white. Approximately 10 auction catalogues, plus 3 price lists each year, $10 annually. Sample copies, $1 each, limited by monthly availability.

Stack's, America's largest public coin auctioneer, acts as a multiservice numismatic organization, also buying and selling directly. Their fixed price list of *United States Gold, Silver & Copper Coins* is handsomely printed, with clear photographs and concise descriptions. Prices are competitive, but can go into the thousands of dollars. If you do not find the coins you seek in their catalogues or auctions, Stack's also has a want-list service.

S-31
THE STAR-SPANGLED BANNER FLAG HOUSE,
Dept. CC
844 East Pratt Street
Baltimore, MD 21202

No catalogue, but flag collectors will be interested in buying a flag from the Star-Spangled Flag House, a National Historic Shrine because it was the 1793 house of Mary Pickersgill, maker of the flag that flew over Fort McHenry, the inspiration for the Francis Scott Key poem that became our national anthem. A fifty-star flag with a certificate stating that it was flown from the pole in the Flag House garden costs $15; a fifteen-star, fifteen-stripe 3' x 5' copy in heavy cotton bunting of Mary Pickersgill's flag, certified to have been flown from the pole on the Flag House, is $20.

S-32
FRANK STEFANO, JR., Dept. CC
39 Remsen Street
Brooklyn, NY 11201

Wedgwood Old Blue Historical Plates, $2.50 plus 25¢ postage, illustrated, black and white.

Between the 1880s and 1950s, Josiah Wedgwood & Sons Ltd. produced a series of plates featuring over 1,000 views of the United States for the Jones, McDuffee & Stratton Co. of Boston. In his comprehensive checklist, Mr. Stefano gives a history of the plates, calendar tiles and pictorial souvenirs and commemoratives. There are three checklists of the historical views: geographic, educational institutions and calendar titles. This is a valuable addition to any Wedgwood collector's library. Ceramic

collectors will be interested to note that Mr. Stefano has two more checklists in preparation: *Pictorial Souvenirs & Commemoratives of North America* and *Rowland & Marsellus, Ceramic Souvenirs.* Write to him for more information.

S-33
STEUBEN GLASS, Dept. CC
Fifth Avenue at 56th Street
New York, NY 10022

The Art of Steuben, $3, 82 pages, illustrated, black and white.

The current edition (Vol. III) of this handsome catalogue, which is published every three years, shows thirty examples of Steuben's famous work in crystal. There are sculptures, bowls, cups, plates and vases. Editions vary in size, and some pieces are unique. For instance, an extraordinary elliptical bowl by Zevi Blum with copper wheel engraving by Roland Erlacher, called *The Hull,* has an arcade with seventy figures of soldiers, cavaliers and a king surrounded by nobles. The figures appear in cameo, in high relief, the glass having been cut away. This is priced at $65,000. A dramatic *Flying Eagle* designed by Paul Schulze, with cut and polished head, engraved eyes and hollow body opening like wing points, 10¼'' x 12½'' x 14½'', is $2,300. *Night Owl* by James Houston, engraved by Roger Selander, a polished crystal disk of an owl sitting on bare branches in starlight with a crescent moon of unpolished crystal, an edition of thirty, is $6,100. An unusual piece is *The Wave,* designed by Eric Hilton, a crystal breaker enclosed in a mirrored box which makes the wave seem like a sea (a light box is concealed beneath the wave and the outer mirrored box has no visible interior when the light is on). This measures 15½'' x 10¼'' x 10¼'' and costs $11,500. Prices range from about $1,000 up.

S-34
THE STEVEN STRAW COMPANY, INC., Dept. CC
30 Green Street
Newburyport, MA 01950

American Selections, $3, published seasonally, 28 pages, illustrated, color.

The Straw Company's beautiful catalogue includes paintings and sculpture by many of the stars of the American art firmament, among them Eastman Johnson, George Inness, William M. Chase, Childe Hassam, Mary Cassatt, Charles Sheeler and Alexander Calder. The last is represented by *The Pregnant Whale,* a 9½' high work in painted steel plate, which was exhibited in the famous "New York Painting and Sculpture: 1940–1970" show at the Metropolitan Museum of Art. The Sheeler is a strong

Above, early American Indian rock art painting serigraph; Gallery of Prehistoric Paintings, G-2. Below left, a cottonwood kachina doll handmade by a Hopi artisan from Colorado River Indian Tribes Museum, C-29. Below right, handwoven baskets from the catalogue on American Indians of the Flint Institute of Arts, F-6.

Above left, woolen wall hanging, "Icicles," by Finnish designer Leena-Kaisa Halme; Stockmann, S-38. Above right, Yalameh wool carpet from Iran; Charles W. Jacobsen, J-1. Below, reproduction hooked rugs from houses at Greenfield Village and the galleries of the Henry Ford Museum; Edison Institute, E-4.

simplification of barns and landscape measuring 12″ x 16″ in tempura on board. Other paintings include a sprightly watercolor of Venice by Maurice Prendergast; *Little Girl with White Ruffled Yoke Dress,* a fine Manctlike Mary Cassatt; an atmospheric *Montclair Meadows* by Inness; and a wonderful panel by L. T. Luther, showing a serpent attacking a man on a horse. Prices on request.

S-35
FRED A. STEWART, INC., ORCHIDS, Dept. CC
1212 E. Las Tunas Drive
San Gabriel, CA 91778

Better Living with Living Beauty, $1, refundable with purchase, published every 2 years, 36 pages, illustrated, color.

Stewart is an orchid breeder and seller of orchid plants either directly at the nursery in San Gabriel or by mail. The catalogue shows a fabulous assortment of Cattleyas, Phalaenopsis and Paphios (including a marvelous Makuli hybrid in rare apple green with light brown dotting on the petals), some very unusual and beautiful hybrids and species, such as the *Angraecum Comorense* from the Comoro Islands in the Indian Ocean, and even the Vanilla planifolia, which forms vanilla beans, a vining plant you can train along a greenhouse wall ($20). Prices range from $7 to $125. Stewart also has these special lists: Cymbidium Treasure list, Cattleya Criterion list, Paphiopedilum stud list, and supplies for orchidists. Plants may be charged to Master Charge or Visa.

S-36
STEWART-MACDONALD MANUFACTURING,
Dept. CC
Box 900
Athens, OH 45701

Banjoist Supplies Catalogue, free, published twice a year, 22 pages, illustrated, black and white.

The catalogue starts with banjo kits, right-handed or left-handed for open-back model ($109.75) or resonator model ($149.50) and then goes into the other supplies available, such as necks, tuning pegs and machines, tone rings, tension hoops, rims, resonators, tailpieces, hardware and fittings, bridges and capos, heads, power tools and saws plus instruction books and courses on records—everything the banjo enthusiast could want. Also offered are engraved banjo components such as the five-star Kershner tailpiece, originally patented in 1916 and used on many high-style banjos of the 1920s ($40.75).

S-37
THE STITCHERY, Dept. CC
Wellesley, MA 02181

The Stitchery, 25 ¢ a year, published 6 times a year, 64 pages, illustrated, color.

All kinds of crafts are featured in this catalogue, from jiffy weaving kits complete with yarns, weaving needle, metal weaving frame and well-diagrammed instructions to the more familiar bargello, crochet, needlepoint, various types of embroidery, latch hook and rya. There's an enchanting Americana sampler quilt (kit includes white cotton percale panels stamped to cross-stitch and quilt, quilt backs and embroidery thread) that ranges in price from $12.95 for a single quilt top, 97″ x 66″, to $17.95 for the king size, 97″ x 97″; other offerings include a needlepoint Aubusson design for a footstool or pillow, and some beautiful oriental and Egyptian needlepoint designs, the latter taken from the Tutankhamun exhibition.

S-38
STOCKMANN, Dept. CC
Export Service Dept.
P. O. Box 220
SF-00101 Helsinki, 10, Finland

Brochures and folders, $3, sent airmail.

Stockmann is Finland's oldest department store, founded in 1862. Although they do not have a catalogue *per se,* they will send an assortment of four-color brochures and folders of products and crafts for $3. Specify interests, if possible. Among the collectibles are jewelry in bronze, silver or gold based on ancient Finnish designs (the *Kalevala-koru* folder); handcrafted Finnish costumes, hats, mitts, potholders, tea cozys, pillows (*Lapin Paja* folder); mobiles, candlesticks, lamps and lamp shades (*Hobby* catalogues); wooden toys (*Jukka* folder). There are wall hangings in kit form from $300—$900 complete—hand mirrors in pine at $10, ceramic candle holders, ceramic items based on old rustic designs, wall plates, dolls in national costumes at $11 each, in Lapp costumes at $20, Lapp slippers, mittens and art reproductions. Many of the works offered are ultracontemporary and quite handsome, and much of the art and craft work is by commissioned artists. For export, the 14 percent purchase tax is dropped from the price. The store accepts major credit cards and will ship, on receipt of payment, by surface mail or sea freight. Stockmann asks that the customer check on customs formalities before placing an order.

S-39
STONEHAND, Dept. CC
245 Centre Street
New York, NY 10013

Brochure and price list, free.

New York's Graphic Boutique, as the owners of Stonehand describe their store, has an unusual and intriguing collection of printing memorabilia. (The name of the store comes from the man who locked up the type on level stone in print shops of yesteryear—the stonehand.) Stonehand recently acquired the contents of a one-hundred-year-old poster printing plant that produced placards and huge billboards for circuses, fairs and political campaigns, and they are selling the hardwood type used by the plant in a variety of faces and sizes ranging from 3″ to 4′ in size. These make great wall decorations because they are all handmade. Prices for Gothic medium-width wood type range from 50¢ for type under 1″ to $20 for 20″; anything over that is $1 for each inch in height. Wood type can be used to make collages. A box of assorted type to make a 12″ x 18″ collage is $35. Stonehand also has hand engraved music sheets; equipment used in old print shops like typesticks, litho stones and hand presses; old cuts in wood, zinc and copper; printer's type drawers; and lots of other goodies. They do not have a complete price list for these, but you can write enquiring about any of the items they carry.

S-40
STRAND BOOK STORE, INC., Dept. CC
828 Broadway
New York, NY 10003

Strand Book Specials, *free, published periodically, around 30 to 40 pages.*

Strand, the largest used-book store in the United States, has nearly two million titles in stock. These are principally out-of-print books, including those of a rare, fine and scholarly nature, although they can also supply a limited quantity of brand-new books at half the published price. Throughout the year Strand publishes catalogues of general and specific interest which are mailed to their list of several million subscribers. You can request to be put

Three charming music boxes from Downs', D-15.

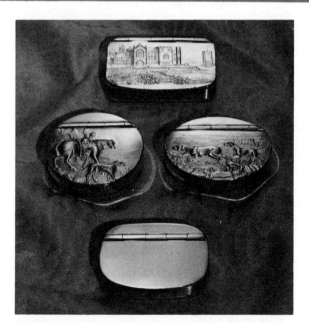

Cornish pewter snuff boxes from G. Smith & Sons, S-22.

on the mailing list. The three catalogues we received covered a wide range of subject matter, listed alphabetically by author. Prices are very reasonable, starting at $1.50.

S-41
STURBRIDGE YANKEE WORKSHOP, Dept. CC
Brimfield Turnpike
Sturbridge, MA 01566

Sturbridge Yankee Workshop, 50¢, published quarterly, 48 pages, illustrated, color and black and white.

The catalogue is subtitled "over 1,000 unique necessaries and gifts for you and your home," which just about sums it up. There's a great variety of furniture, accessories and decorative objects, mostly reproductions or adaptations of early American pieces, peppered with the usual gift items. Among the more interesting are reproductions of old clocks, such as a Seth Thomas Brookfield banjo clock ($229.50), South Jersey glass, antique pewter pieces, a nice selection of bells in colored or clear glass and a collection of hand-painted porcelain soldiers of the Revolution ($27.95 each).

S-42
SUDBERRY HOUSE, Dept. CC
Box 421
Colton Road
Old Lyme, CT 06371

Sudberry House Catalog of Quality Needlework Accessories, $2, published biennially, 24 pages, illustrated, color.

Primarily, Sudberry sells small pieces of furniture and accessories, such as trays, tray tables, game boards, mirrors, picture frames, footstools, boxes, coasters and desk accessories for which you can either buy the needlework designs shown in the catalogue, or others from a list of suppliers who design needlework to fit the Sudberry Products (the list is included with the catalogue). Some of the needlework boxes are especially attractive, such as a round wood box, finished in black or white, with a 5''-round design area ($14.50). There's also a very handy yarn organizer, the Sudberry Yarn Palette, which has holes for twenty-three color categories and a magnet for the needle ($4.95).

S-43
SUNDIALS & MORE, Dept. CC
New Ipswich, NH 03071

Sundials & More, free, published seasonally, 64 pages, illustrated, color.

A charming and varied little gift catalogue, with quite a few things that would be of interest to collectors. First, of course, there's the fascinating and well-chosen selection of about thirty sundials, in various materials—bronze, cast-iron, lemon wood, brass, pewter-finished aluminum, pewter, wrought iron and a stone-like material—with bronze predominating. Many are imports or reproductions of antique sundials from different countries, and there are both outdoor and windowsill models. A reproduction Cannon Sundial, designed so that the sun's rays on the cannon's touch hole at high noon set off a black-powder charge, solid bronze on a simulated ivory base, 5'' high with 7'' cannon, is around $100 ppd. There's a lovely reproduction of a seventeenth-century armillary sundial with wrought-iron bands and copper time band with Arabic numerals and brass arrow shaft, in verdigris green, $85; the Neptune, an equatorial sundial from Sweden that is also a rain gauge, with copper bowl and verdigris base featuring the signs of the zodiac, $45. A Spanish sundial with a base embellished with dragons and floral and vine ornamentation, made of a stone material treated to look as if it came from a centuries-old monastery, would be a handsome addition to any garden, 25'' x 12'' x 12'', $175 ppd. Then there's a faithful reproduction of the sundial made for Governor Endicott of Massachusetts in 1630, the oldest in the United States, in cold cast brass, with a 5½''-diameter dial on a simulated antique ivory base, $55. There are also some good reference books on sundials and a sundial watch. Other interesting pieces are reproductions of Georgian enamel boxes by Crummles of England, 1¾'' x 1'' tall, $30 to $35; three beautiful weather vanes of hammered copper depicting an eagle and arrow, rooster and arrow, and horse; crystal-clear Swedish glass Christmas tree ornaments; and a reproduction of a 125-year-old scrimshaw whale's tooth in the Peabody Museum, Salem, 6½'' high, $65. There is some exceptionally attractive hand-painted stained glass, circles or ovals, with antiqued chain for hanging, of unicorns, a medieval cat, butterflies, a sun-face, a Looking Glass menagerie of Alice and friends (10½'' diameter, around $40) and stained glass squares of the flowers of the four seasons (holly and mistletoe for winter, honeysuckle for spring, the rose for summer and sunflower for fall), a Sundials exclusive, 6'' x 6'', $16 each ppd.

T-1
THE TATTERED BOOT, Dept. CC
Tanglewood Lane
Lamont, FL 32336

Bits and Pieces, 50¢, refundable with purchase, published seasonally, 20 pages, illustrated, black and white.

Reasonably priced lithographs, plain, matted and framed of animals, sea shells, birds, butterflies, mushrooms, seashore and country scenes by artists Lee Evans, Lee Walters, Burk Sauls, Dean Gioia, Ed Jonas and James Johnson. There are also some charming old-fashioned prints from an eighteenth-century herbal, 6'' x 8'', $2.50 each or $14 the set of six, plus $2.50 for green, gray or white mat, $10 for mat and aluminum frame. The majority of the lithographs are $7.50, unmatted and unframed; all are from originals exclusive to The Tattered Boot, and many of the original drawings are also for sale. Postage and handling are extra, and you have fourteen days to return an order, insured, for exchange or refund if you are not completely satisfied.

T-2
TEAM ANTIQUES, Dept. CC
Box 52
Great Neck, NY 11023

Team's Tiffany Treasures, $5 a year, published monthly, 8 pages, illustrated, black and white.

Team Antiques is a rare source for the beautiful, decorative *objets d'art* produced by Louis Comfort Tiffany and his Studio. These are the genuine article, not reproductions, and all pieces are described in detail, authenticated, signed and in mint condition. Pictured in the catalogue are lamps, celebrated for their unique design and color, the famous iridescent and opalescent Favrile glass, and the bronzes, in dark patina or gold doré finish, combined with shells, precious stones or enamel. Prices range from $95 for a pair of 3'' bronze ashtrays—one in gold doré, one in dark patina, with scallop edge—to $9,000 for a cherry-red geranium table lamp, 23'' high with 17''-diameter leaded shade. Smaller Favrile items are under $200. Team also has Tiffany reference books and purchases Tiffany collections.

T-3
THOU ART GALLERY, Dept. CC
P. O. Box 9092
San Diego, CA 92109

Brochure, free, published annually, illustrated, black and white.

This gallery offers originals and prints, and note cards. A pen-and-ink original of *Pan* by Fred Benz is $2,000; the print version (16'' x 20''), $27.95. The sepia original of *Bear Trapper* by Patricia Dobson is $2,500; the print, $27.95.

T-4
TOLEDO MUSEUM OF ART MUSEUM SHOP,
Dept. CC
P. O. Box 1013
Toledo, OH 45697

No catalogue, but you can write for a list of color slides of sculpture, glass and paintings from the Museum's collection, ranging from Egyptian, Greek and Roman sculptures through paintings of every century from the Middle Ages to the present (85¢ a slide) and full-color prints and reproductions of paintings such as Turner's *Venice, Camo Santo*, 21½'' x 23½'' ($6), and Braque's *Still Life with Fish*, 8¼'' x 10'' (50¢). Prices range from 50¢ for the small size to $12 for most of the large sizes. Postcards are also available, at 20¢ each.

T-5
THE TOY FACTORY, Dept. CC
88878 Coast Highway 101
Florence, OR 97439

The Toy Factory Toy Catalogue, 50¢, published annually, 30 pages, illustrated, black and white.

A family business with all kinds of delightful playthings for sale, many handcrafted. There are finger puppets and marionettes; rag dolls and wooden dolls from Poland; wooden puzzles and pull toys; trains, boats and trucks made of wood; musical instruments; doll houses and furniture; folk toys like tops and ball-and-cup; and kites. A circus train has five colorful wooden cars—including an animal cage with a door that lifts up and a calliope car with

Top left, Art Nouveau drop front ladies' desk from Classic Crafts, C-21. Top right, Victorian gentleman's chair in solid mahogany; Martha M. House, H-27. Below, Queen Anne lowboy reproduced from the original in Decorative Arts Gallery of the Henry Ford Museum; The Bartley Collection, B-5.

Top, original drawings from Little Nemo, L-11: at left, a Barry Smith superhero; at right, a 1931 pen-and-ink illustration by John Held, Jr. Below left, La Scala's "Turandot" poster, from the original stone matrix; Fiesta Arts, F-4. Right, Émile Bertrand's original color lithographic poster, 1899, "Cendrillon" (Cinderella); Colbert Gallery, C-24.

a music box. A little armored car made of alder wood doubles as a bank. You can also buy books (including books for parents) and do-it-yourself kits. A Sopwith Camel airplane with a 4-foot wingspan comes in a kit, ready to assemble. A zither comes with music that fits under the strings and shows pictorially which string to pluck. Prices range from $1 to $59 ppd.

T-6
TRAILSIDE GALLERY, Dept. CC
Drawer 1149
Jackson, WY 83001

Trailside Galleries, $5, (refundable with purchase), published annually, 80 pages, illustrated, black and white and color.

As its name implies, the Trailside Gallery is devoted to paintings, sculpture and graphics having to do with the world of cowboys, Indians, pioneers, trappers, cavalry and the West. *Ghost Riders in the Sky* is a vigorous bronze sculpture, 22″ high by 43″ wide, showing two cowboys herding cattle. Another bronze, *Narrow Escape* by Clark Bronson, a hawk attacking two birds, is 37″ high and one of an edition of forty-two. Joe Beeler's sensitive portrait of an Indian, *Nez Percé,* is a pastel, 14″ x 20″. *Taos Valley* is a powerful oil of trees, mountains and horses in winter. There are also works devoted to range life, hunting, historical incidents, birds and portraits. A dramatic sculpture of a cowboy and his horse by Harry Jackson, *Two Champs,* is available in a painted edition of twenty or patined in an edition of forty. Prices on request.

T-7
TREASURE-HOUSE OF WORLDLY WARES,
Dept. CC
1414 Lincoln Avenue
Calistoga, CA 94515

Lists, free (send stamped self-addressed envelope), published periodically, illustrated with black-and-white pencil sketches.

Owner Stevie S. Whitefeather has gathered a very special collection of folk art from all over the world—baskets, pottery, prehistoric items (pottery, stone, shells, tools, mortars), rugs and wall hangings and various artifacts. The two lists we received had a very good range of American Indian baskets and pottery, and though these are one-of-a-kind and the lists change as pieces are sold and new ones added, the following descriptions will give an idea of their quality. A hard-to-find Klamath basket of porcupine quills, redbud, grape and pine roots, 9″diameter, 5½″ high, dating from the early 1900s, was priced at $185. A very rare Miwok shallow tray, basketry in fine condition, 12″ diameter, was $450; a Tlinget basket, 3″ high, 3½″ top diameter, turn-of-the-century, excellent condition, alternating brown and orange triangle design, was $85. An Acoma pot, about 1910, 9″ x 12″, was $185. Listed under Prehistoric Items was a Chiapicuro (Guanajuato) 300 B.C.–300 A.D. pot in perfect condition, 3½″ x 8″, $350.

T-8
TRIEN'S COLLECTORS SHOWCASE, Dept. CC
201 West First Street
Dixon, IL 61021

Original Limited Edition Collector, $1.25 (refundable with purchase), published 6 times a year, 16 pages, illustrated, color.

Trien's specializes in plates decorated with reproductions of works by noted artists and illustrators. They also offer such things as ceramic figurines, pewter thimbles, decorative Easter eggs, trays and even coins. There are Raggedy Ann plates, Hummel plates, Norman Rockwell plates, plates of Leyendecker's charming *Corn Flake Boy* and *Corn Flake Girl,* Snoopy Christmas mugs and ceramic tree ornaments, Rockwell figurines and plates commemorating Valentine's Day or Christmas. Coins include a commemorative Churchill crown and a roll of fifty large English pennies, no longer issued. Prices range from $4.50 to $100.50.

T-9
TRIFLES, Dept. CC
P. O. Box 44432
Dallas, TX 75234

Trifles, free, published seasonally, 34 pages, illustrated, color.

An attractive gift catalogue that usually has one or more things that would interest collectors. In a current issue, there's an antique Chinese porcelain stacking dish from the T'ung Chih period (c. 1861–1875) in *famille rose* design, 3¼″ in diameter, 4″ tall, $50, and an antique Chinese porcelain covered dish, about 9½″ in diameter, $150. Hand-embroidered squares from China, finished and backed in silk to frame or make into pillows, 12″ x 14″, are $30 each. For unicorn collectors, there's a 1″ tall, 14k. gold pendant with unicorn and sparkling two-point diamond on a long gold chain, $200. Another unusual item is the 4″-long "diamond" of faceted lead crystal from Germany that would make a sparkling addition to a paperweight collection.

T-10
TRITON GALLERY, Dept. CC
323 West 45th Street
New York, NY 10036

Theatre Posters, *free, published seasonally, 24 pages, illustrated, color and black and white.*

The Triton Gallery has quickly established itself as *the* source for posters from the theater, ballet, film, opera and related arts. Several hundred titles are listed with separate sections on Broadway theater showcards, and the poster art of David Edward Byrd. Prices range from about $3 to $10. Collectors should note that Triton deals in contemporary theater arts and all material is of recent vintage.

T-11
TROPICRAFTS LTD., Dept. CC
P. O. Box 43
Turkey Lane
Roseau, Dominica, W.I.

Tropicrafts, *free, 24-page booklet and folder of straw rug patterns, illustrated, black and white.*

Tropicrafts is most famous for its hand-woven lacy straw rugs but also makes plaited-straw hats and baskets of all sizes, shapes and weaves. There are appliquéd fabric wall hangings, threadwork wall plaques, all with Caribbean motifs, straw dolls in native costumes and Carib motif straw masks, all made by hand. Prices for the rugs run $1 to $1.20 a square foot. No price list was included with the booklet of other crafts.

T-12
TUCK MEMORIAL MUSEUM, Dept. CC
40 Park Avenue
Hampton, NH 03842

No catalogue or brochure, but the museum, a nonprofit historical organization, offers certain items for sale, one being a historical map of Hampton, 22″ x 28″, suitable for framing, $3 plus postage and handling. They also have historical note paper and postcards of Old Hampton, booklets and publications, prices and descriptions available on request.

T-13
**TURTLE BAY GALLERIES/TURTLE BAY
   TRADING CO.,** Dept. CC
Box 25
Roxbury, CT 06783

Turtle Bay Galleries/Art Graphics, *brochure, 50¢, updated annually, 6 pages, illustrated, color.*

Turtle Bay Galleries offers charming colored lithographs

by contemporary artists of such things as country weddings, church-going, a mill, a Sunday supper or a study of a sailboat on *Moonlit Waters* or several wide-eyed cats, one with a ball of yarn, curled on a quilt, another with a slice of watermelon echoing the shape of a new moon. Prints come in limited and unlimited, signed and unsigned editions, and prices vary from $8.95 to $35.

T-14
21ST CENTURY ANTIQUES, Dept. CC
Hadley, MA 01035

21st Century Antiques Second Collection, *$2.50 plus postage (45¢ third class, 90¢ first class U.S. and Canada, $1.60 overseas airmail), published periodically, 32 pages, illustrated, black and white.*

Owner Peter Rakelbusch has assembled a fantastic collection of 500 examples of what he describes as "the applied art of an epoch recently called the Modern Movement —the Arts and Crafts/Mission, Art Nouveau, and Art Deco periods" and his catalogue is a marvelous source for collectors of these increasingly popular styles. His next project, currently in the works, is to produce a series of Minilogs, smaller and more frequently published Art Nouveau and Art Deco catalogues that will sell for $1 each, which you will receive automatically if you are on the mailing list for the main catalogue. He will also work closely with anyone who has special requests or specific collecting interests in this area and will purchase on commission or sell on consignment.

The current (Second Collection) catalogue contains a varied selection of bronze and copper, silver and brass, pottery and porcelain, china and glass, wood, plastic, leather and chrome objects, ranging from a $650 Lorenzl bronze figurine of a nude leaping dancer, signed Lorenzl 5466-45, to a $1 plastic pencil sharpener; 32 pages of everything from furniture (a "Lips" chair after Dali, 29″ high is $199) to lamps, clocks, figurines, vases, prints, ornaments, mirrors, frames, bookends, desk accessories, ashtrays, dinnerware, kitchenware, bar items, toilet items, fire tools, including those chunky Bakelite radios, chrome cocktail shakers and enameled mesh bags of our not-so-distant past.

An Art Nouveau cracker jar of aged pewter in a flowing fruit design, with a green liner, German or Dutch, circa 1900, is $150; a Mission oak standing shelf, $150; a 1930s adjustable reading lamp in polished nickel chromium by Donald Deskey, one of America's foremost and most prolific Art Deco designers, best known for the interior of Radio City, is $425. Perhaps one of the most pleasant things about this unusual catalogue, in which each item is fully described with dimensions and price, is the wit that occasionally creeps into the copy. An example: "Plaster casting. Cornucopia being mounted by two frolicking maidens. They certainly seem to be having a wonderful time. Painted in naturalistic colors. No Gauguin but not bad either. Ht. 16½"/42 cm. $100."

Since all items are offered subject to prior sale, Peter Rakelbusch says it is easiest to call (evenings are fine, and his number is on the order form). If the item is unsold he will hold it for four post-office days to allow time for the written order to arrive, and he usually ships UPS. Purchases may be charged to Master Charge and Visa.

The arresting shapes of antique musical instruments make an unusual composition on a white wall in this room assembled by Tom Royal. Photographer: Otto Maya.

A shadow-box bed wall of colorfully backed and brightly lighted niches, an easy do-it-yourself built-in for a teenager's room, houses a collection of folk art from the Brooklyn Museum Gallery Shop. Courtesy: Celanese Corporation.

U

U-1
UCHIDA ART CO., Dept. CC
Kumanojinja-Higashi, Sakyo-ku
Kyoto 606, Japan

Art & Craft, free, published seasonally, 34 pages, illustrated, color.

Uchida offers a selection of woodblock prints, printed on handmade rice paper, of subjects ranging from women, the seasons, mountain views, warriors, pagodas in snow, flora and fauna to reprints of Ukiyo-e. They also offer reprints of prints by such masters as Hiroshige, Utamaro and Hokusai; embroidered screens and pictures; contemporary prints; Christmas cards; prints on silk; and frames in mulberry, bamboo and lacquer. Prices run from around $4 for a pure silk fan to $862 for a complete set of Hiroshige's *The 53 Stations of the Tokaido Highway* and are subject to the current rates of exchange. Some works are dutiable.

U-2
THE UNICORN, Dept. CC
12180 Nebel Street—Box 645
Rockville, MD 20851

Textile Books, 50¢, published annually, 14 pages.

A very wide range of publications about weaving, spinning and dyeing is carried by The Unicorn. There are books on history, techniques, individual weavers, costumes, etc. *Clans and Tartans of Scotland* contains 133 illustrations of tartans in color. *Elements of Weaving* covers all aspects of the craft and is co-authored by Jack Lenor Larsen, the famous designer. There are a number of important books listed on Navajo weaving including Charles Amsden's classic study, first published in 1934. Prices vary from 60¢ to $49.95, with a small charge for postage and handling.

U-3
UNICORN CITY, Dept. CC
55 Greenwich Avenue
New York, NY 10014

The Book of Unicorn City, 50¢, published seasonally, 12 pages, illustrated, black and white.

Are you into unicorns? If so, this small but interesting catalogue has a collection of objects from all over the world honoring that mythological, magical creature. From India, there's a unicorn carved on a cowry shell, as delicate as a cameo, for $5.98. A lovely *Unicorn with Flowers,* deeply embossed in Lucite, is $35. There are silver unicorn pendants, a scrimshaw heart-shaped unicorn charm, Irish linen wall hangings, unicorns in leaded glass from the Metropolitan Museum's gift shop, and a beautiful 5″ x 6″ leaded glass adaptation of an engraving from the fifteenth-century book *Hours of the Virgin* of a unicorn with rose shield (the unicorn for purity, rose for love, oak for steadfastness) for $25. Also books on unicorns, a crystal miniature ($4) and, for button collectors, the *Prepare to Meet Thy Unicorn* button-mirror, an original design by Jonathan Fischer in cream plastic with maroon overlay, just $1.

U-4
UNIGRAPHIC ARTS, INC., Dept. CC
82 Wall Street, Suite 1010
New York, NY 10005

How to Start a Rewarding Art Collection, free brochure, published periodically, 8 pages.

Unigraphic Arts specializes in obtaining graphics in all media for collectors, "primarily as a vehicle for capital appreciation." Only original, limited-edition, signed and numbered prints are offered, although sculpture and paintings are dealt with on request. Black-and-white and color photographs of the graphics in question will be sent when

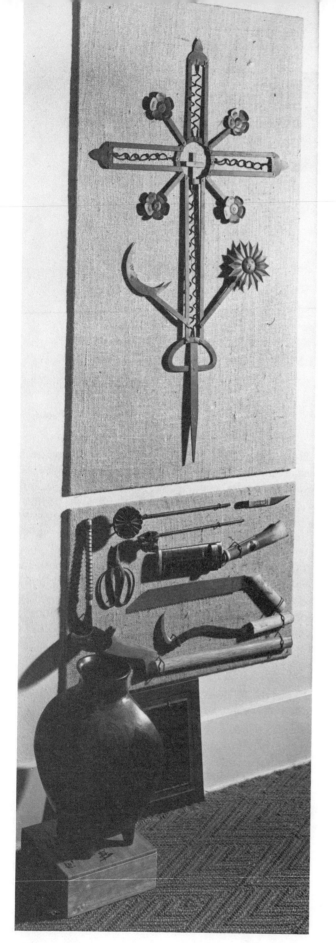

available. Unigraphic usually contacts collectors by telephone and suggests a portfolio to suit their "particular needs, desires and financial circumstance." The toll-free number to call is 800-221-4203. Prices average from $1,000 to $50,000 and include shipping and insurance costs.

U-5
UNIQUE IMPORTS, INC., Dept. CC
800 Slater Lane
Alexandria, VA 22314

Unique Collectibles & Collector Classics, $1, 32 pages, published annually, illustrated, color.

Unique Imports specializes in replica models of weaponry from the Civil War to the present, some available in kit form. The guns have all the characteristics of the originals with one major exception: they are non-firing. Collectors will also find original memorabilia from World War II including combat helmets, Rommel's goggles, medals, badges and insignias. There is also a vast collection of reproduction samurai swords. Books and prints on the military are also available. Prices go as high as $129.95 for an M-16 assault rifle but generally are in the $30 to $60 range. Many of the items are exclusive, and the catalogue makes a point of the fact that these are true collectors' items which will appreciate in value.

U-6
UNIVERSITY OF ALASKA MUSEUM, SALES DESK, Dept. CC
University of Alaska
Fairbanks, AK 99701

Sales list, free, published annually, 2 pages.

A selection of books and booklets on subjects relating to Alaska and the Arctic, the people, flora and fauna. There are booklets on Aleut basket weaving, Alaskan ornamentation, an illustrated key to freshwater fishes of Alaska, and objects from the museum collection. Other items available are an Eskimo doll poster ($1) and various postcards, including sets of Alaska wildflowers ($1 for a set of twelve cards). Prices range from 10¢ to $12.50 for

Japanese tools simply mounted on burlap-covered panels create inexpensive works of art. Photographer: Max Eckert.

Ancient Men of the Arctic by J. L. Giddings, and there is a 75¢ charge for postage and handling, or $1 if sent first class.

U-7
UNIVERSITY OF WYOMING ART MUSEUM,
Dept. CC
P. O. Box 3138 Laramie, WY 82071

100 Years of Artist Activity in Wyoming (1837–1937), $3, 80 pages, illustrated, black and white and color. Hans Kleiber, Artist of the Big Horn, $2, 20 pages, illustrated, black and white. Patterns and Sources of Navajo Weaving, $5, 68 pages, illustrated, black and white and color.

Three examples of the high-quality publications produced by the University of Wyoming Art Museum in connection with its exhibitions program. The *Artist Activity* catalogue is a riveting history of the comings and goings of artists in Wyoming along with a parallel history of events—human and political—that shaped the state and the character of its life. The *Kleiber* catalogue features etchings and aquatints of the Wyoming landscape and wildlife, full of telling observation and sense of place. The *Navajo Weaving* catalogue, an important addition to the increasing number of publications devoted to the extraordinary Indian weavers, includes a concise history of weaving developments along with descriptions and commentary on individual weavings.

U-8
U.S. GAMES SYSTEMS, INC., Dept.CC
468 Park Avenue South
New York, NY 10016

The Best of Cards Catalog, 25¢, published semi-annually, 28 pages, illustrated, black and white and color.

This crowded catalogue must have the most complete selection of tarot cards and fortune-telling cards to be found, as well as ordinary playing cards, double bridge decks, round playing cards, classical, mythological and historical playing cards, accessories for displaying playing card collections (display sheets, mount corners and museum print boxes), and books on tarot, astrology, witchcraft, crystal gazing, palmistry and other arcane subjects. Prices for tarot decks range from around $2 for a beginner's starter set to $30 for the Visconti-Sforza tarocchi deck of over-sized cards, reproduced in color from the earliest extant tarocchi deck (mid-fifteenth century), which once belonged to a ducal family in Milan. There are also I Ching cards, a new visual switch on the Chinese classic, with sixty-four hexagram cards ($6); two limited-edition four-color serigraphs based on mid-seventeenth-century French playing cards, hand silk-screened, pencil signed and numbered in an edition of 450 each ($8 unframed, $25 framed, $15 or $40 for the pair); and sets of four or ten tarot posters. A fascinating collection.

Hand-carved distaffs from Finland. Stockmann, S-38.

Eskimo sculpture from Shishmareff, Alaska. Kennedy Galleries, K-5.

V-1
THE VANCOUVER ART GALLERY SHOP,
Dept. CC
1145 W. Georgia Street
Vancouver, B.C. V6E 3H2
Canada

Publications and price list, free.

The Art Gallery features books by and about Emily Carr, reproductions of her work and postcards. Among the many publications listed are catalogues on *Graphic Art of German Expressionism, Bonnard, Eleven Early British Columbia Photographers, Morandi, Quebec Arts '75, West Coast Lokas* and *Pacific Vibrations.* Prices range from 20¢ to $25.

V-2
SYDNEY B. VERNON, Dept. CC
P. O. Box 387
Baldwin, NY 11510

Military Medals and Decorations, 50¢ a copy or $2.50 a yearly subscription for 8 issues, 16 pages.

The listings in the catalogue cover military medals and decorations from different countries and centuries, among them Great Britain, India, China, Abyssinia, South Africa, Kenya, France, Belgium, Germany, Japan, Poland, Imperial Russia and the U.S. The Order of St. Alexander Nevsky, a breast star, rare, is around $800; a Prussian Iron Cross of 1870 is $85; and the French Legion of Honor, Grand Cross Breast Star, 1870 early-type by Kretly of Paris, $250. Decorations range in price from $7.50 up.

V-3
THE VESTAL PRESS, Dept. CC
P. O. Box 97
Vestal, NY 13850

The Vestal Press, $2 (refundable with purchase), published annually, 64 pages, illustrated, black and white.

Perhaps the best way to describe the books The Vestal Press has to offer is to peruse their table of contents: Significant Books: important books and reference works on a variety of subjects; Pianos, Player Pianos and Or-

DRAMATIC LIGHTING FOR COLLECTIONS

Above, light from built-in eyeball spotlights above, illuminated glass shelf below, washes wall behind a sofa, calling attention to a dramatic contemporary painting and part of a collection of pre-Columbian pottery heads. Courtesy: Bloomingdale's.

Right, five types of lighting were combined by designer Vladimir Kagan to dramatize and accentuate the striking shapes and carving of a collection of primitive art. Spots on the back wall pinpoint three carvings. Flush ceiling lights wash over the wood cabinet wall and silhouette one large figure. Lighted niche allows smaller pieces to hold their own, while the ring of light over the table gives general illumination for dining. Courtesy: Champion-International.

chestrions; service manuals, blueprints and catalogue reprints; Theatre Pipe Organs; Recordo pianos: service information on the piano that plays with expression; Reed organs: service and construction booklets; The Phonograph: catalogs and manuals; Band Organs and Amusement Rides: manuals and catalog reprints; Music Boxes and Music Box publications; Music Boxes from Switzerland; The Mills Violano Virtuoso: the violin playing machine; Ragtime and Nostalgic Music; scores and books; Signs and bumper stickers; The Vestal Press Technical Series on mechanical musical instruments; Old automobiles; Railroads; Posters; Gambling Machines and miscellaneous; Music rolls; Stereo LP records and tapes.'' All in all, a fine collection of books and manuals for the collector and hobbyist.

V-4
VICTORIA TECHNICAL INSTITUTE, Dept. CC
    151-B Anna Road
    Madras 600 002, India

VTI—The House of Indian Arts and Crafts, free, 40 pages, illustrated, color and black and white.

Although a letter with the brochure says the articles for sale in the catalogue are "typical of the country," anyone who has been in India knows that the standard of indigenous crafts is much higher than the type of handcrafts shown here, which are mostly of the tourist- and gift-shop ilk. Carvings of elephants and laughing Buddhas, wooden fruit and salad bowls, leather handbags, an ivory Christ on the cross and garishly colored grass, fiber and bamboo place mats could hardly be called typical. However,

among the junk you'll find some really charming folk-art toys made of light wood, clay and cloth—costume dolls, gaily caparisoned animal dolls, brightly colored Kondapalli wood dolls from Andhra—stone sculpture recreations of the carved votive figures and friezes in South Indian temples, wood temple carvings, a Kerala snake boat and an imaginative fish and parrot made of buffalo horn. As prices, quoted in rupees, are subject to alteration without notice, and the price list we received, dated November 1972, had printed prices crossed out and higher prices inked in, we suggest you request an up-to-date price list with the catalogue. All articles in this catalogue are dutiable.

V-5
VIGNARI ART ENTERPRISES, INC., Dept. CC
    P. O. Box 335
    Ogunquit, ME 03907

Sea, Men and Ships, $2, 36 pages, illustrated, black and white.

Color reproductions of over three centuries of marine art from works by such great artists as Monet, Renoir, Canaletto, Homer, Eakins, Turner, Courbet, Corot, Seurat, Guardi and Sargent down to present-day artists —Dawson, Waugh, Sessions, Hopper, Vickery. Mr. Vignari also offers several of his own works in signed, numbered editions. Some wonderfully powerful images at prices ranging from $6 to $125 (for the hand-signed, numbered prints). Small shipping charge.

The sinuous shapes of Tiffany vases and candlesticks, each with a different-colored candle, are part of Theodoros Stamos' Art Nouveau collection. With his artist's eye for juxtapositions of color and shape, he sets them on a table top with his own red painting from the "Lefkada" series as a backdrop. Photographer: Otto Maya.

W-1

WAKEDA TRADING POST, Dept. CC
P. O. Box 19146
Sacramento, CA 95819

Wakeda Trading Post, 25¢, published every 2 years, 10 pages.

The Trading Post carries many kinds of beads, beading needles, gourds, brass spots, old brass sequins, tin cones, bone-hair pipes, elk teeth, claws, deer tails, porcupine hides, skunk skins, elk hides, sheep hides, turkey spikes, golden pheasant skins, bells, Chilkat blankets, fetishes, knives, and even ''tipis.'' They also offer a large selection of records and tapes of Indian songs. Prices range from 15¢ to $369.

W-2

WAKEFIELD-SCEARCE GALLERIES, Dept. CC
Shelbyville, KY 40065

Wakefield-Scearce Galleries, $3, published annually, 56 pages, illustrated, black and white.

An interesting and handsome catalogue of eighteenth- and nineteenth-century English furniture, mostly Georgian and early Victorian, with some unusual items for collectors, among them a Chinese Chippendale collector's cabinet on stand and a mahogany bagatelle table. Their silver vault, copied from the old London vaults, houses a vast collection of eighteenth- and nineteenth-century sterling and Sheffield plate by such famed silversmiths as Peter and William Bateman, Paul Storr and John Carter. As above items are one of a kind, they are subject to prior sale. Another section of this catalogue is devoted to the porcelain figures of famed artists—Dorothy Doughty, Doris Lindner, Ronald Van Ruyckevelt, Bernard Winskill, Cybis, Boehm, Ispansky and Burgues—with number of the edition and dimensions. All prices on request.

W-3

ALLAN WALLER LTD., Dept. CC
3437 Piedmont Road, N.E.
Atlanta, GA 30305

The Rambouillet Tapestry, $5 (applied to purchase), published annually, 40 pages, illustrated, color.

This firm recreates great tapestries from the past. When the Cluny Museum in Paris granted them the right to reproduce their famous *Lady with a Unicorn,* André Malraux, then Minister of Cultural Affairs, urged other museums to follow suit. As a result, collectors can choose from many works from the world's museums. A panel from the sixteenth-century Unicorn series in the Cluny measures 5' 5'' x 4' 7''. An eighteenth-century design after Tiepolo is 7' 7'' x 6' 1'' including border. From the Kunsthistorisches Museum in Vienna, an example of *Verdure,* a study of floral ''greenery,'' measures 8' 9'' x 6' 8''. All works are silk-screened on handmade canvas blended with flax, cotton and wool, sometimes with gold metallic threads. The color reproduced is that of the tapestries in their present state. Prices on request.

W-4

WALTERS ART GALLERY, Dept. CC
600 North Charles Street
Baltimore, MD 21201

The Walters Art Gallery Museum Store, 35¢, published annually, 30 pages, illustrated, black and white.

The museum store offers for sale a round, stained-glass medieval musician, 4⅛'' in diameter; a cookbook of Baltimore recipes illustrated with works from the museum collection; a catalogue of a show about maps, *The World Encompassed;* facsimile editions of manuscripts; coloring

Wall-hung vanity set against a mirror is lighted to project a sparkling double image of a cluster of beautiful glass paperweights. Photographer: Guerrero.

books; needlepoint; and cards reproducing items in the museum's collection. Prices range from $1.50 to $60 plus shipping charge.

W-5
WALTHER'S EXOTIC HOUSE PLANTS, Dept. CC
R.D. #3, Box 30
Catskill, NY 12414

Living Art Creations, $1 (with plant list), 12 pages, revised quarterly, illustrated, black and white.

The catalogue shows striking, individually designed horticultural art creations by sculptor John P. Walther, arrangements of stone, twig, moss and plants set in California redwood. Most of the plants used are epiphytic Tillandsias, or air plants, which are unique in form and easy to grow. Given good light and occasional mistings, they will go through all the plant cycles, including blooming and reproduction of new plants. There are some wood plaques that can be used hanging or standing, whereas the other arrangements are either centerpieces or sculptural in effect. Plaques range in size from 7″ to 14″ and in price from $15 to $28; a 12″-long centerpiece is $45, and a 12″ sculpture, $38. The list of exotic house plants features bromeliads, cacti and succulents.

W-6
E. G. WASHBURNE & CO., Dept. CC
85 Andover Street
Danvers, MA 01923

Celebrated Copper Weathervanes, 50¢, published annually, 20 pages, illustrated, black and white.

Weathervanes, as Washburne points out in the introduction to their neat little catalogue, are the outgrowth of an Early American folk art of the early 1600s. The colonists wanted to know which way the wind was blowing so they might better carry on their farming and fishing, and they borrowed on their European backgrounds in making weathervanes, adding American touches emblematic of their trade or profession—a sea captain might choose a fish or whale, a farmer a horse or cow. During the 1700s, the original flat silhouette patterns were often given a third dimension to make the figure more lifelike—the most famous weathervane of this type is the copper grasshopper on top of Boston's Faneuil Hall. The craftsmen at Washburne follow the tradition of hammering copper into their original nineteenth-century cast-iron molds, which makes the vanes a survival of an almost lost art and so especially interesting to collectors. Vanes shown in the catalogue, each given in different sizes, include full-bodied and swell-bodied figures of an eagle and arrow, quill, horses, roosters, a deer, dog, fish, sailboat, bull, cow, horse and jockey, and horse and sulky. The complete vane includes steel spire, brass collar, large copper ball, brass cardinals, smaller copper ball and copper weathervane figure, ready for mounting; components are also available separately. You have a choice of finishes—antique verdigris patina, natural polished copper, paint of any color or, at extra cost, 23k. gold leaf. No price list came with the catalogue, so we cannot quote prices.

W-7
FIRMA CHARLOTTE WEIBULL, Dept. CC
Box 43
S-230 47 Akarp
Sweden

Price list, free, published annually, illustrated.

Charlotte Weibull makes enchanting costume dolls in authentic clothes, employing artisans all over Sweden to weave materials and make accessories like wooden shoes, small pieces of silver jewelry, buttons and the traditional silver bridal cross. About a hundred seamstresses are kept busy sewing the various national costumes at home and dressing the dolls. This enterprising little industry started in the Forties, after Ms. Weibull took over the shop for Swedish national costumes in Malmö started by her great-aunt in 1901. When mothers brought their daughters in for a costume, the children wanted a miniature version for their dolls, so she began making costume dolls, and now there are dolls representing twenty-three different districts, which she sells to collectors and tourists and shows in exhibitions. Among the more delightful depicted on the price list sheet are Lucia, the candle-crowned Christmas saint, 6″ tall, $12; pigtailed Tilda and her friend Mats, 8″ tall, each $18; and a wedding couple from Skåne in an honorary arch (8″ tall, bride, $23.50, groom $22.50; 10″ arch, $14). Surface mail for one to three dolls is $2.25. You can also get ten postcards of the Swedish costume dolls for $3, which includes mailing.

W-8
WENDELIGHTING/*Division of Jackson*
International Ltd., Dept. CC
9068 Culver Boulevard
Culver City, CA 90230

Wendelighting Stereo Viewer, $1.50.

Wendelighting is a professional lighting system for illuminating paintings, sculpture and collections. The company recently replaced its twenty-eight-page catalogue with a folding stereo viewer portfolio containing six 18mm color slides showing the lighting effects in various settings. To our way of thinking, this gives no impression at all of the projectors and reflectors themselves, prices for which are listed in a brochure in the portfolio. However, they can be seen at retail stores, although the company also accepts mail orders FOB Culver City, with a half advance payment required, the rest charged COD.

W-9

WESTERN ARBORETUM, Dept. CC
   P. O. Box 2827
   Pasadena, CA 91214

Western Arboretum's New Bonsai Catalogue, $1, published annually, 24 pages, illustrated, black and white.

Everything for the bonsai enthusiast—living exotic trees and shrubs, imported containers and supplies—from a company recommended by botanical gardens and bonsai societies throughout the world. There are also books on bonsai culture and related subjects such as the art of the Japanese garden. For an easy way to start, Western Arboretum sells bonsai kits—starter, intermediate and advanced. A starter kit costs $9.95.

W-10

EDWARD WESTON GRAPHICS, Dept. CC
   6611 Valjean Avenue
   Van Nuys, CA 91406

Loose pages of individual artists' work, $3, refundable with purchase, published seasonally, illustrated, black and white and color.

Prints in all media, some pencil-signed in limited editions, others signed on the stone or plate, by a wide range of artists from Picasso to G. H. Rothe. In the current offering, Philippe Noyer is represented by a suite of five lithographs, signed and numbered in an edition of 225 and titled *Young Sophisticated Leopards & Ladies;* Mark King by silk-screen images of sports events—hockey, horse racing, skiing (signed, numbered, limited editions); G. H. Rothe by signed, numbered, limited-edition prints in drypoint and mezzotint on copper of ballet dancers, butterflies and horses. You can also choose from the caricatures of Charles Bragg; Hilo Chen's super realism; silk-screen scenes by Susan Pear Meisel; Harry Schaare's celebration of the Tall Ships; or serigraphs of country folk by the actress Elke Sommer. Prices range from $10 to several thousand. Certain items are listed with prices on request. There is a minimum order of $50 plus minimum shipping charge of $5.

W-11

WEST RINDGE BASKETS, INC., Dept. CC
   Rindge, NH 03461

Hand Woven New England Baskets, free folder with inserts, published annually, illustrated, some color.

The Taylor family of Rindge, New Hampshire, has been making ash baskets for three generations using essentially the same methods of manufacture as were used 300 years ago. Baskets range from a 9'' x 5'' x 4'' market basket ($5) to a 19'' x 11½'' x 9'' covered picnic basket ($15), with a wide variety of styles in between. Included with the price list is an illustrated booklet detailing the methods used to make these baskets.

W-12

JANE WHITMIRE, Dept. CC
   2353 South Meade Street
   Arlington, VA 22202

Museum Masterpiece Needlework, $1, published annually, 14 pages, illustrated, black and white.

Jane Whitmire has translated designs that have struck her fancy on her travels into suitable designs for needlework. Her kits include fine canvas, often hand painted, the finest wools, silks and even beads and gold cording. There are over sixty designs in the catalogue, including a Byzantine eagle from the eleventh century (16'' x 16''), a portrait of Shakespeare designed for the Folger Library (13'' x 14''), sections of the Bayeux tapestry (16'' x 20''), a design from an Ottoman Turkish plate in the Metropolitan Museum of Art (16'' x 16½''), plus contemporary studies of flowers and fruit and abstractions. The catalogue also offers footstools in Chinese Chippendale, Sheraton and Queen Anne styles made of solid Honduras mahogany, and fire- and candle-screens with a rotating tapestry frame. Prices range from $5 to $125.

W-13

WHITTEMORE-DURGIN GLASS CO., Dept. CC
   P. O. Box 2065-GR
   Hanover, MA 02339

Large number of loose sheets, free, continually updated, illustrated, black and white and color.

Every conceivable need of the worker in glass is offered by this firm—glass stones for stained glass and jewelry work; lampshade forms; cathedral glass; glass remnants and sheets; imported glass; opalescent glass; completely handmade "antique" glass; lead cames for holding pieces of glass together; soldering irons; lead knives; glass cutters; patterns; even glass-handler's gloves. Besides lampshades, there are designs for planters and lamp bases, ready to be finished. Prices for the wide variety of items vary from a few cents to around $300. There is an additional charge for shipping and handling.

W-14
WILDLIFE GALLERY OF NEW ENGLAND,
Dept. CC
172 Bedford Street
Stamford, CT 06901

Limited Edition Wildlife Art Prints, *$1, published annually, 8 pages, illustrated, color.*

The color brochure shows the work of Edward J. Bierly, Don Forrest, Louis Frisino and Walter A. Weber. The subjects of the limited-edition prints, signed and numbered by each artist, are mainly wild birds and dogs retrieving birds. Prices are from $15 to $60, with shipping charges of $3 per order.

W-15
ELSA WILLIAMS, INC., Dept. CC
445 Main Street
West Townsend, MA 01474

The Elsa Williams NeedleArt Collection, *$1, published annually, 84 pages, illustrated, color.*

Elsa Williams, who runs her School of NeedleArt in West Townsend, has produced a stunningly beautiful and unusually informative catalogue that covers the different aspects of needlework—crewel, blackwork, pulled thread embroidery, needlepoint and bargello—a fascinating source for the needle artist. There's even a page that explains how to block your handiwork. The crewel kits include both classic and contemporary designs for pictures, pillows, bell pulls, candle sconces, a footstool, clocks, and a 42″ Tree of Life design printed on 52″ linen, with 18″ repeat, so you can work your own upholstery fabric ($18 a yard for the printed linen, wools and instructions not included). A very inexpensive kit for beginners is a 4″ pin cushion on which you can learn outline stitches, French knots, satin stitches and buttonhole stitch ($2.50). Blackpoint, a tracery of jet black embroidery against white fabric, is seldom seen here, although it has been traditional for centuries in a number of European countries. A blackwork oriental fish, inspired by a cut-paper design, could be used as a picture, table mat or pillow top, 16″ x 10½″ with border ($8.50). The needlepoint kits for everything from carpets to eyeglass cases are varied and delightful. There are pillows with Arabian designs, masterworks of strong color and geometric balance, 12″ square ($18); needlepoint-tramé pictures taken from the works of John Constable; needlepoint Christmas ornaments and stockings. One of the strong points of this catalogue is the inclusion of color charts of the different yarns, close-ups of the various canvases, linens and needles, and all the necessary tools

and accessories, plus a selection of books by Elsa Williams. Custom finishing services are also available.

W-16
WILSHIRE MARKETING CORPORATION,
Dept. CC
5900 Wilshire Boulevard
Los Angeles, CA 90230

The RSVP Collection, *$1, published quarterly, 34 pages, illustrated, color.*

A special selection of things for the home from the company that publishes *Architectural Digest* and *Bon Appetit,* from antiques and reproductions to foods and cookware. The choice is good in terms of style, beauty and value. There are oriental porcelains (a coupe plate with cloisonné pattern, 12¼″ in diameter, is $25); pewter reproductions; an extremely beautiful heavy silver plate *tastevin* (wine taster's cup) with a mask of Bacchus, a reproduction of an 1808 original, just $11; some utterly charming lacquered woven bamboo basket-boxes made only in the Soochow/Shanghai regions, $20 for a tortoise box, $44 for a partridge; a carved and oil-waxed copy of the Egyptian cat in the British Museum, a divinely enigmatic animal, 18″ high, $105; and, in the catalogue we have, a magnificent one-of-a-kind green jade bowl with butterfly handles, of the Ching Dynasty, Chia Ch'ing Period (1796–1820), 11½″ long, 6″ wide, with rosewood stand, for a lofty $9,000. Rare objects such as this are, of course, subject to prior sale.

W-17
RICHARD WOLFFERS, INC., Dept. CC
127 Kearny Street
San Francisco, CA 94108

Auction catalogues of stamps and other philatelic material, issued every 6 weeks, $1.

W-18
THE WOODEN NICKEL, Dept. CC
P. O. Box 1288
Attleboro Falls, MA 02763

The Wooden Nickel, *$2 for 6 issues a year, 12 pages.*

A printed list, updated every six to eight weeks, of the varied collectibles sold by The Wooden Nickel: such things as old tintypes, ambrotypes and photographs; military accoutrements; uniforms; documents and letters; historical documents, books and newspapers; and some offbeat bits of assorted Americana, like a 1900s hand-strength tester and a silk cigar-band pillow quilt (unfinished cotton-cloth backing and ten loose silk bands, $18.50). Plucking at random from the current, and lengthy, list, we found a Sandwich glass marble ($14.50), an 1807 London theater handbill ($8.50), an accountant's hand-written case book of the 1700s, a cartridge box and flag holder from the Indian Wars, G.A.R. medals, a 1946 Terry & The Pirates coloring book ($6.50) and a twenty-one-piece Lionel train set ($32). An amusing list with some unusual items.

W-19
WORLD'S WINDOW, Dept. CC
    12 Holly Lane
    Plainview, NY 11833

    World's Window, free, published annually, 12 pages, illustrated, black and white.

Collectors' accessories abound within the pages of World's Window. Display stands in wood, acrylic and metal for eggs, rocks, shells and plates; illuminators for crystal and glass; picture and sculpture lights; pedestals; glass domes; plate hangers; frames; easels and wall shelves in styles to suit every kind of decor. In addition, the company offers glass paperweights, lead crystal sculpture, brass candlesticks, crystal bells, cheese platters, Victorian coat hangers, china bird napkin rings, place card holders, pin cushions and wickerware. Prices are very reasonable.

W-20
WORLD WIDE GAMES, INC., Dept. CC
    Box 450
    Delaware, OH 43015

    World Wide Games, free within the U.S. only, elsewhere $3 airmail, published annually, 28 pages, illustrated, color.

An unusual, high-quality catalogue from a company that began in 1953 as an at-home family business. Warren and Mary Lea Bailey saw a need for handcrafted, well-constructed family games that would be fun to play, challenging to the mind, handsome to look at and capable of standing the test of time and use. In this they have certainly succeeded. Their line of games is both beautifully designed and interesting for collectors, as you'll find here all kinds of old, traditional games like diabolo (which originated in China and was played at the French court), checkers and backgammon, English skittles, oriental and African board games, such as Gomoku from Japan and Adi from Ghana, and modern games based on sports. Some of the games were crafted by the students at Berea College; others are made abroad. The games are notable for quality workmanship in woods such as cherry, birch, birch and mahogany plywood, walnut and maple, and range in price from $1.25 for simple pocket puzzles for children to around $75 for a table golf game called Fore-Par, with the board games running mostly under $10. Chinese checkers (actually a Swedish game), with solid cherry or black walnut board made at Berea College, costs around $15 in cherry, around $17 in walnut. A handcrafted walnut and birch backgammon set, with instruction book, costs around $25. Adi, a fascinating game we have played in the West Indian islands, is around $17 in walnut, less in other materials. There are also tables and stands, games cabinets, game kits, books on world-wide games, tanagram puzzles, hand shadows, string figures and folk dances and a couple of games that can be played outdoors—Pillo Polo (played by field hockey rules, but with foam balls and sticks with foam heads) and Toppleball, which combines the batting of cricket, the throwing of dodgeball and the passing and team play of basketball. One of the unique features of the World Wide Games catalogue is that many of the traditional board games are designed with the blind or physically handicapped in mind.

"Snake," Hebi, sixth sign of the oriental zodiac, symbol of woman's jealousy, reproduced from the nineteenth-century original. The Peabody Museum of Salem, P-7.

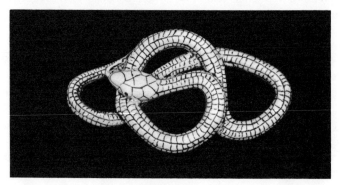

Y

Y-1
YESTERYEAR TOY COMPANY, INC., Dept. CC
Box 4383
Charleston, WV 25304

1875–1900 Wooden Entertainments, 50¢, published annually, 8 pages, price list and inserts, illustrated, black and white.

A delightful little catalogue of most unusual hand carved and hand painted wooden toys made in the tradition of the 1875–1900 era, based on original Appalachian mountain designs. The Yesteryear Toy Company, which was formed in 1971 by a sculptor, a mechanical engineer and a dress designer, is the sole industry of Davis Creek and employs local artisans to make the toys, which are so special and enchanting that they would delight both children and collectors of rural Americana. Our favorites are the Hackett family of 10″-tall, clog-dancing "West Virginia Stomper" dolls that come with their own dance platform. Zachary Quincy Hackett, a mountain man in overalls, floppy hat and beard, his wife Sarah Beth in calico and sailor hat, and their kinsfolk, Cousin L. O. Twittle Hackett, Boysenberry Hackett, Gamblin' Dan Hackett and Rip Van Hackett, plus Chauncey, the Hackett horse, all dance to snappy tunes with a dowel inserted in their backs for support. History and instructions are included with the dolls, which are $12.50 each. Or you can buy life-size versions of Zachary and Sarah Beth for $250 each. Then there are animated circus toys, a seven-car circus train and an 1875 six-car French train, various games and entertainments, boxes, amusing, primitive wooden ornaments ($3 each, $3.50 for the Santa Claus) and the Davis Creek Grenadier Set with officer, enlisted soldier, cannon and drum ($12.50).

Y-2
THE YOSEIDO GALLERY, Dept. CC
5-5-15 Ginza, Chuo-ku
Tokyo 104, Japan

Catalogue, $5 (plus $2.50 for airmail), published annually, 120 pages, illustrated, black and white and color.

A wide variety of prints by contemporary Japanese artists, including examples of traditional printmaking like woodblocks, lithographs, intaglio prints along with more modern techniques such as serigraphs, cement and mimeograph prints. In the catalogue we saw, No. 13, every kind of imagery is represented—realistic, abstract, stylized, folk, surreal landscapes, figure studies, still-life studies, fantasies, the theater. Editions run from 25 to 150 and prices from $13 to $1,042, subject to the current rate of exchange. A number of unlimited-edition prints are available from $21 to $33.

Reproduction blue Canton teapot. The Peabody Museum of Salem, P-7.

Almost any available space can be used to display a collection. In this foyer dining area, Frank Hines grouped Imari, lacquerware and Waterford crystal that do double duty on the table among old and new books, creating a lively interplay of shapes and colors. While one contemporary painting is conventionally posed over a desk, large-scale etchings fill in the area below the bookshelves to provide ground-level eye interest.

Members of the Antiquarian Booksellers' Association of America, Inc.

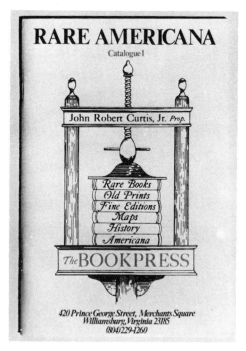

A catalogue of Rare Americana. The Bookpress, page 197.

A-TO-Z BOOK SERVICE
P.O. Box 610813
N. Miami, FL 33161
Paperbacks, Biography, First Editions, Science Fiction, Poetry, Children's Books (Mail order only)

ABRAMS, HARVEY DAN—
BOOKSELLER
3878 Vermont Rd. N.E.
Atlanta, GA 30319
Georgia, Southern & Confederate Americana, Maps & Prints

ACRES OF BOOKS, INC.
633 Main St.
Cincinnati, OH 45202
Science & Technology, Travel, History, Literature (Fiction)

ADELSON, RICHARD H.—
ANTIQUARIAN BOOKSELLER
N. Pomfret, VT 05053
Americana, Rare Voyages & Travels, Polar Exploration (Arctic & Antarctic), Natural History, Fishing & Sporting

ALBATROSS BOOK COMPANY
166 Eddy St.
San Francisco, CA 94102
Illustrated Books, General O.P., Jack London, San Franciscana, Science Fiction

ALDREDGE BOOK STORE
2506 Cedar Springs
Dallas, TX 75201
Texas, Southwest, Fine Bindings, General Non-Fiction

ALLEN, D. C.
Box 3
503 N. Elm St.
Three Oaks, MI 49128
Commerce & Industry, Midwest, 19th Century American Literature, Social History

ALLENSON, ALEC R., INC.
Box 31
635 E. Ogden Ave.
Naperville, IL 60540

Chicago Loop Branch
29 W. Jackson Blvd.
Chicago, IL 60604
Theology, Philosophy & History of Religions, Church History, Bibliography of Theology

ALTA CALIFORNIA BOOKSTORE
P.O. Box 296
Laguna Beach, CA 92652

1407 Solano Ave.
Albany, CA 94706
Antiquarian Ephemera, Mexicana, Photographica, Americana, Californiana

AMERICANIST, THE
1525 Shenkel Rd.
Pottstown, PA 19464
Black Studies, Early American Imprints, Americana, American Literature, Pennsylvania

AMTMANN, BERNARD, INC.
1529 Sherbrooke St. W.
Montreal, Quebec
H3G 1L7 CANADA
Canadiana

ANGLER'S & SHOOTER'S BOOKSHELF
Goshen, CT 06756
Sporting Art, Shooting, Hunting, Derrydale Press, Angling

ANTIQUUS BIBLIOPOLE
4147 24th St. / San Francisco, CA 94114
General Antiquarian & O. P.

APPEL, PAUL P.
119 Library La. / Mamaroneck, NY 10543
Little Magazines (1920–1950), Reprint Publisher, Literary Autographs, 20th Century First Editions

APPELFELD GALLERY
1372 York Ave. / New York, NY 10021
Fine Bindings, Standard Sets, English & American Literature, Autographs, Appraisals

ARGONAUT BOOK SHOP
792 Sutter St.
San Francisco, CA 94109
Early American Exploration, California, Maps, Prints, Voyages, Western Americana, Fine Books in All Fields

ARGOSY BOOK STORE, INC.
116 E. 59th St. / New York, NY 10022
Out-of-Print, Early Maps & Prints, Americana, Rare Medical Books, First Editions

ARGUS BOOKS
2741 Riverside Blvd.
Sacramento, CA 95818
Social Movements, Fine Press, Western History, Californiana

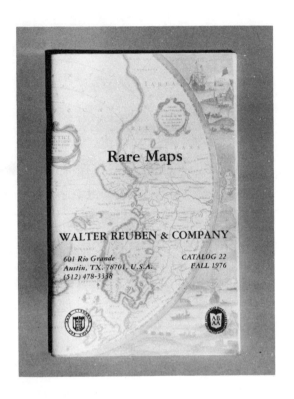

ARNOLD'S OF MICHIGAN
511 S. Union St.
Traverse City, MI 49684
American & British Literature, Hunting & Fishing, Children's Books, History

ATLANTIS BOOKS
6513 Hollywood Blvd.
Hollywood, CA 90028
American History, Russian & European History, Social & Political Radicalism, Money & Economic History, History of World War II

BARKER, CONWAY—
AUTOGRAPH DEALER
4126 Meadowdale Lane
P.O. Box 30625 / Dallas, TX 75320
Autographs & Historical Manuscripts

BARTFIELD, J. N.
45 W. 57th St. / New York, NY 10019
Paintings, Bindings, Sets, Rare Books, Color Plate Books

BEAVER BOOK STORE
1027 S.W. 5th Ave.
Portland, OR 97204
General O. P. Stock

BEIL, DOROTHY—BOOKS
2712 9th St. N. / P.O. Box 7045
St. Petersburg, FL 33734
Floridiana, General O. P., Americana, Fine Press, First Editions

BENJAMIN, WALTER R.,
AUTOGRAPHS, INC.
P.O. Box 255 / Scribner Hollow Rd.
Hunter, NY 12442
Autograph Letters & Manuscripts: Historical, Literary, Musical, Presidential

BENNETT & MARSHALL
8214 Melrose Ave.
Los Angeles, CA 90046
Rare Books, Science, Early Printing, Americana, Travel & Voyages

BERLIAWSKY, LILLIAN—BOOKS
23 Bay View St.
Camden, ME 04843
General Americana, European History & Biography, Literature, Music & Art

BERNETT, F. A., INC.
2001 Palmer Ave.
Larchmont, NY 10538
Fine Arts, Architecture, Archaeology

BEST BOOKS
P.O. Box 701
Folkston, GA 31537
Americana, Book Binding, Repair

BIBBY, G. A.
1225 Sardine Creek Rd.
Gold Hill, OR 97525
Natural History, Horticulture, Gardening

BIBLION, INC.
P.O. Box 9
Forest Hills, NY 11375
History of Medicine, History of Science, Rare Books, Scientific Periodicals

BLACK SUN BOOKS
667 Madison Ave.
New York, NY 10021
19th & 20th Century First Editions, Press Books, Books About Books, Manuscripts, English Paintings

BLEDSOE, WILLIAM—BOOKSELLER
P.O. Box 763
San Carlos, CA 94070
Business & Economics, Foreign Affairs, Government, Industrial & Labor Relations, Political Theory (Mail order only)

BLEIWEISS, ROY—FINE BOOKS
2277 Westwood Blvd.
Los Angeles, CA 90064
Fine Printing, Private Presses, Literary First Editions, Western Americana, Law, Tobacco & Smoking

BOND, NELSON
4724 Easthill Dr.
Roanoke, VA 24018
Literature, Association Books, First Editions, Virginiana, James Branch Cabell

BOOK CHEST, THE
19 Oxford Place
Rockville Centre, NY 11570
Natural History, Scarce Botanical & Zoological Books, Geology, Naturalists' Biographies, Travels

BOOK GALLERY, THE
512 Mamaroneck Ave.
White Plains, NY 10605
Fine & Applied Arts, Illustrated Books, Architecture, Photography, Search Service

BOOK SAIL, THE
1186 N. Tustin
Orange, CA 92667
Press Books, Western Americana, Rare Books, Illustrated Books, Manuscripts

BOOK SHOP, THE
352 Miller Ave.
Mill Valley, CA 94941
T. E. Lawrence, Art Books, Illustrated Books, Fine Bindings

BOOK STALL, THE
126 N. Church St.
Rockford, IL 61101
Wisconsiniana, Illinoisiana, Americana

BOOKED UP
1214 31st St. N.W.
Washington, DC 20007
Literature, Travel, First Editions

BOOKPRESS, LTD.
Box KP
420 Prince George St.
Williamsburg, VA 23185
Americana, Printing, Old Prints & Maps, Rare Books, 18th & 19th Century Travel

BOOKS FOR COLLECTORS
60 Urban St.
Stamford, CT 06905
Books About Books, Western Americana, Connecticut, Marine, Limited Editions Club

BOOKS-ON-FILE
Box 195
Union City, NJ 07087
General Search Service, Mail Order, Out-of-Print Books

BOOKWORM & SILVERFISH
P.O. Box 516
Wytheville, VA 24382
Americana, Southern States, Civil War, Appalachia

BOSWELL, ROY V.
P.O. Box 278 / Gilroy, CA 95020
Voyages & Travels, Discovery & Exploration, Atlases, Maps, History of Cartography

BRADLEY, VAN ALLEN, INC.
P.O. Box 578
Lake Zurich, IL 60010
Literary First Editions, Americana, Chicagoana, the West

BRATTLE BOOK SHOP
5 West St. / Boston, MA 02111
General Used & Rare, Over 350,000 Books

BRENTANO'S
586 Fifth Ave. / New York, NY 10036
Sets, Bindings, Color Plates, First Editions, Private Presses

BREWER, HARVEY W.
Box 322 / Closter, NJ 07624
Fine & Applied Arts, Textiles, Color Plate Books, Photography, Architecture

BRICK ROW BOOK SHOP
251 Post St., #608
San Francisco, CA 94108
Latin America, English & American Literature, Mexico, Bibliography

BROMER BOOKSELLERS
127 Barnard Ave.
Watertown, MA 02172
First Editions, Illustrated Books, Fine Printing, Juveniles, Miniatures

BROMSEN, MAURY A.,
ASSOCIATES, INC.
770 Boylston St.
Boston, MA 02199
Autographs & Manuscripts, Americana, Latin Americana, Paintings & Prints, Appraisals

BROUDE BROTHERS LIMITED
56 W. 45th St. / New York, NY 10036
Early Books on Music, Fine Facsimile Reprints of Music, Music Books & Music Literature

BROWN, ROBERT K.—ART & BOOKS
120 E. 86th St. / New York, NY 10028
20th Century Fine & Applied Arts Illustrated Books, Original Posters

BURGER & EVANS
Gloria Lane / P.O. Box 832
Pine Grove, CA 95665
Western Americana, American Paintings & Prints, Historical Manuscripts, Autographs

BURSTEIN, HAROLD M.
16 Park Place
Waltham, MA 02154
Books About Books, Bibliography & Reference, American Juveniles, 19th Century American Literature, General Americana

BUSCK, HARRY—BOOKSELLER
710 N. Humphrey Ave.
Oak Park, IL 60302
Out-of-Print, General

BUTTERFIELD, ROGER, INC.
White House, Rt. 205
Hartwick, NY 13348
Americana, New York State, Fine Printing, Literature, First Editions, Books About Books

CALER, JOHN W., PUBLICATIONS
CORPORATION
7506 Clybourn Ave.
P.O. Box 1426
Sun Valley, CA 91352
Humanities & Art Books & Periodicals, Sets & Issues of General Periodicals

CANTERBURY BOOKSHOP
29 E. Congress Parkway
Chicago, IL 60605
The Arts, Books About Books, English & American Literature, Hunting, Fishing, Literary Biography & Criticism

CARAVAN BOOK STORE
605 S. Grand Ave.
Los Angeles, CA 90017
Western Americana, Military and Naval History, Railroads, Early Travel & Exploration, Antiques & Rare Books

CARAVAN-MARITIME BOOKS
87-06 168th Place
Jamaica, NY 11432
Naval History & Science, Shipping & Ship Building, Voyages & Piracy, Whaling, Yachting (Mail order only)

CARLOS BOOK STALL
1115 San Carlos Ave.
San Carlos, CA 94070
Rare & Scarce Books, General, Californiana, Fore-Edge Paintings

CARRY BACK BOOKS
Haverhill, NH 03765
New England Americana, Vermontiana, Literary Libraries, White Mountains, Hemingway

CARTOGRAPHER, THE
114 E. 61st St. / New York, NY 10021
Atlases, Maps, Books on Cartography, Travel, Americana

CASSIDY, WILLIAM J.
109 E. 65th St.
Kansas City, MO 64113
Dance, Labor, Sociology, Political Science, Economics

CELLAR BOOK SHOP, THE
18090 Wyoming / Detroit, MI 48221
Sub-Saharan Africa, Southeast Asia, Worldwide City Planning, Pacific Area, Philippines

CELMER'S BOOK STORE
4433 N. Broadway
Chicago, IL 60640
Books About Books, Bibliography and Bibliomania, Early American Humor, Rare Books & Prints, Early Comic Books & Art

CHEROKEE BOOKSHOP, INC.
6607 Hollywood Blvd.
Hollywood, CA 90028
Fine Bindings, Literary First Editions, Children's Illustrated Books, Military, Americana

CHILTON'S, INC.
938-944 Conti St.
Mobile, AL 36604
Old Prints, Natural History, Old Maps, Americana

CHISWICK BOOK SHOP, INC.
Walnut Tree Hill Rd.
Sandy Hook, CT 06482
Calligraphy, History of Printing, Illustrated Books, Private Press Books, Rare Books

CLARE, ROY W.—ANTIQUARIAN AND UNCOMMON BOOKS
47 Woodshire S. / Getzville, NY 14068
Incunabula, Early Woodcut Books, Early Medicine & Science, Early Books in English, Witchcraft

CLARK'S, TAYLOR, INC.
2623 Government St.
Baton Rouge, LA 70806
Louisiana Books & Prints, Audubon Prints & Books, Natural History, Color Plates, Bird Prints

COGITATOR BOOKSTORE, THE
1165 Wilmette Ave.
Wilmette, IL 60091
General Stock, Literary Biography & Criticism, First Editions, Children's Books, Search Service

COLEMAN BOOK LOCATORS
257 E. Market St.
Long Beach, CA 90805
General Antiquarian, Search Service

COLLINS, LOUIS—BOOKSELLER
898 Carolina St.
San Francisco, CA 94107
Anthropology, Modern Firsts, Literature, American Bohemian, Collection Development

COLOPHON BOOK SHOP
700 S. 6th Ave. / La Grange, IL 60525
First Editions, Press Books, Bibliography, Manuscripts

CORNER BOOK SHOP
102 4th Ave. / New York, NY 10003
Cookbooks & Wine (Old), Drama, Textiles, Herbals

COUNTRY LANE BOOKS
38 Country Lane
Collinsville, CT 06022
Americana, Arctic, First Editions, Juvenile, Medical & Science

COUTANT, GRACE H.
R.D. 4, Box 342
Amsterdam Rd.
Scotia, NY 12302
Dolls, Back-Number Magazines, Needlework

COWEN, NATHANIEL
2196 Stoll Rd. / Saugerties, NY 12477
General Antiquarian

CURRENT COMPANY, THE
12 Howe St.
P.O. Box 46
Bristol, RI 02809

No. 9, The Arcade
Providence, RI 02903
Letters, Autographs & Manuscripts, Voyages & Travels, North & South Americana, English & American Literature, Rare & First Editions

CURREY, L. W., INC.
18 Church St.
Elizabethtown, NY 12932
19th Century American Literature & History, Modern First Editions, Fantasy & Science Fiction, Fine Printing

DABNEY, Q.M. & CO., INC.
P.O. Box 31061
Washington, DC 20031
Military, History, Americana, Government Publications, Law

DAILEY, VICTORIA KEILUS & WILLIAM
303 N. Sweetzer Ave.
Los Angeles, CA 90048
Prints, Art Reference, Illustrated Books, Rare Books, Press Books

DALY COLLECTION, THE CHARLES
66 Chilton St. / Cambridge, MA 02138
Natural History, Exploration & Discovery, Hunting, Firearms, Fishing

DAME, NATHANIEL & CO.
127-133 Walden St.
Cambridge, MA 02140
Fiction, Juveniles, New & Remainders

DAUBER & PINE, INC.
66 Fifth Ave. / New York, NY 10011
History, Americana, American & English Literature, Art, Fine Bindings

DAVIES, OWEN—BOOKSELLER
1214 N. La Salle St.
Chicago, IL 60610
Maritime History, Railroad Literature

DAVIS ART BOOKS
1547 Westwood Blvd.
Los Angeles, CA 90024
Modern Art, Original Art, Appraisals & Research, Art & Architecture, Search Service

DAWSON'S BOOK SHOP
535 N. Larchmont Blvd.
Los Angeles, CA 90004
Western Americana, Books About Books, Miniature Books, Mountaineering, Oriental Art

DECKER, PETER
45 W. 57th St. / New York, NY 10019
Travel in America, Voyages & Explorations, Canadiana, Western Americana, Americana

DREW'S BOOK SHOP
27 E. Canon Perdido
Box 163
Santa Barbara, CA 93101
Prints, Literary Criticism, Maps, Literature, Ephemera, Americana

DRISCOLL, EMILY
P.O. Box 834
Shepherdstown, WV 25443
Autographs, Manuscripts, Drawings, Illustrations, Association Books

DUNAWAY, R.—BOOKSELLER
6138 Delmar Blvd.
St. Louis, MO 63112
Bibliography, Literary Biography & Criticism, First Editions, Out-of-Print

DUPRIEST, M. INC.
434 Hudson St. / New York, NY 10014
Press Books, Illustrated Books, Literature, Caribbean & Latin America, Florida & The South

DUSCHNES, PHILIP C. INC.
699 Madison Ave.
New York, NY 10021
Fine Bindings, Illuminated Manuscripts, Fine Press Books, Fine Printing, First Editions

DWYER'S BOOKSTORE, INC.
44 Main St. / P.O. Box 426
Northampton, MA 01060
Printing, Rare Books, Autographs, Press Books, Illustrated Books

DYKES, JEFF—WESTERN BOOKS
Box 38
College Park, MD 20740
Western Americana, J. Frank Dobie, Outlaws & Rangers, Western Illustrators, Range Livestock

EAST AND WEST SHOP, INC.
4 Appleblossom Lane
Newtown, CT 06470
Middle Eastern, Asian, East Asian & African History

EDGEWATER BOOK STORE
1204 W. Thorndale Ave.
Chicago, IL 60660
General, Used, Chicagoana, Search Service, Out-of-Print

EDMUNDS, LARRY, BOOKSHOP, INC.
6658 Hollywood Blvd.
Hollywood, CA 90028
Theatre, Cinema

EMDIN, JACOB L.
11 Euclid Ave. / Summit, NJ 07901
First Editions, Art Books, American Literature, Poetry, Autographed Material

ERIE BOOK STORE
717 French St.
Erie, PA 16501
General Used Books, Early Pennsylvania Oil, Great Lakes, Western Pennsylvania

ESTATE BOOK SALES
1724 H St. N.W.
Washington, DC 20006
Select Books in All Fields from Estate Libraries of the Washington Area

FALES, EDWARD C.
P.O. Box 56 / Salisbury, NH 03268
Manuscripts, Crafts, Cookery, Gardening, Americana

FAMILY ALBUM, THE
R.D. 1, Box 42
Glen Rock, PA 17327
Fine Americana, Pennsylvania, Photographica, Early American and European Imprints, Incunabula

FLEMING, JOHN F., INC.
322 E. 57th St.
New York, NY 10022
First Editions, Rare Books, Manuscripts

FONDA BOOKS
P.O. Box 1800
Nantucket, MA 02554
Nantucketiana, Marine Manuscripts of all Nations and Periods

FORDHAM BOOK CO.
Box 6 / New Rochelle, NY 10801
Literature, General History, Philosophy

FRASER, JAMES
309 S. Willard
Burlington, VT 05401
Wall Street, Stock Market, Economics, Business History, Americana (Business)

FRENCH, PALMER D.—
ANTIQUARIAN BOOKSELLER
2104 MacArthur Blvd.
P.O. Box 2704 (all mail)
Oakland, CA 94602
Fine & Decorative Arts, Fine Crafts, Graphics & Illustration, Social & Cultural History, Travel & Exploration (Afternoons only)

FRISCH, HOWARD
Livingston, NY 12541
19th Century Fiction

FROHNSDORFF, DORIS
P.O. Box 2306
Gaithersburg, MD 20760
Original Illustrative Art, Miniature Books, Illustrated Books, Early & Rare Children's Books, 20th Century Children's Books

FRONT, THEODORE—
MUSICAL LITERATURE
155 N. San Vicente Blvd.
Beverly Hills, CA 90211
Music, Books on Music

FRONTIER AMERICA CORPORATION
P.O. Box 3698
Bryan, TX 77801
Mexico & Mexican War, Texas, Photographica, Ranching, Cattle Industry, Western Americana

GACH, JOHN—BOOKSERVICE
3012 Greenmount Ave.
Baltimore, MD 21218
Rare Books, Black Studies, Africa, First Editions, Psychoanalysis, Freud

Gach, John—Bookshop
3322 Greenmount Ave.
Baltimore, MD 21218
General Stock

GAISSER, KENDALL G.—BOOKSELLERS
1242 Broadway / Toledo, OH 43609
Rare Books, Military History, History, General, Art

GARDINER, AVIS & ROCKWELL
60 Mill Rd. / Stamford, CT 06903
Americana, Atlases & Maps, Travel, American Newspapers, Trade Catalogues

GARNETT, ANTHONY—FINE BOOKS
Box 4918
St. Louis, MO 63108
Fine Printing, First Editions, Press Books, English Literature

GATES, W.C.—BOOKS
1279 Bardstown
Louisville, KY 40204
Americana, Kentucky, Indiana, American Fiction to 1900, American First Editions, Illustrated Books

GENNS, W.T.—BOOKS
Studio 1, 116 E. De La Guerra St.
Santa Barbara, CA 93101
General Books, California & The West, Fine Press Books, Literature, First Editions

GILMAN, STANLEY
237 E. 9th St.
P.O. Box 131 Cooper Station
New York, NY 10003
Newspaper History, Literature, American History, Out-of-Print

GINSBERG, MICHAEL—BOOKS, INC.
P.O. Box 402
Sharon, MA 02067
Western Americana, American History, Canadiana & Arctic, Voyages & Travels, Manuscripts & Autographs, Scholarly Journals

GLASER, EDWIN V.
P.O. Box 1394
New Rochelle, NY 10802
Literature, History of Science, Voyages & Travels, Rare Books

GLENN BOOKS, INC.
1227 Baltimore
Kansas City, MO 64105
General–Old, Rare & Out-of-Print, Printing & Typography, Manuscripts, Press Books, Western Americana

GLOBE BOOKSTORE, THE
P.O. Box 69218
Los Angeles, CA 90069
Comparative Religion, Occult, Alchemy, Mysticism, Astrology

GOLDSCHMIDT, LUCIEN, INC.
1117 Madison Ave.
New York, NY 10028
Fine Arts, French Literature, Illustrated Books (15th-20th Century), Prints, Drawings

GOODSPEED'S BOOKSHOP, INC.
18 Beacon St. / Boston, MA 02108

2 Milk Street / Boston, MA 02108
Autographs, Americana, Genealogies, First Editions, Prints

GORE, MARIAN L.—BOOKSELLER
Box 433 / San Gabriel, CA 91775
Beverages, Wine, Cookery, Gastronomy, Hotels, Inns

GOTHAM BOOK MART & GALLERY, INC.
41 West 47th St.
New York, NY 10036
Literary Art & Photographs, Literary Manuscripts, Archives & Correspondence, Modern First Editions

GREEN THOUGHT BOOKSELLERS
283 Lee Ave.
Yonkers, NY 10705
Manuscripts, Autograph Letters, First Editions, Classical Literature, History

GREENE, PAULETTE—RARE BOOKS
140 Princeton Rd.
Rockville Centre, NY 11570
19th & 20th Century American & English Literature

GREGORY, K.
222 E. 71st St.
New York, NY 10021
Illustrated Books, Decorative Old Prints, Horticulture, Valentines & Greeting Cards Before 1875, Playing Cards

HALL, NORMAN ALEXANDER
Normandie Rd.
Dover, MA 02030
Appraisals

HAMILL & BARKER
400 N. Michigan Ave., Room 1210
Chicago, IL 60611
First Editions, Literary Autographs, Early Illustrated Books, Incunabula

HAMMER, MILTON—BOOKS
819 Anacapa St.
Santa Barbara, CA 93101
Literature, Americana, Californiana, Maps, Prints

HAMPTON BOOKS
Rt. 1, Box 76
Newberry, SC 29108
Aerospace, Movies, Old Photography, South Caroliniana, Television & Radio

HANNS, EBENSTEN & CO.
55 W. 42nd St.
New York, NY 10036
Baedeker Travel Guidebooks, Travel Guidebooks

HANRAHAN, J & J, INC.
67 Bow St.
Portsmouth, NH 03801
Rare Books, New Hampshire, Mosher Press, Early Music, Americana

HARDING, DOUGLAS N.
35 E. Pearl St.
Box 361
Nashua, NH 03060
Alaska, Arctic, Antarctic, Canadiana, Antiques

HARDY, GRAHAME—BOOKS
Box 449
Virginia City, NV 89440
Railroadiana, Automobiliana, Trade Catalogues, Western Americana, Nevadiana

HARPER, LATHROP C., INC.
22 E. 40th St.
New York, NY 10016
Incunabula, Illuminated Manuscripts, Illustrated Books, Early Science, Medicine & Natural History, Humanism, Americana (pre-1820)

HARRIS, DORIS—AUTOGRAPHS
Room 907
5410 Wilshire Blvd.
Los Angeles, CA 90036
Autograph Letters & Manuscripts, Association Books

HAYMAN, ROBERT G.—
ANTIQUARIAN BOOKS
R.F.D. 1
Carey, OH 43316
Americana, Midwest Americana, Great Lakes Area, Ohio Valley States, Western Americana

HEINMAN, W.S.
P.O. Box 602, Ansonia Station
1966 Broadway
New York, NY 10023
Africana, Dictionaries, Reference, Special Imports, Technical

HEINOLDT BOOKS
Central & Buffalo Avenues
South Egg Harbor, NJ 08215
American Colonial Period, American Revolution, Early American Travels, Western Americana, American Indians

HELLER, F. THOMAS
308 E. 79th St.
New York, NY 10021
Early Science, Medicine & Natural History, Psychiatry, Psychoanalysis

HENNESSEYS, THE
4th & Woodlawn
Saratoga, NY 12866
Americana, Art, History, Literature, Sporting Books

HERITAGE BOOKSHOP, INC.
847 N. La Cienega Blvd.
Los Angeles, CA 90069
Rare Books, California, Press Books, Manuscripts, First Editions

HERTZ, ALEXANDER, & CO., INC
88-28 43rd Ave.
Elmhurst, NY 11373
Russia & Eastern Europe, General Slavica, Baltic and Balkan Countries

HICKOK, ERNEST S.
382 Springfield Ave.
Summit, NJ 07901
Angling, Hunting (A.B. Frost, F. Benson, R. Clark)

HIRSCH, DANIEL—BOOKS
P.O. Box 315
Hopewell Junction, NY 12533
Children's Literature, Illustrated Books, 19th Century Literature, Rare Books

HOFMANN & FREEMAN
P.O. Box 207 / Cambridge, MA 02138
English Books Before 1700, 18th & 19th Century English Literature, Literary Manuscripts & Autographs, Early Historical Manuscripts, Early Continental Books

HOLLANDER, MICHAEL S.
P.O. Box 3678
San Rafael, CA 94902
Illuminated Manuscripts, Color Plate Books, 19th Century Technology & Literature

HOLLYWOOD BOOK SHOP
6613 Hollywood Blvd.
Hollywood, CA 90028
Art, Literature, Anthropology, Americana, Vintage Periodicals

HOLMAN'S PRINT SHOP, INC.
28 Court Square / Boston, MA 02108
Historical Prints, Fine Prints, Marine Prints & Drawings, Engraved Portraits, Old Maps

HOLMES BOOK COMPANY, THE
274 14th St.
Oakland, CA 94612

22 Third St.
San Francisco, CA 94103
Americana & Western Americana, Rare, Scholarly, General & Out-of-Print Books

HOUSATONIC BOOKSHOP
Salisbury, CT 06068
General Literature, First & Rare Editions, Scholarly (New & Old)

HOUSE OF BOOKS, LTD.
667 Madison Ave.
New York, NY 10021
20th Century First Editions, Autograph Material

HOUSE OF EL DIEFF, INC.
139 E. 63rd St. / New York, NY 10021
Manuscripts, Rare Books

HOWARD, VERNON—
BOOKS/GAMUT BOOKSHOP
723 California Dr.
Burlingame, CA 94010
Mountaineering, Western Americana, Literature, Criticism, Exploration & Travel

HOWELL, JOHN—BOOKS
434 Post St.
San Francisco, CA 94102
Americana & Californiana, English & American Literature, Fine Prints & Paintings, Illuminated Manuscripts, Incunabula, Medicine & Science, Rare Books in all Fields

HOWEY, RALPH T.
Hampton House 10B
Narberth, PA 19072
(By appointment only)

HUNLEY, MAXWELL
225 S. Los Robles Ave.
Pasadena, CA 91101
Western Americana, American & English First Editions, Early Juveniles, Fine Press Books, Early American Plays and Poetry

HURLEY BOOKS
Rt. 12 / Westmoreland, NH 03467
General Stock, Animal Husbandry, Theology, Horticulture, Agriculture

INMAN'S BOOK SHOP
50 E. 50th St.
New York, NY 10022
First Editions, Rare Books, Fine Bindings

INTERNATIONAL BOOKFINDERS, INC.
Box 1
Pacific Palisades, CA 90272
Search Service, Americana, Western Americana, First Editions, Rare Books

INTERNATIONAL UNIVERSITY
BOOKSELLERS, INC.
101 Fifth Ave.
New York, NY 10003
Periodicals (in all fields), Reference Materials & Book Collections

JACOBS, DOUGLAS M.
P.O. Box 363
Chestnut Ridge
Bethel, CT 06801
Autographs & Manuscripts, Unique Books, Americana, First Editions, Old and Rare Books

JELTRUPS'—BOOKS
51 ABC Company St.
Christiansted
Saint Croix, VI 00820
Virgin Islands Books, West Indian Books

JENKINS COMPANY, THE
Box 2085
Austin, TX 78767
Texas, Western Americana, Literary First Editions, Bibliography, Autographs

JOHNSON, JOHN
R.F.D. #2
North Bennington, VT 05257
Natural History, Botany, Birds & Mammals, Reptiles & Fish, Insects

JOHNSON, WALTER J., INC.
355 Chestnut St.
Norwood, NJ 07648
Scientific Periodicals & Books, Medical, Liberal Arts, All Languages

A single central niche in a bookwall acts as a shadow box for a restrained museum-like arrangement of precious, tiny objects mounted on plinths. Photographer: Guerrero.

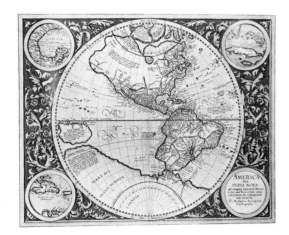

"America Sive India Nova" map by Michael Mercator, 1595. W. Graham Arader, III, A-17.

JOSEPH THE PROVIDER—BOOKS
903 State St. (Suite 201)
Santa Barbara, CA 93101
*Modern Literature: Manuscripts, Letters,
Signed and Association Copies, First Editions*

JOYCE BOOK SHOPS, THE
Box 310
Martinez, CA 94553

Gull Book Shop
538 15th St.
Oakland, CA 94612

Joyce Book Shop
2187 Salvio St.
Concord, CA 94519
*Wholesale, Rare and Antiquarian, Out-of-
Print, Foreign Language, Fiction*

KAPLAN, CAROLYN
P.O. Box 201
Laguna Beach, CA 92652
Theater, Plays, Drama

KARMIOLE, KENNETH—BOOKSELLER
P.O. Box 464
Santa Monica, CA 90406

2255 Westwood Blvd.
Los Angeles, CA 90064
*General Antiquarian, History of the Book,
Modern Fine Printing, History of Religion*

KATZ, SAMUEL W.
10845 Lindbrook Dr. #6
Los Angeles, CA 90024
*Illustrated Books–15th to 20th Century, Callig-
raphy, Incunables, Mexico and Mexican Art,
Rare Books (By appointment)*

KEATS, IRVING
280 Del Mesa Carmel
Carmel, CA 93921
*Color Plate Books, Fine Bindings, Fine Press
Books, First Editions*

KEBABIAN, JOHN S.
2 Winding Lane / Scarsdale, NY 10583
Appraisals

KENNEDY'S BOOKSHOP
P.O. Box 191 / 1911 Central St.
Evanston, IL 60204
Scholarly, General, Out-of-Print

KLEMM, GAIL—BOOKS
P.O. Box 551
Ellicott City, MD 21043
*Early & Contemporary Children's Books,
Western Americana, Californiana, Printing,
Papermaking & Typography*

KRAUS, H. P.
16 E. 46th St. / New York, NY 10017
*Incunabula, History of Science, Cartography,
Americana, Medieval Manuscripts*

KRAUS PERIODICALS CO.
Rt. 100 / Millwood, NY 10546
*Scholarly Periodicals, Bibliographies, Refer-
ence Works, Antiquarian Books*

KREBS, EDGAR
5849 N. Talman Ave.
Chicago, IL 60659
*Americana, Art, History, Literature, Out-of-
Print*

KRONOVET, DR. MILTON
881-C Balmoral Ct.
Lakewood, NJ 08701
*Literary, Theatrical & Presidential Auto-
graphs, Musical First Day Covers, Historical
Documents*

LA CHANCE, DONALD
P.O. Box L
4325 Bridge St.
Cambria, CA 93428
Search Service

LEEKLEY BOOK SEARCH
P.O. Box 337
711 Sheridan Rd.
Winthrop Harbor, IL 60096
*Theory & Practice of Education, Popular
Culture, 20th Century Poetry, Mid-West
Americana, Search Service*

LEFKOWICZ, EDWARD J.
43 Fort St. / P.O. Box 630
Fairhaven, MA 02719
Rare Books & Mss. Relating to the Sea, its Islands & Nautical Science (Primarily mail order)

LEHR, JANET
45 E. 85th St. / New York, NY 10028
Stereograms, Photograph Albums, Photographic Reference works, Photographs, Related Autographs, Photographically Illustrated Books

LENNIE'S BOOK NOOK
8125 W. 3rd St.
Los Angeles, CA 90048
Out-of-Print, General Stock, History, Theater, Cinema, Biography

LEVIN, BARRY R.—SCIENCE FICTION & FANTASY LITERATURE
2253 Westwood Blvd.
Los Angeles, CA 90064
Science Fiction & Fantasy, Fine & Scholarly Books

LEVINSON, HARRY A.—RARE BOOKS
Box 534 / Beverly Hills, CA 90213
Early Illustrated Books, Early Science & Medicine, Incunabula, Early & Medieval Manuscripts, Wing & STC Books

LEWIS, R. E., INC.
P.O. Box 1108 / San Rafael, CA 94902
Illustrated Books, 19th-20th Century Prints, Old Master Prints, Japanese Prints, Indian Miniatures

LIEBMANN, WILLIAM B.
211 E. 70th St.
New York, NY 10021
Autographs, Manuscripts, Press Books, Rare Books, Appraisals (By appointment only)

LOWE, JAMES—AUTOGRAPHS, LTD.
667 Madison Ave., Suite 709
New York, NY 10021
Autograph Letters, Manuscripts, Documents, Signed Editions, Americana

LUBBE, ERNEST—BOOKS
280 Golden Gate Ave.
San Francisco, CA 94102
Western Americana

LUBRECHT & CRAMER
Rt. 42 & Forestburgh Rd., R.F.D. 1
Monticello, NY 12701
Botany & Biology

M & S RARE BOOKS, INC.
Box 311 / 45 Colpitts Rd.
Weston, MA 02193
Americana, American Reform, Early American Literature, Science & Medicine, Early American Thought

McGILVERY, LAURENCE
P.O. Box 852
La Jolla, CA 92038
Art, Art Periodicals

MacEWEN, AIMEE B.
Victorian House
Stockton Springs, ME 04981
Americana, Maine

MacKENZIE, ISOBEL—
RARE BOOKS & PRINTS
900 Sherbrooke St. W., Suite 23
Montreal, Quebec
H3A 1G3 CANADA
Plate Books, Children's Books, Fishing, Canadiana, Prints, North and South Americana (By appointment)

MacMANUS, GEORGE S., CO.
1317 Irving St. / Philadelphia, PA 19107
English & American Literature, Pennsylvania, Local History, Americana

MAGEE, DAVID
2475 Filbert St.
San Francisco, CA 94123
Rare Book Consultant (By appointment only)

MAGIC, INC.
5082 N. Lincoln Ave.
Chicago, IL 60625
Ventriloquism, Punch & Judy, Puppetry, Conjuring, Playing Cards

MARSHALL FIELD & CO
111 N. State St. / Chicago, IL 60690
Prints, Old Maps, First Editions, Fine Bindings, Illustrated Books

MAXWELL SCIENTIFIC
INTERNATIONAL (MSI)
Fairview Park / Elmsford, NY 10523
Backfiles in Education, Liberal Arts & Social Science, Science, Technology, Medicine, Mathematics

MEMORABILIA, LTD.
7624 El Camino Real
Carlsbad, CA 92008
American History, Judaica, Napoleonic, Classical Composers, French & English Authors

MENDOZA, ISAAC, BOOK CO.
15 Ann St. / New York, NY 10038
Science Fiction, Modern First Editions, Detective Fiction

MINKOFF, GEORGE ROBERT, INC.
Box 147 / Rowe Rd.
R.F.D. #3
Great Barrington, MA 01230
Modern First Editions, Original Drawings, Press Books, Illustrated Books, Manuscripts & Letters

MINTERS, ARTHUR H., INC.
84 University Pl.
New York, NY 10003
Architecture, Fine Arts, Photography, Modern Literature, Modern Illustrated Books

MOORE, EARL
P.O. Box 243
Wynnewood, PA 19096
Historic Documents, American Maps, Prints, Americana, Autograph Letters

MORRILL, EDWARD & SON, INC.
15 Kingston St.
Boston, MA 02111
Science, Sports & Nature, Reference Books, Travel, Americana

MORRISON, W.M.—BOOKS
Box 3277
Waco, TX 76707
The West, Texana

MOTT, HOWARD S., INC.
S. Main St.
Sheffield, MA 01257
Caribbean, Juveniles, British & American Literature, Literary & Historical Autographs, Americana

MUNS, J.B.—FINE ARTS BOOKDEALER
1162 Shattuck Ave.
Berkeley, CA 94707
Photography, Fine Arts, Music, City Planning, Architecture (By appointment only)

MURRAY, SAMUEL
477 Main St.
Wilbraham, MA 01095
Color Plate Books, Prints, Rare Books, Miniature Books, Juvenilia (By appointment)

NEBENZAHL, KENNETH, INC.
333 N. Michigan Ave.
Chicago, IL 60601
Atlases, Prints, Maps, Voyages & Travels, Rare Americana

NEEDHAM BOOK FINDERS
2317 Westwood Blvd.
Los Angeles, CA 90064
Search Service, General Stock

NESTLER, HAROLD R., INC.
13 Pennington Ave.
Waldwick, NJ 07463
Americana, especially New York, New Jersey, New England & Delaware Valley (By appointment only)

NORMAN, JEREMY & CO., INC.
442 Post St.
San Francisco, CA 94102
Medicine, Science & Technology, Natural History, Voyages & Travels, Art & Illustrated Books

NORMILE, JAMES—BOOKS
6888 Alta Loma Terrace
Los Angeles, CA 90068
Oriental Art, Primitive Art, Drawings, First Editions, Prints

NORTH, PAUL H., JR.
81 Bullitt Park Pl.
Columbus, OH 43209
American History & Travel, Ohioana, First Editions, Manuscripts, Paintings

NORTHWEST BOOKS
3814 Lyon Ave.
Oakland, CA 94601
Western Americana, Fine Arts, Fine Prints, Oriental Art, Color Plate Books

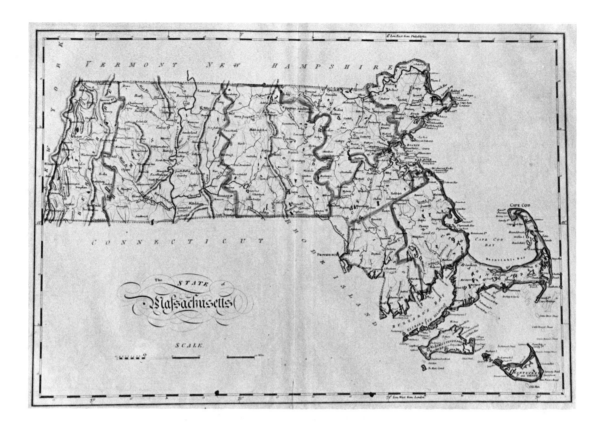

O'BRIEN, F. M.—
ANTIQUARIAN BOOKSELLER
    34 & 36 High St.
    Portland, ME 04101
Early Education, Early Science, Americana, General Literature, Maine Literature & History

OELGART, ISAAC J.—
RARE & SCHOLARLY BOOKS
    30 Milk Street
    Newburyport, MA 01950
Sporting Books, Natural History of Sporting Interest, Falconry & Hawking Literature, Naval Americana, American Civil War

OFFENBACHER, EMIL
    84-50 Austin St.
    P.O. Box 96
    Kew Gardens, NY 11415
Early Medicine, Early Science, Rare Books

O'GARA, JOSEPH—BOOKSELLER
    1311 E. 57th St.
    Chicago, IL 60637
Ancient History, Religion & Theology, European History, American & English Literature

OLD BOOK HOME, THE
    P.O. Box 7777 / Rosewood Station
    Spokane, WA 99208

    W. 3217 Cora
    Spokane, WA 99205
Appraisals, Bibliography, American First Editions, Books About Books, Western Americana

OLD DRAGON'S BOOK DEN, THE
    P.O. Box 186 / 352 W. Cuba Rd.
    Barrington, IL 60010
Dogs, Horses, Hunting, Shooting, Sporting

OLD HICKORY BOOKSHOP
    Brinklow, MD 20727
Old & Rare Medical Books, Out-of-Print Medical Books

OLD MYSTIC BOOKSHOP
    58 Main St.
    Old Mystic, CT 06372
General Americana, Canadiana, Marine

OLD OREGON BOOK STORE
    610 S.W. 12th St.
    Portland, OR 97205
Northwest Material, General, Old & Rare Books, Scholarly Books

OLD PRINT SHOP, INC., THE
    150 Lexington Ave.
    New York, NY 10016
American Maps, Old Prints, American Watercolors, American Oil Paintings, Currier & Ives.

OLD SETTLER BOOKSHOP
    Walpole, NH 03608
Mountain Climbing, American Literature

O'NEAL, DAVID L.—
ANTIQUARIAN BOOKSELLERS
    Box 13 / Sharon Road
    Peterborough, NH 03458
American Literature, Printing History, Fine Books, First Editions, Typography

O'SHEA, JUNE—BOOKS
    6222 San Vicente Blvd.
    Los Angeles, CA 90048
Criminology, Psychiatry, Psychology

OTTENBERG, S. & N.—BOOKSELLERS
    P.O. Box 15509
    Wedgewood Station
    Seattle, WA 98115
Africana, Primitive Art

PACIFIC BOOK HOUSE
Kilohana Square
1016G Kapahulu Ave.
Honolulu, HI 96816
18th & 19th Century Literature, Hawaiiana & Pacificana

PAGEANT BOOK CO.
59 4th Ave. / New York, NY 10003
General Literature, Art & Illustrated Books, Old Maps & Prints, Americana, Fiction

PAINE, ALFRED W.—BOOKS
Wolfpits Rd. / Bethel, CT 06801
Whaling, Voyages, Naval History, Nautical Science, Americana

PANGLOSS BOOKSHOP
1284 Massachusetts Ave.
Cambridge, MA 02138
Fine Arts, Scholarly Books, Literature, History, Social Sciences

PARNASSUS BOOK SERVICE
Rt. 6A / Yarmouth Port, MA 02675
Russia, Caribbean, South America, Central America, Maritime

PARNASSUS BOOK SHOP
26 Montgomery St.
Rhinebeck, NY 12572
Scholarly Books, Photography, Modern First Editions

PAULSON, ROBERT A.
39 Downing Place
Harrington Park, NJ 07640
Books About Books, Adirondack Mountain History, New Jersey History, Rockwell Kent, Signed Books

PHIEBIG, ALBERT J., INC.
P.O. Box 352 / White Plains, NY 10602
Foreign Books & Periodicals, International Congresses, Irregular Serials, Building Special Collections

PINKNEY, WILLIAM & LOIS M.—
ANTIQUARIAN BOOKSELLERS
240 N. Granby Rd.
Granby, CT 06035
New York, First Editions, Americana, Western Americana

POTTER, NICHOLAS
203 E. Palace Ave. / Santa Fe, NM 87501
Southwestern History, Modern First Editions, Photographic Books

PRINTER'S DEVIL, THE
One Claremont Court
Arlington, MA 02174
History of Medicine, Science, Sporting, Natural History, Illustrated Books (Mail order & by appointment)

RAMER, RICHARD C.
225 E. 70th St.
New York, NY 10021
Luso-Brasiliana, Spain & Latin America, Americana, Nautical Science, Voyages & Travels

RARE BOOK COMPANY
P.O. Box 957
Freehold, NJ 07728
Christian Science Literature

REED, THEODORE—
ANTIQUARIAN BOOKS
P.O. Box 34
Agua Caliente Springs, R. Br.
Julian, CA 92036
General Antiquarian

REGENT HOUSE—PUBLISHERS &
BOOKSELLERS
108 N. Roselake Ave.
Los Angeles, CA 90026
British Literature, American History, American Literature, Foreign Affairs, Psychology

REISLER, JO ANN
360 Glyndon St., N.E.
Vienna, VA 22180
Children's Books, Illustrated Books, Juveniles

RENDELLS, THE, INC.
154 Wells Ave. / Newton, MA 02159
Illuminated Manuscripts, Autographs & Manuscripts, Inscribed & Association Books, Appraisals

REUBEN, WALTER, INC.
American Bank Tower / Suite 410
Austin, TX 78701
Americana, Atlases, Rare Maps, Texana

REYNOLDS, J. E.—BOOKSELLER
3801 Ridgewood Rd.
Willits, CA 95490
Press Books, Western Americana, Californiana (Catalogues only)

RICHARDS, PAUL C.—AUTOGRAPHS
High Acres / Templeton, MA 01468
Autographs & Letters, Signed Photographs, Signed First Editions, Documents

ROBERTS, LESTER—
ANTIQUARIAN BOOKS
P.O. Box 6094
San Rafael, CA 94903
Californiana, Out-of-Print Books, Rare Americana, First Editions

ROBINSON, CEDRIC L.—BOOKSELLER
597 Palisado Ave.
Windsor, CT 06095
Americana, Architecture, Connecticut, Naval History, Travels

ROSENBERG, MARY S., INC.
100 W. 72nd St.
New York, NY 10023
German & French: Humanities, Children's Books, Linguistics, Psychology, Psychoanalysis, Judaica

ROSENTHAL, BERNARD M., INC.
251 Post St.
San Francisco, CA 94108
Bibliography, Humanities, Incunabula & 16th Century, Manuscripts Before 1600, Paleography

ROSS, ROBERT H.—RARE BOOKS
P.O. Box 985
Hanover, NH 03755

Trumbull Lane (shop)
Norwich, VT 05055
American & English Modern First Editions, Press Books

ROSTENBERG, LEONA—RARE BOOKS
Box 188 Gracie Station
40 E. 88 St.
New York, NY 10028
Renaissance, Political Theory, Ephemera, Aldine Editions, France (By appointment)

RUBINFINE, JOSEPH
R.F.D. #1 / Pleasantville, NJ 08232
American Historical Autographs

SABBOT, RUDOLPH WM.—
NATURAL HISTORY BOOKS
5239 Tendilla Ave.
Woodland Hills, CA 91364
Mammalogy, Ornithology, Herpetology, Ichthyology, Entomology

SACKHEIM, BEN—
RARE BOOKS & FINE ART
5425 E. Fort Lowell Rd.
Tucson, AZ 85712
Modern First Editions, Limited Editions, Art Books, Art: Limited Edition Prints

SALLOCH, WILLIAM
Pines Bridge Rd.
Ossining, NY 10562
Music, Rare Books, Manuscripts, Incunables, Medieval, Renaissance, Baroque History & Literature, Classics, Emblem Books

SAN FRANCISCIANA
Cliff House / 1090 Pt. Lobos Ave.
San Francisco, CA 94121
Stereopticon Cards, Prints & Posters, Photographs, Postcards & Tradecards, San Francisco Memorabilia

SCARLET LETTER BOOKS
Candlewood Mountain Rd.
New Milford, CT 06776
Children's, Americana, Presidents, Medical, Illustrated

SCHAB, WILLIAM H., GALLERY, INC.
37 W. 57th St.
New York, NY 10019
Manuscripts, Americana, Science, Woodcut Books, Prints & Drawings

SCHATZKI, WALTER
160 Stratford Rd.
Brooklyn, NY 11218
Illustrated Books, Illuminated Manuscripts, Fine Bindings, Autographs, Early Juveniles

SCHILLER, JUSTIN G., LTD.
36 E. 61st St.
New York, NY 10021

P.O. Box 1667, FDR Station
New York, NY 10022
Posters, Juveniles, Illustrated Books, Drawings, Bibliography

SCHNASE, ANNEMARIE
120 Brown Rd. / P.O. Box 119
Scarsdale, NY 10583
Music, Periodicals (Scientific), Academy Publications

SCHNEIDER, WILLIAM—BOOKS
212 17th St.
Pacific Grove, CA 93950
Rare Books, First Editions, O. P.

SCHUMAN, HENRY, LTD.
2211 Broadway
New York, NY 10024
History of Science & Medicine

SCHUYLKILL BOOK & CURIO SHOP
873 Belmont Ave.
Philadelphia, PA 19104
General, Prints, Autographs, Manuscripts, Out-of-Print

SCHWARZ, KURT L.—
FINE AND RARE BOOKS
738 S. Bristol Ave.
Los Angeles, CA 90049

Northern Calif. Office:
736 Coventry Rd.
Kensington, CA 94707
Fine Printing, Orientalia, History, Social & Racial Problems, Fine Arts

SCIENTIFIC LIBRARY SERVICE
29 E. 10th St. / New York, NY 10003
Music Autographs, Early & Rare Music, Science & Mathematics

SCOPAZZI, JOHN—FINE & RARE BOOKS
278 Post St., Suite 305
San Francisco, CA 94108
Art Books, Private Press Books, Maps & Prints, General Literature, Fine & Rare Books

SCOTT, BARRY
15 Gramercy Pk. / New York, NY 10003
Literary Manuscripts, 20th Century First Editions

SCRIPTORIUM, THE
427 North Canon Dr.
Beverly Hills, CA 90210
Autograph Letters & Documents, Manuscripts, Motion Picture Memorabilia, Signed Books & Photographs, Appraisals

SERENDIPITY BOOKS INC.
1790 Shattuck Ave.
Berkeley, CA 94709
Archives (Literary), Mss. & Letters (Literary), First Editions (20th Century), Fiction (Modern), Poetry (Modern)

SESSLER, CHARLES, INC.
1308 Walnut St.
Philadelphia, PA 19107
Rare Books, Autographs, Prints & Paintings, Current Books

SEVEN GABLES BOOKSHOP, INC.
3 W. 46th St. / New York, NY 10036
Early American Literature, Bibliography, Children's Books, Early English Literature

SHAPIRO, OSCAR
3726 Connecticut Ave., N.W.
Washington, D.C. 20008
Chess, Music Autographs, Violin Books, Early Music, American Music (Mail order only)

SHOREY BOOK STORE, THE
110 Union St. / Seattle, WA 98101

P.O. Box 21626 / Seattle, WA 98111
General Stock, Americana (All Types), Natural History, Alaska & Arctic, Western Americana

SLATER, WILLIAM
80 E. 11th St. / New York, NY 10003
Alchemy, Occult, Astrology, Hermetic, Yoga (By appointment only)

SLIFER, ROSEJEANNE
30 Park Ave. / New York, NY 10016
Autographs, Documents, Antique Maps, Atlases & Maps (By appointment only)

SMITH, PATTERSON
23 Prospect Terrace
Montclair, NJ 07042
Social History, Criminology

SMITH, SYDNEY R.—SPORTING BOOKS
Canaan, NY 12029
Horses, Dogs, Guns, Shooting, Fishing

SOTHEBY PARKE BERNET INC.
980 Madison Ave. / New York, NY 10021
Auctions

SPECIALTY BOOK CONCERN
11 Dundas St., E.
Waterdown, Ontario
LOR 2HO CANADA
Canadiana, Arctica

STANOFF, JERROLD G.—
ORIENTAL BOOKSELLERS
P.O. Box 39788
2717 Lakewood Ave.
Los Angeles, CA 90039
Lafcadio Hearn, Rare Japan & China, Orientals in America, Japanese & Chinese Arts, Antique Maps of the Orient (By appointment only)

STARR BOOK CO., INC., THE
37 Kingston St. / Boston, MA 02111
Fiction, Standard Sets, American & English Literature, General O. P.

STARR BOOK SHOP, INC.
29 Plympton St.
Cambridge, MA 02138
American Literature, Out-of-Print, Sets, Americana, Press Books

STEELE, GEOFFREY, INC.
Lumberville, PA 18933
Color Plate Books, Art, Architecture

STERNE, PAULA BOOKS
Huckleberry Rd., R.F.D. #2
W. Redding, CT 06896
Americana, Sporting, Dogs, Guns

STEVENS, HENRY, SON & STILES
Albee Ct. / Larchmont, NY 10538
Americana, Books & Maps

STINSON HOUSE BOOKS
Quincy Rd.
Rumney Village, NH 03266
Natural History, White Mountains, Americana, New Hampshire

STONEHILL, C. A., INC.
282 York St. / New Haven, CT 06511
Manuscripts, Incunabula, History, English Literature, Appraisals

SUN DANCE BOOKS
1520 N. Crescent Heights Blvd.
Hollywood, CA 90046
California Gold Rush & Early California Material, Indians & Eskimos of the Americas, Mexico, Central & South America (By appointment only)

SWANN GALLERIES, INC.
104 E. 25th St. / New York, NY 10010
Auctioneers & Appraisers

TALISMAN PRESS
Box 455 / Georgetown, CA 95634
California History, Nevada History, Books & Pamphlets, Manuscript Material, Ephemera

TAMERLIS, VICTOR
911 Stuart Ave.
Mamaroneck, NY 10543
Art, Prints, Early Printing, Illustrated Books, Scholarly Books

TAYLOR, W. THOMAS
P.O. Box 5343 / Austin, TX 78763
American Literature, Typography, Incunabula, Press Books, English Literature

TEMPLE BAR BOOKSHOP
7 Boylston St. / Cambridge, MA 02138
Photography (Books & Images), First Editions, New Trade Books

TITLES, INC.
Box 342 / 1931 Sheridan Rd.
Highland Park, IL 60035
First Editions, Private Press, Poetry, Fine Bindings, Americana (Chicago)

TOTTERIDGE BOOK SHOP
667 Madison Ave., Suite 305
New York, NY 10021
First Editions, Rare Books, Press Books, Bindings, Illustrated Books

TRACE, TIMOTHY
Red Mill Rd. / Peekskill, NY 10566
Antiques, Crafts & Trades, Decorative Arts, Architecture

TUNICK, DAVID
12 E. 80th St. / New York, NY 10021
Original Old Master & Modern Engravings, Etchings, Woodcuts & Lithographs, Illustrated Books, Sets of Fine Prints

TURNER, DAVE—BOOKS
P.O. Box 2104
Menlo Park, CA 94025
Science Fiction, Detective Fiction, Jazz, Western Fiction

TUTTLE, CHARLES E. CO., INC.
P.O. Drawer F
Rutland, VT 05701
Vermontiana, Atlases & Maps (American), Americana, Town & County Histories, Genealogies

TWENEY, GEORGE H.—BOOKS
16660 Marine View Dr. S.W.
Seattle, WA 98166
Western Americana, Alaska & Canada, Voyages & Western Exploration, Maps, Manuscripts

UNIVERSITY BOOK RESERVE
75 Main St. & 815 Nantasket Ave.
Hull, MA 02045
Philosophy, Religion, Literature, Social Sciences, Drama

UNIVERSITY PLACE BOOK SHOP
821 Broadway / New York, NY 10003
Africa & Antilles, Black Studies, Chess, Communism & Socialism, Incunabula

URBAN BOOKS
295 Grizzly Peak Blvd.
Berkeley, CA 94708
Political Science, Economics, Americana, Californiana, Urbanism, Business History

URSUS BOOKS LTD.
667 Madison Ave. / New York, NY 10021
Art Reference, Illustrated Books, Books About Books, Fine Printing

VALLEY BOOK CITY
5249 Lankershim Blvd.
N. Hollywood, CA 91601
Art, Cinema, General Scholarly Books, Photography, Black Studies

VALLEY BOOK SHOP
122 Hamilton St. / Box 533
Geneva, IL 60134
Railroadiana, Illinoisiana, Western Americana, Catholic Americana, Architecture

VAN NORMAN BOOK COMPANY
422-424 Bank of Galesburg Bldg.
Galesburg, IL 61401
Midwest Americana, Western Americana, Illinois, Abraham Lincoln, American & English Literature

VERBEKE, CHRISTIAN F.—
RARE BOOKS INC.
7 Pond St.
Newburyport, MA 01950
Appraisals, Graphic Arts, Illustrated Books, 19th Century English Literature, Continental Books

VICKEY, HENRY J.
9 Brook St. / Stoughton, MA 02072
Out-of-Print

VICTORIA BOOK SHOP
307 Fifth Ave., Rm 1400
New York, NY 10016
Illustrated Books, Children's Books

VOLKOFF & VON HOHENLOHE
1514 La Coronilla Dr.
Santa Barbara, CA 93109
Rare Books & Manuscripts, Science & Medicine, Political Science & Philosophy, European History, Polonica & Slavica

WAHRENBROCK'S BOOK HOUSE
649 Broadway / San Diego, CA 92101
First Editions, Contemporary Fiction, Voyages & Travel, Mormon History, Southern California History, Baja California

WALTON, RAY S.—RARE BOOKS
502 Westwood Terrace
Austin, TX 78746
Western Americana, Texas & the Southwest, Overland Narratives, Photographica, Press Books, Literature

WEISER, SAMUEL, INC.
734 Broadway / New York, NY 10003
Occult, Theology, Egyptology, Astrology, Orientalia

WEISS, BERNICE—RARE BOOKS
36 Tuckahoe Ave.
Eastchester, NY 10707
First Editions, American & English Literature, Poetry, Private Press Books, Association & Inscribed Books

WESTERN HEMISPHERE, INC.
1613 Central St.
Stoughton, MA 02072
Western Americana, Canadiana, Voyages & Travels, American History, Economics & Related Fields

WEYHE, E., INC.
794 Lexington Ave. / New York, NY 10021
Art, Architecture

WHITLOCK FARM BOOKSELLERS
20 Sperry Rd. / Bethany, CT 06525
Americana, Children's Books, Rare Books, Maps, Prints

WILSON BOOKSHOP, THE
3005 Fairmount St.
Dallas, TX 75201
Texana, Fine Bindings, Sets, Confederacy, American Southwest

WITHERSPOON ART & BOOK STORE
12 Nassau St. / Princeton, NJ 08540
Rare, Out-of-Print, Fine Sets, Reference Works

WITTEN, LAURENCE—RARE BOOKS
181 Old Post Rd. / P.O. Box 490
Southport, CT 06490
Illustrated Books, Medieval & Later Manuscripts, Incunabula & 16th Century, History of Printing, Fine Bindings

WOFSY, ALAN—FINE ARTS
150 Green St.
San Francisco, CA 94111
Bibliographies, Private Press Books, Art Reference, Old Master & Modern Prints, Illustrated Books

WOLFE, WILLIAM P.
222 rue de l'Hopital
Montreal, Quebec
H2Y 1V8 CANADA
Canadiana, Americana, Alcoholic Beverages

WOOD, CHARLES B., III, INC.—
ANTIQUARIAN BOOKSELLERS
The Green / S. Woodstock, CT 06267
Technology (19th Century), Architecture, Photography, American Art

WOODBURN, ELISABETH
Booknoll Farm
Hopewell, NJ 08525
Horticulture, Herbs, Landscape, Beverages (Wine, Beer, etc.), Agriculture, Early Farming

WOOLMER, J. HOWARD—RARE BOOKS
Gladstone Hollow / Andes, NY 13731
Author Collections, Autograph Letters & Manuscripts, Modern First Editions, Poetry, 20th Century Literature

WREDEN, WILLIAM P.—
BOOKS & MANUSCRIPTS
200 Hamilton Ave. (cor. Emerson)
Box 56 / Palo Alto, CA 94302
General Antiquarian Books, English & American Literature, Western Americana, Printing, Manuscripts

XIMENES: RARE BOOKS, INC.
120 E. 85th St.
New York, NY 10028
First Editions, Rare Books, Literature, Americana, Voyages & Travels

YANKEE PEDDLER BOOKSHOP
94 Mill St. / Pultneyville, NY 14538
Americana, Civil War, Illustrated Books & Prints, New York State, the West

YOUNG, WILLIAM & CO.
Box 282
Wellesley Hills, MA 02181
Modern Manuscripts, First Editions, Modern First Editions, Roaring Twenties

ZAMBELLI, ALFRED F.
156 Fifth Ave. / New York, NY 10010
Rare Books, Paleography, Philosophy, History (Medieval, Renaissance, Reformation) Bibliography

ZEITLIN & VER BRUGGE
815 N. La Cienega Blvd.
Los Angeles, CA 90069
Early Science, Natural History, Fine Arts, History of Medicine, Fine Press Books

ZEITLIN PERIODICALS COMPANY, INC.
817 S. La Brea Ave.
Los Angeles, CA 90036
Back-Issue Periodicals, Reprints, Geological Publications, Microforms, Appraisals

ZUCKER, IRVING—ART BOOKS
256 Fifth Ave. / New York, NY 10001
Typography & Printing, Old and Rare Books, Modern French Illustrated, Fine & Applied Arts, Color Plate Books

Some Collectors' Clubs

Source: ENCYCLOPEDIA OF ASSOCIATIONS, 12th Edition (1978), published by Gale Research Company.

Antiques:

Questers
210 South Quince Street
Philadelphia, PA 19107

Art:

Association for the Study of Dada and Surrealism
c/o Michael Riffaterre
Dept. of French
Columbia University
New York, NY 10027

Art Glass:

American Custard Glass Collectors
4129 Virginia Avenue
Kansas City, MO 64110

International Carnival Glass Association
R. R. Two
Warren, IN 46792

Autographs:

Manuscript Society
1206 N. Stoneman Avenue, No. 15
Alhambra, CA 91801

Universal Autograph Collectors Club
562 Lakeview Avenue
Rockville Centre, NY 11570

Automobiles:

Antique Automobile Club of America
501 West Governor Road
Hershey, PA 17033

Barbed Wire:

Texas Barbed Wire Collectors' Association
1019 Cedar Trail
Cedar Hill, TX 75104

Bells:

American Bell Association
Route 1, Box 286
Natrona Heights, PA 15065

Bookplates:

American Society of Bookplate Collectors and Designers
1206 N. Stoneman Avenue, No. 15
Alhambra, CA 91801

Books:

Caxton Club
60 West Walton Street
Chicago, IL 60610

Grolier Club
47 East 60th Street
New York, NY 10022

Great Books Foundation
307 North Michigan Avenue
Chicago, IL 60601

Buttons:

National Button Society of America
P.O. Box 39
Eastwood, KY 40018

Coca-Cola:

The Cola Clan
3965 Pikes Peak
Memphis, TN 38108

Coins:

American Numismatic Association
P. O. Box 2366
Colorado Springs, CO 80901

Collectors of Numismatic Errors
Box 126
Dresden, OH 43821

Comics:

Academy of Comic Art Fans and Collectors
487 Lakewood
Detroit, MI 48215

Dolls:

International Rose O'Neill Club
Box 668
Bronson, MO 65616
(Rose O'Neill created the Kewpie doll in 1909.)

Embroidery:

Embroiderers Guild of America
6 East 45th Street, Room 1501
New York, NY 10017

Jazz Records:

International Association of Jazz Record Collectors
7200 Cresheim Road, Apartment B-6
Philadelphia, PA 19119

Locks:

American Lock Collectors Association
14010 Cardwell
Livonia, MI 48154

Marbles:

Marble Collectors Society of America
P. O. Box 222
Trumbull, CT 06611

Matchcovers:

Rathkemp Matchcover Society
1311 East 215th Place
Carson, CA 90745

Medals:

Orders and Medals Society of America
3828 Ronnald Drive
Philadelphia, PA 19154

Token and Medal Society
611 Oakwood Way
El Cajon, CA 92021

Military Insignias:

American Society of Military Insignia Collectors
744 Warfield Road
Oakland, CA 94610

Milk Bottles:

Milkbottles Only Organization (MOO)
P. O. Box 5456
Newport News, VA 23605

Miniatures:

National Association of Miniatures Enthusiasts
P. O. Box 2621
Anaheim, CA 92804

Musical Instruments, Automatic:

Automatic Musical Instrument Collectors Association
P. O. Box 666
Grand Junction, CO 81501

Music Boxes:

Musical Box Society, International
Box 202, Rte. 3
Morgantown, IN 46160

Newspapers:

International Newspaper Collector's Club
P. O. Box 7271
Phoenix, AZ 85011

Paperweights:

Paperweight Collectors' Association
47 Windsor Road
Scarsdale, NY 10583

Playing Cards:

Chicago Playing Card Collectors
9645 South Leavitt Street
Chicago, IL 60643

Playing Card Collectors' Association
1511 West Sixth Street
Racine, WI 53404

Political Items:

American Political Items Collectors
66 Golf Street
Newington, CT 06111

Association for the Preservation of Political Americana
P. O. Box 211
Forest Hills, NY 11375

Postcards:

Deltiologists of America
3709 Gradyville Road
Newton Square, PA 19073

International Postcard Collectors Association
Suite 907, 6380 Wilshire Boulevard
Los Angeles, CA 90048

Radio:

North American Radio Archives
1615-A Emerson Street
Honolulu, HI 96813

Association of North American Radio Clubs
557 North Madison Avenue
Pasadena, CA 91101

Railroads:

National Model Railroad Association
Box 2186
Indianapolis, IN 46206

Railroad Enthusiasts
P. O. Box 133
West Townsend, MA 01474

Train Collectors Association
P. O. Box 248
Strasburg, PA 17579

Spoons:

The Spooner
Route 1, Box 61
Shullsburg, WI 53586

Stamps:

American Academy of Philately
58 West Salisbury Drive
Wilmington, DE 19809

American Philatelic Society
P. O. Box 800
State College, PA 16801

Steins:

Stein Collectors International
P. O. Box 16326
St. Paul, MN 55116

Tin Containers:

Tin Container Collectors Association
P. O. Box 4555
Denver, CO 80204

Toys:

International Toy Buff's Association
425 East Green Street, Room 500 W
Pasadena, CA 91103

Watches:

National Association of Watch and Clock Collectors
P. O. Box 33
Columbia, PA 17512

Wooden Nickels:

International Organization of Wooden Money Collectors
P. O. Box 395
Goose Creek, SC 29445

Index of Collectibles

Within the text, all museums, galleries, shops and other sources for collectibles are in numbered alphabetical sequence. The index is keyed to the alphabetical number for the source and not to page number.

*A-14 refers to the Antiquarian Booksellers' Association, a general description of which appears in the main entry. A complete list of the members of the Association, their addresses and specialities will be found starting on page 195.

books (*cont.*)

on archaeology, A-14, D-14
on the Arctic, U-6
on arms and armor, A-10, A-14, H-26
on art and architecture, A-7, A-10,
    A-14, A-22, C-22, D-13,
    E-8, H-19, H-26, M-30
    forgeries, M-21
    Oriental, A-14, C-10, C-19, C-22,
      G-4
    painting, A-14, B-10, G-4, N-4,
      R-12
atlases and maps, A-14, A-17, C-8,
    F-16, H-26
on Audubon prints, A-14
on autographs, A-14, H-3, H-26
on automobiles, A-7, A-14, V-3
on barbed wire, H-26
biographies, A-7, A-14, B-25, H-19
on birds, A-14, B-8, D-16
on boats, O-1
on books, A-10, A-14, H-26
on bottles, H-26
on bumper stickers, V-3
on buttons, H-26
children's books, A-14, A-22
on China, A-7, H-26
on china and porcelain, A-10, H-19,
    H-26, P-17
on cinema, A-14, A-22
on the Civil War, A-7, A-14
on clocks and watches, A-7, A-14,
    E-8, G-9, H-26
on coins, B-1, H-19, H-26
on collecting, D-13
comic books, A-14
cookbooks, A-7, B-1, B-29, C-13,
    C-33, M-27, N-18, P-10,
    S-28, W-4
on costume, H-19
on Currier & Ives, A-14
on dance, A-14, D-3, R-3
on decorative arts and crafts, A-7,
    A-14, A-22, B-1, D-13, E-8,
    H-1, H-26, S-10
on decoys, H-26
dictionaries, A-14, B-1, B-25
on dogs, A-14
on dolls and doll houses. *See under*
    books: on toys
on Egyptology, A-7, A-14
on Fabergé, C-22
field guides, N-3, N-18
fine bindings, A-7, A-14
first editions, A-14, H-20
on fish, C-25, P-1, U-6
on food and drink, A-14, C-33
on fossils, P-1
on furniture, A-7, A-10, H-26
on gambling machines, V-3
on games, A-14, E-8, H-26, W-20
on genealogy, A-14, D-4
on geography, C-8
on glass, A-7, A-10, H-26, T-2
on hallmarks, A-10
on Hispanic culture, H-19
on history, A-7, A-14, H-1
on icons, C-19
illuminated manuscripts, A-14

books (*cont.*)

on insects, A-14
on ironwork, A-10, H-26
on jewelry, A-10, E-8, H-19
on keys, A-10
on kitchenware, A-10, H-26
on lace, H-19
on locks, A-10
McGuffey's Pictorial Eclectic Primer,
    B-29
manuscripts, A-14, W-4
on marbles, H-26
on maritime subjects, A-7, A-14,
    M-34, P-7, P-26, R-14, S-28
on military subjects, A-7, A-14, S-26
on mineralogy and gems, C-36, E-8
miniature, A-14
on miniatures, A-14, E-9
on music, A-14, B-24, B-25, E-8,
    O-7, V-3
on musical instruments, A-10, C-4,
    H-26, V-3
on music boxes, A-10
on Napoleon, A-14
on natural history, A-14
on nautical instruments and naviga-
    tion, H-20, P-7, R-14
on needlework, A-7, A-14, H-26
on netsuke, H-26, P-7
on occult subjects, A-14, E-8, I-8,
    U-8
old and out-of-print, A-14, M-17,
    S-40
on opera, B-25, O-7
on Oriental rugs, C-19, C-39, G-9, J-1
on paperweights, H-26, S-11
on Pennsylvania Dutch subjects,
    M-13
on pewter, C-28, C-41, H-26
on photography, A-14, A-21, A-22,
    D-10, I-6
on postcards, H-26
on posters, A-7, A-26, V-3
on pottery marks, A-10
on quilts, A-7, D-7, H-26, S-16
on railroads, A-7, A-10, A-14, B-2,
    H-26, V-3
rare, A-14, A-21, H-20, S-40
on sciences, A-14, C-36, D-3, D-14,
    F-12, P-1
on sculpture, A-22, C-19, C-22, D-7,
    G-9, H-19
on the Shakers, S-14, S-15
on shells, C-25, H-26, J-2
on silver, C-28, H-26
on spinning, S-10, U-2
on stamps, A-14, H-10, H-26
on steins, A-10
on sundials, S-43
on technology and industry, A-14,
    F-12, H-1, H-20
on textiles, A-14, H-19, M-21
on theater, A-14, R-3
on thimbles, H-26
on tinware, A-7, C-28, H-26
on toys, A-7, A-14, D-11, E-9, H-26
on unicorns, U-3
on United States, A-7, H-26
    cities, A-14, M-27, S-28

books (*cont.*)

    counties, F-16, R-13
on United States
    regions, A-14, C-13, E-10, S-21
    states, A-14, C-5, F-16, N-12,
      N-18, P-10, P-14, P-16,
      R-13, U-6, U-7
on valentines, A-14
on Washington, George, A-7, M-26
on weaponry, A-10, S-26
on weaving, S-10, U-2, U-7
on Wedgwood, B-31
on Western subjects, A-7, A-14,
    G-11, H-26, N-18, P-14, R-8
See also exhibition catalogues
Bosch, Hieronymus, P-25
Botticelli, N-4, P-25
bottles, L-15
    chicha gourd, I-5
    Coca-Cola, P-2
    commemorative, H-23
    milk bottles, D-1
    reproductions, E-4, H-23
    silver, G-17
    snuff, G-17, N-19
    whiskey, L-15
Bowditch, Nathaniel, P-7
Bowie, William, S-9
bowls, A-7, P-22
    Americana, A-7
    antique
      Himalayan, H-25
      Saxon, L-1
    Ching Dynasty, W-16
    crystal, S-33
    glass, H-2
    Hawaiian silver dollar, S-6
    pewter, H-22
    porcelain, H-25
    silver, L-8, M-16
    stone, M-28
boxes, M-13, N-15, O-10, Y-1
    Chinese, H-4, S-19, S-24
    dispatch case, O-10
    enameled, B-26, S-43
    eighteenth-century, B-26
    English tin, O-10
    gold-plated, B-26
    letter, G-14
    map cases, O-10
    Mexican, S-19
    miniature, P-18
    Nepali, N-11
    pewter, B-28, S-19
    porcelain, H-4, M-32, P-22
    quillwork, R-22
    Shaker, G-25
    shell, C-23, S-19
    silver, C-23, K-6
    snuff, S-22
    South American Indian, I-5
    wooden, K-1, O-10, O-13, P-13
    See also shadowboxes
Boyle, Carla, R-16
brackets, G-5
Brady, Mathew, N-2, P-28
branding irons, N-19
Braque, Georges, C-24, M-22, P-12, T-4
Brasilier, André, O-9

215

marine. *See* nautical

marionettes, T 5

marrow scoops, K-6, L-8

masks, I-5, I-9, K-1, N-11, R-10, T-11

matchbox sleeves, L-15

Matisse, A-25, M-22, P-12

Matta, C-24

medals, D-5, G-14, M-27, S-26, U-5, V-2, W-18

meerschaum pipes, C-11

Meisel, Susan Pear, W-10

Meissen. *See under* chinaware and porcelain

Melrose, Andrew, E-10

menorahs, J-4

Mesopotamian antiquities, L-1

Mexican

    crafts, D-14, H-13, N-19, S-19

    jewelry, A-9

    maps, D-17

mezuzahs, J-4

microscopes, F-12, H-20

military items, D-5, G-14, S-26, W-18

    armbands, D-5

    buckles, S-23, S-26

    buttons, S-26

    flag holder, W-18

    helmets, C-20, P-2, S-26

    insignia, P-2, U-5

    medals, U-5, V-2

    music, S-26

    prints, F-5

    stirrups, S-26

    uniforms, W-18

    World War II, U-5

    See also firearms; swords

milk cans, D-1

Millais, Sir John Everett, O-3

Miller, John, D-8

Milton, Peter, E-5, I-3

minerals, C-25, D-10, D-14, M-3, N-19, R-20

miniatures

    animals, N-3

    baskets, F-2

    bathroom sets, H-6

    bicycles, F-2

    boxes, P-18

    bronzes, K-2

    cabinetmaker's samples, P-18

    Christmas, G-10

    Chrysnbon, H-6, M-4

    clocks, F-2, P-20

    English pub, C-35

    firearms, P-18

    furniture and furnishings, C-15, C-38, D-11, E-9, F-2, H-6, H-14, M-4, M-13, M-32, N-5, P-18, S-7, S-8, S-24, T-5

    general-store, F-2, H-6

    glassware, F-2

    musical instruments, C-35, F-2, H-6, M-7

    nativity group, C-34

    paintings, C-15

    paper models, H-11

    porcelain, C-15, E-9, P-18

miniatures (*cont.*)

    silver, C-27, E-9, M-16, M-20

    stained glass, G-13

    theaters, R-3

    See also doll houses; dolls

Minton. *See under* chinaware and porcelain

Miró, Joan, C-24, C-26, I-7, L-13, M-22, O-9

mirrors, E-4, G-5, P-2

    Art Nouveau, T-14

    Federal period, E-4

    pub, R-7

    Shaker, G-25

    with stained-glass panels, H-14

    zodiac, R-7

Mission period arts and crafts, T-14

mobiles, A-4, A-18, H-11, S-38

models. *See* airplane models; automobiles: models of; railroad models; ship models

Modigliani, Amedeo, H-18

Mohawk paintings. *See under* American Indian arts and crafts

Mojave tribe. *See under* American Indian arts and crafts

molas, A-5, P-3

Monet, Claude, C-22, P-12, V-5

moon, maps of, H-5

Moore, Henry, A-22, C-17, I-7, L-13

Moran, Thomas, L-11

Moses, Grandma, A-3, B-10

Moskowitz, Ira, B-23

Motherwell, Robert, P-12

Moti, Kaiko, C-26

Mucha, Alphonse, I-1, R-16

mugs, C-30, F-8, L-8, M-11, S-5, S-20, S-26

Munch, Edvard, C-24

Murillo, Bartolomé Esteban, P-25

museum reproductions

    American Museum of Natural History, A-9

    Bennington Museum, B-10

    Bishop Museum, B-15

    Boston Museum of Fine Arts, B-18

    British Museum, B-27

    Brooklyn Museum, B-28

    Buten Museum, B-31

    Cleveland Museum of Art, C-22

    Cleveland Museum of Natural History, C-23

    Cluny Museum (Paris), W-3

    Colonial Williamsburg, C-28

    Freer Gallery of Art, F-14

    Grandma Moses Schoolhouse Museum, B-10

    Greenfield Village/Henry Ford Museum, B-5, E-4

    Hale Farm and Village, H-2

    Historic Charleston, H-22

    the Jewish Museum, J-4

    Kunsthistorisches Museum (Vienna), W-3

    the Louvre, M-28

    Mercer Museum, M-13

    Metropolitan Museum of Art, M-16

    Minneapolis Institute of Arts, M-21

museum reproductions (*cont.*)

    Municipal Museum of Baltimore, M-27

    Museo del Prado, P-25

    Museum of the City of New York, M-32

    the Museum of Modern Art, M-30

    National Gallery of Art, N-4

    National Museum of Anthropology, A-23

    National Museum of Denmark, N-6

    Ohio River Museum, O-1

    Oriental Institute, O-8

    Peabody Museum of Salem, P-7

    Peter Matteson Tavern Museum, B-10

    Philadelphia Museum of Art, P-11

    Phillips Collection, P-12

    Remington Art Museum, R-8

    Rijksmuseum, R-12

    Saint Louis Art Museum, S-1

    Smithsonian Institution, S-24

    Toledo Museum of Art, T-4

    Walters Art Gallery, W-4

music

    Arabic, R-4

    manuscripts, L-9, S-39

    military, S-26

    for recorders, A-13

    song sheets, B-29, M-32

    See also musical instruments; opera; recordings

musical instruments, A-24

    African, C-7

    American Indian, I-9

    antique, M-23

    automatic, A-8

    bagpipes, M-1

    balalaikas, H-32

    banjos, H-16, H-32

        kits for, S-36

    Chinese, C-7

    clavichords, M-23

    drums, C-4, I-5

    dulcimers, H-16, H-32

    electronic keyboards, A-24

    flutes, C-4, I-5

    fortepianos, H-31

    guitars, H-32

        left-handed, L-5

    harps, C-4, H-32, M-23

    harpsichords, G-24, H-31

    horns, C-4, C-7

    hurdy-gurdys, C-4

    Indian, C-7

    Japanese, C-7

    kalimbas, H-32

    kazoos, C-4

    kits for, C-4, H-16, H-31

    lutes, C-4, R-9

    lyres, H-32

    mandolins, H-32

    maracas, I-5

    organs, A-8

    padded bags for, A-24

    pianos, G-24, H-31, M-23

        player, A-8, P-19

    piccolos, A-24

    psalteries, H-16

    recorders, A-13, K-8

musical instruments (*cont.*)
    reeds, C-4
    reproductions, H-31, M-23
    South American Indian, I-5
    spinets, G-24, H-31, M-23
    synthesizers, A-24
    thumb pianos, H-16
    tubas, A-24
    virginals, M-23
    West Indian, C-7
    whistles, C-7
    zithers, C-4
    See also bells
music boxes, A-8, D-15, M-15, N-5, S-5
    movements for, M-7
    recordings of, M-15
mustard pots, L-8
Muybridge, Eadweard, A-22

N

napkin rings, C-23, W-19
Nast, Thomas, F-15, L-9
nautical
    antiques, N-13, R-14
    figureheads, R-14, S-17
    gear, G-5, P-26, S-18
    instruments, P-26, R-14
    name boards, S-17
    paintings and prints, M-34, P-6, R-14,
      V-5
    pilot wheels, C-20, S-18
    reproductions, M-34, P-7, S-18
    See also ship models
Navajo tribe. *See under* American Indian
    arts and crafts
Nazi items, C-20, D-5, H-3, P-2, U-5
necklaces. *See under* jewelry
needlepoint
    accessories, S-42
    boxes, P-13
    frames, P-13, S-25
    furniture to cover with, S-42, W-12,
      W-15
    kits and designs, B-18, C-28, C-38,
      F-13, F-14, F-15, H-22,
      L-12, M-16, N-7, P-5, P-11,
      S-24, S-37, W-4, W-12,
      W-15
      Christmas ornaments, W-15
      Della Robbia design, P-5
      Egyptian designs, S-37
      Eskimo designs, I-2
      heraldic, F-13
      on Jewish themes, J-4
      Oriental designs, C-38, N-10, P-5
      Pennsylvania Dutch, F-15, S-25
      Persian, F-13
      from tapestries, F-13
    See also embroidery
Nègre, Charles, A-22
Neiman, LeRoy, E-5, O-9
Nepali handcrafts, N-11
Nesbitt, Lowell, C-32
netsuke, G-17, P-7
Netzsch, Uwe, E-2
New England handcrafts, N-13
Nisbet, Peggy, E-9
Noland, Kenneth, C-32

Northrup, George, R-16
numismatics. *See* coins

O

Obin, Philomé, N-1
occult items, I-8, O-11, U-8
Ojibway crafts. *See under* American In-
    dian arts and crafts
O'Keeffe, Georgia, M-22, P-12
opera
    figurines, B-17
    posters, C-24, F-4, T-10
    programs, H-3
    scores, autographed, H-3
orchids, A-19, G-20, H-12, J-5, M-12,
    S-13, S-35
    See also under flowers
organs. *See under* musical instruments
Oriental. *See under* Chinese *and* Japanese
Orlando, Peter, L-13
Orrefors. *See under* crystal; glass
owls
    bronze, B-22, C-16
    carvings, A-2, B-22, N-11
    crystal, G-26, N-8, S-19, S-33
    jewelry, C-26, M-28
    mobile, card, A-18, H-11, N-9
    paperweight, M-28
    pewter, M-28
    porcelain, A-28, B-17, B-30, E-2
    prints, C-31, F-10, G-15, G-19,
      M-19, O-12

P

Pacifica
    crafts, B-15
    maps, C-8
    shells, C-25
    See also Hawaiian
paintings
    acrylics, L-11
    American, H-18, S-6, S-34
    American Indian, I-9
    antique, I-9, O-3, S-6
    Chinese, on silk, N-14
    Ecuadorian, I-5
    folk art, H-18
    Haitian, N-1
    Hudson Valley, A-3, S-6
    Impressionists, H-18, S-6
    landscapes, M-24, P-6, S-34
    marine subjects, M-34, P-6, R-14,
      V-5
    military, P-6
    Nepali, on fabric, N-11
    New England, N-13
    portraits, A-3, H-18, M-24, O-3, S-6
    railroad, P-6
    Southern American, M-24
    sporting scenes, M-24, P-6
    still-lifes, H-18, M-24, S-6
    Victorian, G-22, S-6
    watercolors, G-22, H-18, I-9, K-5,
      N-14, P-6, S-34
    Western subjects, T-6
    wildlife, C-26, E-7, K-5, M-9, P-6
    See also prints *and artists' names*

paper scale models, H-11
paperweights, M-3
    acrylic, D-10
    D'Albret, S-11
    antique, S-11
    art glass, B-18, K-1
    Art Nouveau, R-22, S-11
    Baccarat, P-17, S-11
    Banford, S-11
    barrel-bung, L-15
    brass, N-3
    butterfly, C-25
    campaign, C-1
    cataloguing kit for, S-11
    Clichy, S-11
    commemorative, H-23
    crystal, C-26, H-4, M-16, P-17, S-11,
      T-9
    glass, C-2, E-4, H-2, K-1, S-11,
      W-19
    Lalique, H-4
    Lundberg Studios, S-11
    metal, H-1
    military, S-26
    millefiori, S-24
    mineral, M-3
    owl, M-28
    Perthshire, S-11
    porcelain, B-17
    railroad, B-2
    Saint Louis, S-11
    scarabs, H-4
    sea life, C-25
    Stankard and Whittemore, S-11
    sulphide, S-11
    tomahawk, P-15
    whale, N-3
Parnall, Peter, C-31
Parrish, Maxfield, G-23, I-1, S-6
Pasmore, Victor, C-17
Passover plates, J-4
patches, D-5, L-5, S-23
Peale, James, C-32
Peale, Rembrandt, S-6
pendants. *See under* jewelry
Pène du Bois, Guy, K-5
Pennsylvania Dutch
    Amish, A-17, P-29
    Christmas plate, R-18
    crafts, M-13
    embroidery kits, F-15, S-25
    fraktur, H-14, M-13
    kitchenware, M-13
    quilt patterns, L-6
    toys, P-11, R-18
Persian art, C-22
    See also Iranian
Peruvian pottery, R-22
Peters, Jurgen, E-5
Peterson, Roger Tory, M-19
petrified wood, R-5
petroglyphs, B-15, G-2, M-8
pewter and pewter reproductions, C-28,
      E-4, G-26, H-22, M-16,
      S-24, W-16
    Art Nouveau, T-14
    bowls, B-28, H-22
    boxes, S-19